Morale, Culture, and Character: Assessing Schools of Hope

Morale, Culture, and Character: Assessing Schools of Hope

Douglas H. Heath

Conrow Publishing House

Published by Conrow Publishing House
P.O. Box 1411, Bryn Mawr, PA 19010
www.conrowpub.com

Printed in the United States of America
by Thomson-Shore, Inc., Dexter, Michigan

Cover: John Davis Gummere
Book Design: Eva Fernandez Beehler

Library of Congress Catalog Card Number: 98-94949

ISBN 0-9641727-2-0 (hardcover)
ISBN 0-9641727-3-9 (paper)

First Edition

*To David
and the Memory of Emily*

Contents

Section V: Applying Measures of Morale and Culture for Understanding Contemporary Educational Issues

Section VI: Rethinking Character Education

Section VII: Holding Schools Accountable

Preface

What should be the educational agenda for the 21st century? Among other proposals: create smaller elementary classrooms and build more schools to house them, increase student choice by creating 3000 charter schools, introduce national standards, hold schools more accountable. Meritorious? Yes. The best solutions? Questionable. Successful implementation of each proposal depends on the "devil in the details"—as politicians are wont to say.

Consider what I believe to be the key proposal: accountability. But accountability for what? Achievement test scores? They so pervasively define today's standards for accountability that, in William Spady's words, "genuinely alternative perspectives are being ignored."[1]

My alternative perspective is that schools should strive for human, not just academic, excellence. If they are to produce enduring effects on their students, they must educate for the healthy growth of mind *and* character, integrated by a maturing self.

What prescriptions does such a value commitment suggest for holding schools accountable? We must view schools more systemically, not just as collections of academic disciplines. We must search for principles of assessment and standards for evaluating the quality of schools' learning environment. We must assess achievement of their school-wide goals, typically attributes of character. Standards for evaluating students' healthy growth are not arbitrary, whimsical, or relative. They are much more significant and demanding than evaluating only achievement test performance. Why? Because extensive research shows that academic grades and achievement test scores do not predict the most significant adult outcomes for many students. Measures of students' healthy growth or maturity do.[2]

Please don't misunderstand me. Of course, academic grades and test scores showing students' mastery of the three R's, other skills, and information are important. I monitor my grandsons' academic progress by them.

However, when conventional test scores are **the** primary index of schools' excellence, they sell schools dreadfully short. They measure neither the rich cognitive strengths that define academic excellence nor schools' potential maturing effects. What do you think reflective students spontaneously describe to be their schools' principal effects? They never cite what achievement tests measure: "I can now solve a quadratic equation and write a well-structured sentence"—as important as such skills may be. No, they write instead about just the strengths for which I hold my grandsons' schools accountable: intrinsic curiosity, joy in learning, self-educating attitudes and skills, imagination, compassion, empathy, social insight, collaborative skills, honesty, and a host of other strengths. These strengths describe students who grow in wholeness and so in health. If you don't believe me, scan now Appendix B to learn what reflective students spontaneously write about their growths in school. No current achievement or scholastic aptitude test measures them.

Are measures of academic achievement good for anything? Yes. Academic grades, ironically, predict *adult* perseverance, hard work, purposefulness, and self-discipline—just the character strengths needed to use one's intellectual talents and do well in school. The Japanese know that development of academic talents depends upon such strengths, which is why they value character more than level of innate ability.[3] That is also why some persons with undistinguished SAT scores and school grades rise to greatness.

Schools therefore must be held accountable not just for attaining academic excellence, when comprehensively measured, but also for contributing to the character maturation necessary to achieve academic excellence.

Background of the Book

What is the evidence for such out-of-favor statements? I have followed the legendary path of the 5th century B.C. Greek philosopher Diogenes who searched for years with his lamp to find a good man. I too have searched for years to understand the Greek ideal of arete or human excellence—the historic goal of liberal educators. What are men and women like who live fulfilled, authentic, whole-hearted, mature, self-actualized, healthy, and virtuous lives? And my lamps? Interviews, questionnaires, personality tests, even the Rorschach ink blots, judges knowledgeable about each person. I have followed college freshmen and their partners when in their early 30s through their 40s, and most recently into their late 50s.

My search speaks to the first of three questions every parent-educator must answer: What is the ideal of healthy growth for which to educate? What truths have I discovered? *Fulfilling Lives: Paths to Maturity and Success* and its subsequently revised and updated *Lives of Hope: Women's and Men's Paths to Success and Fulfillment* describe what I found. Schools' mission statements typically include some, though not all, of the attributes my research has identified that define human excellence or psychological maturity.

The second question? What are the attributes of schools that educate for the ideal of human excellence? *Schools of Hope: Developing the Mind and Character of Today's Youth* brought together the results of my diogeanen search and my concurrent 35 years of work with hundreds of elementary to graduate schools throughout America and abroad. It identifies from research the attributes and the standards that define a school of hope—a school likely to have enduring impacts on both mind and character.

Overview of the Contents

The more practical third question is the focus of this book: How can we hold a school accountable for fulfilling the standards of a school of hope and educating its students to become more psychologically mature? Chapter 1 describes the standards of a school of hope. Chapter 2 illustrates *how* one adventurous public school district, Michigan's Bloomfield Hills, sponsored an alternative school, called the Model

High School (MHS). Chapters 3 and 4 then describe *how* to hold a school accountable for creating a learning environment that encourages the healthy psychological growth or maturity of its students. They describe the principles of assessment that guided its evaluation and why it is a school of hope.

Chapters 5 through 8 describe the novel but simple and economical methods used to assess Model High School's teachers' and students' morale, its culture of values—the principal contributors to an organization's health and effectiveness. Chapters 9 through 13 illustrate how generic measures of morale and culture have illuminated organizational issues of larger significance: why urban minority schools have been so difficult to improve; how a university's culture contributed to its students' disruptive behavior; how a non-educational organization misunderstood its board and executive conflicts; what the inner world of students predisposed to drop out of school but who remain—psychic dropouts—tells us why today's schools fail so many; and what comparisons of private and public school students and teachers warn us about building more and more large schools and give us the information needed to make wise decisions about publicly financing private schools.

Chapters 14 to 16 focus specifically on how to assess character, especially ethical behavior, its educational roots, and the conditions necessary for moral education to be effective.

Finally, Chapter 17 asks you to hold yourself accountable for what the book may have taught you. If you wish to test what you have learned, why not rate what you believe are the more and less important proposals for improving our schools on pages 238-40. Identify the most important ones you might include in your State of the Union speech if you were president, or if you have less grandiose fantasies, are a school board member or superintendent. Write your answers on a separate piece of paper to be able to honestly compare your ratings when completing this book. Do not read my priorities and reasons for them, given in Appendices C and D, until you have read the book and then re-ranked your priorities. Test how you have changed your own values. I am playfully testing your educability and, incidentally, commitment to the principle of accountability.

I approach the end of my consulting career, whose lessons this book summarizes. So I am mindful of those who have urged me to pass on to others the diagnostic methods, attitudes, and skills I've learned with which to hold organizations accountable. Some readers may wish to acquire the knowledge and develop further the skills necessary to become more accomplished institutional diagnosticians. I have prepared a supplementary and technical self-teaching manual, titled *Assessing Schools of Hope: Methods, Norms, and Case Studies (ASH)*. It includes more detailed commentaries about some chapters and their tabular results, copies of the unpublished surveys this book describes, step-by-step directions about their administration, stable and provisional norms for many of them, and case studies of schools that illustrate typical problems for which the heads of schools and colleges have asked for help. The manual is designed to be used in conjunction with this book. Notations in the text refer you to ASH's corresponding commentaries or methods, i.e., "ASH 1:" refers to the manual's commentary # 1. The manual can be secured from Conrow Publishing House.

I must now warn you. The methods created to assess morale and culture can be distressingly revelatory. Because of the methods' sensitivity, I have never revealed the names of the schools and colleges with which I have worked. Please don't try to figure out the ones the book describes. Except for some of their insiders who may recognize their schools, you will be wrong. I have disguised all but four to be unrecognizable to outsiders.

I honor the four for what they have taught me, for their integrity and courage to permit me to name them, and for their heads' humaneness. Gary Doyle is Superintendent of Michigan's Bloomfield Hills' public school district; Cindy Boughner is the head of the district's pioneering Model High School, which Chapters 2 to 4 describe. Raymond Smyth is the former and Kenneth Dragseth the current superintendent of Minnesota's Edina school district. Chapters 15 and 16 rely upon their pioneering work to understand their students' ethical behavior and identify the principal institutional contributors to moral education. Finally, I honor Jon O'Brien, former, and Tad Roach, current head of Delaware's St. Andrew's School, and Bert Okma, founder and principal of Michigan's International Academy. These two schools are described in *Assessing Schools of Hope (ASH)* and used to test your diagnostic and evaluative skills.

Acknowledgments

I have waited decades to acknowledge my indebtedness and appreciation to the anonymous thousands who have taught me. The list of the names I now gratefully recall, and the one's I wish I could, would be much too long to mention. The book has been materially improved by the critiques of those who represent the readers for whom I wrote the book: superintendents of public schools—Gary Doyle of Michigan's Bloomfield Hills; school administrators—Anne Janson, former principal of Pennsylvania's Radnor High School; and Jan Jacobi, former head of Missouri's Mary Institute-Country Day's elementary and now head of its middle school; adventurous public school heads creating variants of charter schools—Cindy Boughner, Director of Bloomfield Hills' Model High School; national leaders deeply knowledgeable about public and independent schools—Ron Brandt, former editor of ASCD's *Educational Leadership* and Steve Clem, Executive Director, Association of Independent Schools in New England; advanced education graduate students—Patricia Harned of the University of Pittsburgh; teachers interested in studying their schools—Steve Siwinski, Head of Maryland's Gilman School's Science Department; teachers and counselors of other countries—Michael Murray, Mexico City's American School. Their searching and detailed critiques have been most helpful.

I am also grateful to Holley Webster, Eva V. Beehler, and John D. Gummere. Each worked under a severely tight publication schedule to produce this book without compromising a commitment to excellence. The book's remaining faults are solely mine.

I affectionately dedicate the book to David Mallery, Director of Professional Development of the National Association of Independent Schools, and to the memory of Emily Kingham. He opened many of the school-doors that enabled me to secure the information which this book reports. Emily was my secretary for more than 30 years. She died of breast cancer shortly after entering into our computers the last of more than 5,000,000 numbers from more than 14,000 students and 4,000 teachers and after reading this dedication. Her devotion and integrity were exemplary, her loyalty and commitment irreplaceable.

223 Buck Lane,
Haverford, PA 19041   Douglas H. Heath

Legend

(Selected Key School Examples)

Adelphi — Suburban independent upper school: pure academic culture whose mission was to educate for human excellence but whose senior class collectively cheated on its exams

Appalachia — Rural liberal arts college: fraternities partying entering freshmen frustrating their faculty worried about its disappearing best students

Belmont — Rural-small town consolidated public high school: excellent reputation but persistent psychic dropout problem for which faculty did not wish to assume responsibility

Bloomfield Hills — Suburban public school district, Bloomfield Hills, Michigan: visionary leadership sympathetic to alternative charter-type schools

Broward — Suburban independent K-12 girl's school: faculty passively protesting an authoritarian head's efforts to make a strong academic school even stronger

Countryside — Urban Montessori independent elementary-middle school: a loving faculty of high morale so idealizing its students that it did not recognize painful quality of students' peer relationships

Edina — Suburban public school district, Edina, Minnesota: at parents' request initiated development of survey to assess its students' ethical behavior

Marathon — Suburban independent elementary school: board meeting to fire new head who had seemingly created low faculty morale by disrupting the old guards' cozy relationships

Marlboro — Suburban independent boy's K-12 day school: requiring tackle football to make men of its boys who were resisting

Model (MHS) — Bloomfield Hills, Michigan's alternative public high school: a charter-type self-renewing school of hope

Neufield — Suburban lighthouse public high school: principal unable to lead a contentious seditious faculty clique that sabotaged school's assessment

Parkworth — Suburban independent Parkway and Worth upper schools: combined to provide large enough groups to compare to Belmont's students to determine generic meaning of a psychic dropout

Prairie — Private coed college: a despairing, paralyzed, and dying faculty who found hope in its collective anger about being confronted with its despair

Reagan — Suburban public high school: a model of academic excellence whose contented faculty's students paid some psychic prices

Rosemont — Suburban public middle school: faculty with high morale whose teacher-centered school was rejected by its students

Sandia — Urban Hispanic and Afro-American public high school: a school of despair courageously exploring itself, seeking hope

Washington — Urban minority public junior-high school: "We are losers."

Wentworth — Urban white and Afro-American public high school: faculty deeply frustrated by its school's lack of identity and whose black and white students verged on resegregation

SECTION I

Self-Renewing Schools

Chapter 1

————•◦•————

"HEALTHY, GROWTH-PRODUCING CULTURES" [1]

". . . organizations are more than technical systems. Apart from anything else, they are also social systems. They are about people and about the way people behave and interact with each other in groups. They are about the attitudes, the aspirations and the motivation of people in work situations." [2]

W. Edwards Deming's well-known philosophy of Total Quality Management (TQM) [3] prodded business leaders to think of their offices and factories primarily as social not technical systems. Customer satisfaction with the quality of the products that met their needs is the touchstone to success; workers should be consulted about how to improve quality; attention to workers' morale is indispensable to achieve quality; poor quality is due more to managerial inadequacies and organizational rigidities than to workers' sloth; everyone—even secretaries and janitors—should be held accountable for achieving their organization's goals; continuous objective monitoring of the processes producing a quality, not just a completed, product is essential.

Deming insisted that a firm's social organization is the major contributor to quality. Some economists believe similarly. Social capital contributes to economic well-being. Social capital refers to a community's "intricate web of relationships, norms of behavior, values, [and] obligations. . . .Within groups and regions, its presence may boost productivity and income, while its absence may hinder growth." [4]

American businesses, like its General Motors, ignored these principles of social organization or capital. Japanese ones, like its Toyotos, did not.

The General Motors lost market share. The Toyotos increased theirs. The Japanese attribute their world-class products to Deming's principles.

Japan's economic success stimulated educators to ask if TQM's principles were as generic as Deming insisted. If so, then schools' more important resources are not their physical (for example, computers and classrooms) and human ones (for example, faculty-student ratios and SAT averages). They are their social system's "relationships, norms of behavior, [and] values" which decisively contribute to quality.[5]

TQM has not proved to be "the magic bullet" for which some educators and legislators wistfully search.[6] Students are more than customers, schools more than factories. But its emphasis on hard-to-measure, subjective, organizational attributes offers the more humane, hopeful, and "genuinely alternative perspective" about accountability that Spady has called for.

Schools should be "healthy, growth-producing cultures" for everyone who works and learns in them. This succinct prescription, paraphrased from *The Self-Renewing School,* is what its authors (Bruce Joyce, James Wolf, and Emily Calhoun) distilled from hundreds of studies about schools' curricula, teaching strategies, and standards. Focusing on schools' "healthy growth-producing cultures" reflects Deming's views that their relationships and values or culture affect the quality of their curricular and classroom outcomes.

So how shall we go about discovering what a school's "intricate web of relationships, norms of behavior, values and obligations" is? How can we learn what "healthy growth" means? John Dewey's advice about how to learn what liberal education means also applies about how to learn what an effective social system and healthy growth mean. He told us, "the only way which does not lead us into the clouds . . . is discovery of what actually takes place when education really occurs."[7] Avoid committees and authorities that speculate about what such systems are and how students grow healthily. Instead, go into schools to discover what actually happens to students being educated and why.

I heeded Dewey's advice. I listened to and studied in depth how high school and college students changed while being educated and identified their schools' attributes that contributed to their changes.[8]

Schools of Hope summarizes, and this chapter illustrates, the eight core attributes of schools that my and others' research suggested produce enduring effects on their members.[9] They rephrase and make more pointed Deming's, Joyce's and other commentators' criteria defining an effective school.[10] Abstract terms like "system" or "self-renewing schools" are slippery, even vacuous, ideas to some. Medical researchers have wrestled with similarly elusive terms like "health" and "well-being." What can we learn from them about *how* to begin to understand such ideas in a way that prefigures how to measure them? Historically, researchers began to define health, especially mental health, by what it was *not*.

I begin to understand schools as "systems" by examining instances of their breakdown. I focus on what is systemically dysfunctional for students and teachers for whom I have reliable normative information. I do not have comparable norms from administrators, staff,and boards, as TQM proponents would have hoped.

Attributes of a School of Hope

1. *A school of hope has a <u>distinctive vision</u> of its liberally-educating goals that is widely shared by all members of the school and parents.*

TQM advocates speak of a focussed philosophy or objective, the fulfillment of which increases "the satisfaction of all those concerned with the organization."[11] I have long maintained that an effective school is like a Catholic monastery. Everyone is committed to similar core values and cannot escape them wherever they are, whether in its kitchen, library, or cloisters.

St. Ignatius College illustrates how a faculty divided about its core values became mired in a fruitless and increasingly bitter debate. Its president called to say that his faculty's morale was low because of arguments between its religious and secular faculty. He felt the acrimony was more intense than the argument's focus merited. The secular scientific and some social science faculty wanted to require students to work with computers. Highly-structured curricular requirements permitted no time for such work, so they had proposed that a two-semester prescribed course in theology and morals be reduced to one semester. The priests were incensed. The President asked, "Were other reasons fueling the growing split? How does one heal such divisions?"

Study of the faculty's morale and the college's culture revealed that morale was not as low as everyone believed. Moreover, many of the secular faculty were not emotionally committed to the college's theology but were to its ethical expectations. On the other hand, the religious faculty believed students' religious commitment and morals would suffer if the curricular requirement were reduced.

The President's intuition was correct. Less available to awareness and resolution were the different emotional meanings of a vocation. The religious felt that their core identity, their calling as Catholic priests to serve God, was being attacked and denigrated. The secular faculty, committed to its vocation as seekers of truth, could not empathize with colleagues who put devotion to God above what the former believed should be the primary value of a teacher. The divisive issue was not the computer course requirement. The faculty quickly resolved it once the underlying source of the argument's intensity was recognized. The faculty agreed about the college's moral vision. It remained uneasily divided about its theological mission.

2. *A school of hope has adults who are as committed to the maturation of its students' character and selves as to their minds.*

Schools should be person-centered, not merely mind-centered. Schools of hope do not ignore or dismiss the maturation of students' interpersonal relationships and values; they seek to encourage the integration of character and mind by assisting students to get command of themselves. TQM advocates worker empowerment; educators such as Joyce, Whitehead, Dewey, and Montessori agree.

Adelphi, a nationally prestigious private high school, illustrates a faculty unanimously committed to mind's but not character's maturation. The school's head asked me to discover what its faculty, students, board, and parents really thought about Adelphi. A preceding head had asked for a similar study a decade earlier. An extraordinary 90 to 100% of every constituency now agreed about 13 values defining the school's culture. It was academic, hard-working, demanding, and intellectually rigorous among other academic attributes. I know of no other school that has such a distinctively "pure" academic culture which everyone is satisfied with and rightly proud of.

However, during the previous year the school had been seared by wide-spread academic cheating among its seniors. Not one student had notified administrators or teachers about the cheating. Why does

Adelphi not join my select list of schools of hope? Not because of the cheating episode itself. Such adolescent frailties can occur even in exemplary schools. No, Adelphi was divided about its primary mission. It publicly proclaimed it was devoted to both academic and character excellence. However, the apparently unmonitored process of becoming an intellectual power-house overshadowed its goal to encourage character excellence. Its students failed to learn for what purposes their academic power should be used. The restudy showed that many of the newer faculty were not emotionally committed to its goal of character maturation.

3. *The leader of a school of hope must above all else be the steward and articulator of the school's vision.*

Leadership is not synonymous with administration. Ronald Reagan was considered by many to be a persuasive leader who marshaled widespread support for his vision, but most knowledgeable observers believed he was a poor administrator. On the other hand, an effective administrator or manager may be a poor leader. Too often, administrators' immediate tasks usurp their leaderships' primary role. Jimmy Carter was considered to be a detailed hands-on administrator but a failed leader. According to Deming, administrative style more often than not is the cause of leadership and organizational failure. Today, workers, such as teachers, are too often unjustly blamed for poor quality or their organizations' failures. Most failures, Deming claims, result, more often than not, from top-down authoritarian or too laissez faire decision-making. System rigidities rather than workers' laziness or incompetence also contribute to poor quality.[12]

Neufield, one state's "lighthouse" public school district, shows us the disruptive effects that can occur when administrators are not leaders.

After I had agreed to the superintendent's request to assess the districts' seven schools I received a telephone call from an anonymous high school teacher, vaguely warning me that her faculty was in turmoil. Preoccupied by the details of the district's study, I failed to heed her advice. I incautiously accepted the high school faculty's rated morale as reliable. It had the highest morale of any public high school faculty I have ever assessed. Its morale was also higher than that of the district's elementary and middle school teachers, who usually are more satisfied with their schools and vocations.

I subsequently learned in a raucous meeting with the high school faculty that I had been sand-bagged. A sizable group of aggressively rebellious members, led by several articulate, charismatic social science teachers, had cowed other members. They had also refused to complete the surveys. So I inaccurately reported to the district's full faculty that its high school faculty scored higher in satisfaction than every other public high school faculty that I had studied. The malcontents used my favorable interpretation to attack publicly, with great intensity, the credibility of the entire study which they opposed.

At no time did the principal exercise leadership. He neither publicly reaffirmed the school's vision, which the study sought to evaluate, nor prepared for or forthrightly conducted the meeting to maintain civility. He too had been cowed. Excerpts of his letter to me said the "faculty is stubborn . . . unable to work with each other . . . resistant to change."

Perhaps shamed by their incivility or now exorcised by the cathartic discharge of their frustration and anger about their impotent principal, the seditious faculty has unexpectedly remained silent since.

For Deming, leaders who tolerate and fail to deal with contentiousness, divisiveness, competitiveness, and intimidation among their workers destroy their organization's effectiveness.[13]

4. *A school of hope has teachers who empathically understand the interpersonal world of their students as their students perceive it.*

We must understand our students from the inside-out if we are to serve them effectively. We must listen, listen, and listen, though not always assent. We must master the arts of listening, even when words are unspoken, as with children or because they may hurt too much if expressed. A core TQM principle is to seek out and genuinely listen to what those for whom one is responsible really believe.

Countryside, one of our country's oldest and most prestigious Montessori schools, was a challenge to understand. Its faculty viewed its students very differently than its students viewed each other. Its principal had heard me lecture. She was intrigued by how children could be "heard" in ways to secure quantitative indices of their inner lives and relationships. She invited me to study her fifth, sixth, and seventh graders and then visit her school to speak to her teachers and parents. I accepted immediately. After all, Maria Monstessori was the first TQM educator! She observed how children grew when teaching themselves. She created a learning environment that permitted disciplined observations of a student's continuing growth. Montessori teachers are rigorously trained to observe, listen, and then follow a child's lead about the learning opportunities most appropriate for the child. Deming similarly recommends that we learn how to make disciplined observations but objectify them using quantitative indices when possible, as materials now available make possible for children as young as 11 or 12.

One of Countryside's principal results perplexed and humbled me. It taught me how much more I had to learn about interpreting the congruence of teachers' and students' perceptions. Countryside's teachers viewed their students radically differently than their students viewed their peers. The discrepancies were too great to be believable—especially for Montessori teachers. With unexampled agreement, the teachers believed that their children had already achieved the highest stages of perfection. For example, 96% of the faculty believed that their typical student was enthusiastic, capable, cooperative, creative, curious, energetic, honest and so on. Only 52% of the fifth and sixth graders believed that their peers were enthusiastic, 48% were creative, or 41% were curious.

Since love does blind, I wondered if the teachers' love for their children blinded them to how their children actually behaved. A most implausible idea, but how to explain why their consensual idyllic view far outshone the normative view of other teachers of pre-pubertal children? The teachers also wondered if they were living in "la-la" land, as one teacher impulsively uttered, after learning the survey's results.

Analysis of the students' view of their peers and then of the students' and their teachers' morale provided a hunch. The children's' beliefs about their peers were similar to my elementary school norms. Their independently measured level of satisfaction about the school was also similar to the average of my elementary student norms. On the other hand, the faculty's morale stretched far beyond similar teachers' normative range. Did the faculty have such a strong calling to a Montessorian view of their students that they identified their typical student as an exemplar of Montessorian values? Had their commitment become an ideology that shaped their view of reality?

5. *Adults and students in a school of hope have alive relationships that are growth-inducing for both—trusting, caring, adventurous, and intellectually exciting.*

A social system is a matrix of relationships. Members of self-renewing schools seek to help others grow.[14] I have asked teachers to identify from a list of 150 traits those of their colleagues that contribute most to their own healthy growth. Traits like trusting, caring, adventurous, and intellectually exciting usually head their lists.[15]

Nation-wide, neither the majority of teachers nor of students believe that their peers possess most of these traits. What sustained meaningful school renewal will occur when so few teachers believe their peers are, for example, adventurous (29%), intellectually exciting (33%), trusting (35%) though caring (86%)? Or when so few public high school students believe that their peers are adventurous (47%), intellectually exciting (17%), trusting (25%), and caring (39%)?

Faculty and students have the potential to demonstrate such strengths. Educators just have not created the culture and practices that encourage such traits to emerge. Developing a self-renewing culture must begin by nurturing such potentials. Deming would agree. He estimated that about 90% of the causes of poor quality were due to manager-generated systemic rules and practices—not to worker commission. He said TQM had to begin by reforming an organization's social system to empower workers' self-education and cooperative relationships. Genuine collaboration requires trust. I've described elsewhere how schools could begin to generate more trust among their members.[16]

6. *Schools of hope have teachers and students for whom teaching and learning are a calling, rather than a job, and whose morale about their work is high.*

A telling sign of a school of hope is a high level of satisfaction among all of its members in their school and their work. Enid Brown, a TQM consultant, agrees. A school should not focus on measuring its students' mastery of bits of information but on making learning a satisfying and joyful process.[17]

Rosemont is a junior high school that feeds its students into a large traditional and conservative academic high school. It illustrates that a great discrepancy between the morale of a school's different constituencies is a red flag. The superintendent initiated a study of the district's schools. Because the high school faculty envied the reputedly high morale of one of the junior high school faculties, he wanted to know why. Rosemont's principal was not keen to reveal her "secret"; she failed to secure information about the faculty's view of the school's culture. Ordinarily, people who have high morale describe their organizations very positively. Failure to secure the faculty's view of her school meant that I could not confirm the faculty's exceptionally high morale or understand its sources directly.

Two results, however, told me something was amiss in Rosemont. The morale of its students told a different story. Like the morale of Countryside's students, theirs barely approached the average score of their peers nationally. Furthermore, their satisfaction with 30 different attributes of their school and their role as students did not differ statistically from the comparable morale scores of the district's high school students. I therefore felt confident that Rosemont's students' results were trustworthy.

The second fact was that Rosemont's faculty was very disenchanted with its students. How could a faculty with such high morale be so turned off by its students? Though Countryside's and Rosemont's discrepancies were similar they obviously had radically different meanings. The middle schoolers' pattern of satisfactions matched that of the high school students. Compared to the high school students' view of their teachers, Rosemont's viewed their teachers more negatively. Two-thirds reported that their teachers bored them. They believed that their teachers were less helpful and responsible but more moody and impatient. No students believed that their teachers were curious or giving; no more than 17% believed that they were energetic, joyful, loving, or sympathetic. Aren't these attributes that teachers need to work effectively, especially with pubertal children? Tentative hypothesis: The middle school was teacher-, not student-centered. Emotionally called to be more prestigious high school teachers, they taught as if they were, ignoring the special needs of pubertal children.

One lesson Rosemont teaches us is that the meaning of a test score depends upon the context of other different measures. Survey or test results should always be confirmed by other types of measures and be interpreted contextually for dependability and interpretive consistency. Chapter 6 returns to probe more deeply for the sources of what I now call the Rosemont paradox: unusually high faculty and much lower student morale and high faculty discontent with its students.

7. *Teachers and students in a school of hope emotionally own not only its goals but also the means of implementing them within the school and the classroom.*

Surely the potential for emotional ownership must be present if the ideas of Deming, Joyce, Schlecty, and other advocates of a more holistic or systemic understanding of schools are to "take."[18] Each assumes that teachers and students are emotionally committed to continued growth, self-education, self-renewal, and school improvement. A Deming would ask for objective evidence about faculty and student commitments.

Of the numerous schools and colleges for which I now have such evidence, only six had teachers committed to developing, for example, self-educating students, which is a widely shared goal by schools. Four of them were Montessori, including Countryside. The harsh fact is that most teachers want and so teach their students to need them—not to create a school and classroom culture that empowers their own and draws out their students' self-renewing potentials.

Reagan high school shows us that academic excellence, when it includes empowering students to enjoy learning and become self-educating, does not occur when faculty and students are not committed to such a goal. Reagan is nationally known as one of the country's more affluent and prestigious suburban high schools. Highly-educated professional, business, and artistic parents move to the area because of the school's exemplary academic reputation. Its teachers have numerous advanced degrees, are among the highest paid in the country, and rate themselves to be more competent teachers than faculty do of every other of the schools I have studied. All of its students graduate, receive numerous awards, and many go on to our country's most academically demanding colleges. So not surprisingly 94% of its students and 92% of its teachers identify "academic" as the high school's most salient value. Chapter 15 examines the consequences of such academic excellence for the school's moral climate and the healthy development of its students.

Before examining how emotionally committed Reagan's students and faculty are to their continuing self-education and self-renewal, we must ask what are the traits of such persons? Do they describe Reagan's students and faculty? Table 1-1 lists some of the principal indices of a lifelong learner and compares the students' and faculty's views of the typical student, students' own self-concepts and view of the faculty as self-renewing people.

Table 1-1 Reagan's High School Students' and Faculty's Views of Their Typical Student, Students' Self-Concepts and Faculty as Lifelong Learners

Attribute	% Students' View Peers	% Faculty View Student	% Students' Self-Concept	% Students' View Faculty
Curious	33	16	55	15
Deep interests	36	11	49	21
Self-confident	38	21	50	25
Self-disciplined	20	11	44	26
Self-educating	18	5	34	26
Self-motivating	31	5	49	26
Self-reliant	22	11	41	18

Clearly, Reagan's students and faculty do not believe that an academically excellent school necessarily creates self-educating students or faculty. Why don't more students believe their faculty are curious, self-motivated, and self-educating people? Deming would answer that the system's expectations, values, patterns, and rigidities, more than just individual faculty malaise and contentment, are the causes. Forty-three minute periods, assigned procrustean texts, and state curricular requirements, for example, can destroy curiosity. The greatest resistance to continued growth occurs in some of our most academically accomplished schools. One Reagan teacher's attitude is not atypical for such schools. "We are teaching at the best high school in the country. We have no dropout problem. Students achieve at high levels and get into top colleges. Why do we need to change?" He told me that even after the faculty had learned that only 18% of its highly capable students believed the faculty was intellectually excit-ing and only 20% that it was excellent. Was there not some room left

for faculty growth—at least in the students' view? Humans are not
Japanese cars. Attaining human rather than technological excellence
may be only for saints, but how many of us strive throughout our
lives to approach that exalted state?

More importantly, does Reagan increase its students' desire and
will to become self-renewing persons? Do they value becoming self-
educating and self-motivating people? If they don't, then how can
we expect mandates to develop such people be implemented? The
results are clear. Less than a majority of Reagan's students are
committed to becoming self-educating themselves as well as also
expecting their peers and faculty to become so. You may find these
results distressing, if not unbelievable, and singular. But they are more
typical than atypical of contemporary students and faculty. They reflect what the Department of Education's own studies have shown:
Students (and many faculty too) have lost a sense of the ideal for
themselves[19] and for others, or I would add, of character perfection
for themselves and others. What grabs emotional commitment is an
achievement test score, not the perfection of character which the attributes of self-renewing persons describe.

8. *Schools of hope are sustained by adults and students who value
risking together to discover more effective ways to achieve their
goals, who are willing to hold themselves accountable for their
success and failure, and who reflect about why their school and
classroom climates and methods have not been as effective as they
had hoped.*

A five- or seven-yearly self-study just won't ensure quality.
TQM advocates believe continuous reflective monitoring of what one
is doing is necessary to maintain and improve quality. Deming taught
Japanese managers to encourage their workers to stop their assembly
lines to correct a mistake when they first noticed it. I relied on continuous student reflections about how well our course was proceeding
and altered it as we proceeded.

The principal of a combined junior and high school named Washington cornered me, after a workshop, to ask what she could do to turn
her school around. Washington has more than 1,000 students, 75% of
whom are minority students—predominantly Afro-American. It is
located in one of the poorest sections of a large city. Set in the middle of

a large forlorn and cluttered wasteland, the 80-year-old school is the neighborhood center of drug dealers who pressure its seventh and eighth grade students to run drugs for them. Surprisingly no iron fence circled the area. Trash, discarded needles, even condoms, littered the schoolyard. Windows are barred in its early 1900 brick walls. Guards patrol the school's corridors and are posted at every corner where they can be seen by another guard. Each has a walkie-talkie radio to coordinate their supervision. At her urging, some faculty agreed to patrol the halls and bathrooms between bells. Bathroom stalls had no doors; the presence of toilet paper was unpredictable; a few staff brought rolls for the bathrooms they supervised; unprintable graffiti enlivened the walls. The janitors apparently were on vacation the days of my visit.

Washington has been publicly identified to be one of the state's academically "worst" schools. It had been ordered by the state's education department to raise its students' test scores. I ploughed through the extensive test score data sent me before my visit. They revealed considerable unrealized potential.

The principal had eagerly—"desperately" is probably more accurate—accepted my suggestion to study and then visit the school to share the study's results with the faculty. She planned to release the students the last period for the faculty to learn about their and their students' morale. After a short break, I was to then present the students' views of the school for discussion about their implications.

Throughout the day I asked teachers and students to tell me the first words that came to mind when I said "Washington." Most— even seventh graders—spontaneously answered with words like "loser" and "worst." To prove his point, one student said their teams could never win a game. An advertised meeting to talk about the results with parents attracted only a husband and wife much to the principal's embarrassment.

Her enthusiasm had attracted, however, a number of dedicated teachers who had felt called to work at Washington. Their morale brought the collective faculty's morale to the average of suburban public high school teachers.

At the general faculty meeting, more than a few teachers angrily disputed that their morale was the same as privileged suburban public school teachers. "Inconceivable," they insisted. The collective faculty image as losers, reinforced by the state's label of "worst,"

imposed mandates, and failure to provide toilet paper defended them
from any suggestion that they had the potential to improve.

I was not prepared for the next illuminating event, though I should
have been from my work with other faculties working under time-
constrained contracts. After a break only **ten** of the more than 70
faculty returned to learn about their students' views of them, the
school, and their peers. The principal and her small group felt de-
feated. She later confessed that the faculty's behavior confirmed a
hunch that she had not wanted to face, the reality of the real issue
with which she had to cope. Most of her faculty viewed their work as
a job, not a calling.

The next year a city-wide shuffle of personnel resulted in her transfer to head a middle school; her team of supporters was dispersed.
Washington's children attended the same school.

I was chastened by the realities of the meaning of work as a
job. Becoming aware of the potentiality of children for growth and
of one's school for creating a growth-producing culture can be too
threatening to bear. Deming's philosophy meets its ultimate test in
our large impersonal schools. How can faculty who collectively believe that they are losers and whose leaders have no control over
scarce resources realistically lift themselves and their students out of
despair into hope?

What sources sustain hope for our schools? Accumulating research
identifies the attributes of schools and colleges that do make a difference in their students' lives: thousands and thousands of dedicated
and caring teachers called to work with our youth; increased regula-
tory flexibility to encourage the development of small adventurous
charter schools which have the opportunity (if they realize it) to create alternative ways for students to grow healthily; the emergence of
schools of hope that model such alternative ways and which alert us
to both the potential pitfalls as well as rewards along the way. Like
Deming, I believe that schools can achieve high standards of excellence appropriate for the 21st century's demands. The next chapter
describes how one public school district thoughtfully created a school
of hope, a self-renewing school that empowered many of its students
to become their own self-teachers. Its reflective, on-going monitoring of itself illustrates how humanizing accountability measures can
prefigure steps to improve a school.

SECTION II

---·◆·---

Creating and Assessing
A School of Hope

Chapter 2

———••••———

CREATING MODEL HIGH SCHOOL:
A CASE STUDY

Schools of hope take many forms. Eight generic attributes are, however, their common signature. Such schools may be more numerous
than we know; the restless 60s and 70s spawned numerous alternative schools. How many survived I don't know; the ones I knew well
died. Why? Their adventurous and courageous—some might say "ro-
mantic and foolhardy"—leaders did not have the discipline to build
their schools on the core attributes that we have since learned make
an effective school.

Established schools must be even more adventurous and courageous to examine themselves honestly, non-defensively, and then
actually take sustained steps to renew themselves. Since the publication of *A Nation at Risk,* we have discovered just how daunting a task
it is to change a school's entrenched culture—its patterns of relationships, attitudes, aspirations, and motivations. Especially the cultures
of high schools. Even more so of colleges.

It is much easier to begin afresh, especially with younger children.
It is riskier to begin with adolescents who are seeking their own paths.
The recent ground swell of small charter schools is potentially hopeful; they fulfill calls for more publicly-supported alternative schools.
They may increase the number of schools of hope. Why be hopeful
given that so many past efforts failed? For two reasons. Today's cre-
ators can now build on the past two decades of research about the
attributes of effective schools. They also can learn from the reflections and advice of faculties that have successfully created schools
of hope, like the one this chapter describes.

School founders must ask themselves whether they really understand and emotionally own a school of hopes' generic eight attributes. Do they have the patience and discipline to devote the time and effort to read the research, visit pioneering schools, and consult with those experienced with the problems they will face? Do they have the courage to face honestly why they begin to stumble? Do they have the humility to listen to others—especially their students—and the commitment to persist and persist? Have they initiated the self-reflective processes necessary to improve themselves continuously? The next chapter describes how they can assess whether or not they have begun to create the healthy growth-producing culture necessary to become a school of hope.

Or like their forebearers, the alternative schools of the 1970s and 80s, will most new schools just plunge in, ignoring what the history of previous pioneers could teach them? Believing that they really know how to build Dorothy's yellow brick road to education's Oz will they still just die along the way? Or, to change the metaphor, will the remaining few imperceptibly detour back into the educational establishment's eager and safer but suffocating arms from which they had so bravely set forth?

Bloomfield Hills' Model High School

This chapter describes a small experimental public high school creating itself. The next two chapters illustrate how it sought to hold itself accountable. Bloomfield Hills' Model High School (MHS) teaches us that there are "genuinely alternative perspectives" about how to educate today's students to enjoy learning and develop a calling to be a self-educating student. It also teaches us how to understand healthy growth and hold a school to the standards of a school of hope.

Michigan's Bloomfield Hills' administration and board are an inspiring example of adventurous and courageous public school leaders willing to start afresh with high school students. Gary Doyle, then Deputy but now Superintendent of its nationally honored schools, believed that the district needed to provide more educational choices for its two high schools' students. He proposed an experimental school empowered to decide its own program, administrative and teaching procedures, budget allocations, and curriculum. The school was even invited to try programs that might fail. The Board agreed. It also agreed to stay the course for the school's first five years, at which time it would reevaluate the scope of its support.

In 1988 three youthful adventurous Bloomfield Hills' teachers began their search for innovative ideas to create a new school. Their year-long search took them to Sizer's Coalition of Essential Schools, Alverno College's competency-based curriculum, and TQM's principles, among other ideas. By the fall of 1990 they had created their vision; planned how to realize it; applied for and received a RJR Nabisco Foundation Next Century Schools' grant; found and renovated six empty rooms in a former elementary school; advertised their school; recruited 10 full and part-time faculty, one counselor, and 78 students; established an up-to-date computer laboratory; and opened with high hopes—only to face chaos, uncertainty, and two quite skeptical district high school faculties.

I rely throughout the chapter on the discerning, final Next Century Schools report written by Cindy Boughner, the current head of MHS. A former ceramics teacher, she is the school's perceptive educational philosopher and eloquent spokesperson for Model's faculty. She shared the administrative leadership in the school's early years with Shannon Flumerfelt.

The Next Century Schools grant required a detailed statistical assessment of the school's effects, which I was asked to make, since for several years I had served as a consultant to the district. An earlier study of the two high schools' students and faculty provided baseline information to which to compare MHS's climate and students.

MHS's Primary Goal

What was the faculty's vision and how did it go about achieving it? Very simply, MHS sought to engage its students in their growth by assuming "personal responsibility for their own education." Certainly not a unique goal. Schools world-wide now recognize they must more self-consciously assist their students to acquire the attitudes, motives, and skills to be lifelong learners. What is rare is Model's specification of the generic skills and attitudes required, persistent efforts to create a unique structure to ensure their development, and participation in an assessment specifically targeted for their acquisition.

Competency Outcomes

Drawing on Alverno's pioneering competency goals,[1] the MHS faculty agreed that a self-educating person needed to know how to

- inquire about and investigate issues,
- solve problems and make decisions,
- communicate effectively in different modes, such as written, oral, technological, and aesthetic,
- relate to others by developing skills such as listening, understanding opposing viewpoints, and acting in a socially responsible way in group and community activities,
- act with courage, integrity, and empathy as well as live a physically and emotionally healthy life, and finally,
- develop what the faculty labeled aesthetic skills, a catchword for attributes of quality: reflectiveness, personal standards of excellence, intrinsic motivation, and appreciation of the arts.

Such a rich variety of imposing outcomes confused both the students and me. Students did not know what the faculty's abstract terms meant. I did not know the faculty's intent in enough detail to develop objective means to measure them. When pushed even the faculty itself did not know what the terms meant. So in 1991, the faculty began the laborious task of explaining to itself and others what its competencies meant.

Compelled to bring their abstract goals down to earth, in the words of Boughner, "produced high anxiety, initial confusion, engagement in hard work, a need to pull work together to get closure on a period of study, an understanding of what it means to account for one's work."

In a later section of her report, she expands on the personal costs of their intense labor which

> created mountains of difficult work, many attempts to find good systems to manage these processes [for assessing the competencies], a decrease in efficiency, a decrease in our free time outside of school, lost hours of sleep, increased skill at counseling anxious students, and lots of headaches (literally). We learned that we needed to provide students with examples of exemplary performance so that they had a general notion of what to shoot for.

The faculty's labor produced consensual agreement about their outcomes. They defined each competence by seven to eleven indices, a total of 47 indices—a prohibitive number for which to educate and a nightmare to track and assess. For example, one index of Inquiry was "Student makes use of, and can describe the reasons for use of the proper conventions of formal research writing and formal research presentation." For the elusive Aesthetic competence, the sixth index was "Student can articulate personal criteria for excellence and demonstrate, in the development of his or her work, how he or she has attempted to reach these standards."

Boughner subsequently reflected that "the best thing we did was create a highly complex learning environment. The complexity laid out an array of possibilities so that people could attach to the aspects of the overall vision what they most needed at any given moment in time."[2] A truly Montessorian understanding of how a responsive learning environment could facilitate a student's healthy growth.

I was impressed by how thoughtfully the weary and rightfully proud faculty had worked to develop its own standards of excellence. I did not have the heart (courage?) to hint at, even if only gently, the next practicable steps necessary to generate assessable measures. They needed to prioritize their competencies and indices. They then needed to specify them further by examples that could prefigure the instructional strategies likely to encourage their attainment.

The faculty discovered that the process of collaboratively clarifying its outcomes contributed to their own growth as professionals. It produced

> a marked increase in creative energy, sense of responsibility, sense of accomplishment, and increased self-esteem and ability to self-assess. . . .Despite the apparent negatives, none of us would retreat from [our] commitment because it was simply worth it in terms of the positive effects it had on student growth. It turned assessment from an often punitive power play and threat into a genuine occasion for growth. The rewards from this facet of the work have been rich.

TQM is at its heart a philosophical attitude, not just about collaborative quality circles, numerical ratings, or statistical evaluations, (which the faculty abandoned anyway after the Nabisco grant expired!). Boughner captured TQM's essence this way:

> We had to become a self-assessing organization, willing to hold anything we did up to examination and questioning. Faculty had to become self-disclosing about our personal and group assessment and decision-making processes and, in our assessment interactions with students, we had to learn to be both deeply honest and supportive. When possible, we asked ourselves to do what we expected of students.

This philosophical attitude could only be held and lived by professionals profoundly called to help their students become their own teachers, even if at the expense of their own egos. So with groans but without paralyzing complaints teachers met daily, frequently after school and during vacations, to reflectively assess what was and was not working for each student. They planned how to consistently implement their vision. They pursued every practicable way to assess the quality of their and their students' work for which they and their students held themselves accountable. Their self-conscious attention to the educational process deepened their awareness of how much growth requires risk. They also developed a clearer understanding of how a school's structure and culture encourages growth. As one teacher reflected about their growth,

> . . . more than anything, we've learned the importance of listening to and being open enough to really hear students. That's what they need at this stage in their lives—to be heard, recognized, and respected. When they feel they have been heard, then they open up enough to begin hearing what we have to say.

Assumptions about Ways to Achieve Model's Goals

The creation of a pioneering school inevitably draws upon values and assumptions frequently not explicitly recognized and articulated by their innovators. Not the MHS faculty. It early and self-consciously clarified its values and assumptions about what a healthy learning environment should be like.

1. Abandon the traditional role of the teacher as an authority to become a facilitator, mentor, co-learner, learning generalist, and catalyst to spur growth.
   The faculty's changed role freed them to be

   > more human, real, and present with students. We all learned how to listen much better and how to offer meaningful support to students. The overall effect was a wonderful increase in our own rates of learning and humanistic growth . . . we learned how to collaborate, we became much more honest with ourselves and others both inside and outside of MHS . . . our sense of ourselves as professionals skyrocketed.

2. Risking growth requires safety and trust
   Studies of the district's two high schools and the faculty's own experience convinced them that Model had to be a safe place. Students and faculty had to believe that others would support their own efforts to take risks. The district had installed a ropes course designed by Project Adventure, Inc. which provided individual and group-trust building experiences. Faculty and new students participated together in the course. Model also adopted Project Adventure's "Full-Value Contract" as the school's interpersonal ethic:

   > . . . to accept responsibility for each other's physical and emotional safety, to give up using put-downs, to grant each other the full-value of our experiences (i.e., avoid rescuing or doing something for someone on the assumption that it's too difficult for him or her to accomplish), and to confront each other if we engage in devaluing others.

3. Growth occurs as a consequence of making choices for which one is held responsible.
   The faculty believed that adults greatly underestimate the responsibility that students can assume. One just needs to observe Montessorian pre-kindergarten children to learn how much responsibility even that age can fulfill well. The faculty also believed that faced with a rich variety of choices, students would discover their own potential interests. As Dewey emphasized, our interests are the roots of intrinsic motivation.

Not unexpectedly, students accustomed to being told what courses to take, what to learn and how to behave (even to need a pass to go to the bathroom), fall apart when given freedom. Some MHS students did also. The faculty expected students to identify and design individual projects during the first weeks of school. I spoke to new students during this period. I heard what I had heard from some students at the end of their year at a 70s alternative school: frustration, anxiety, anger that the teachers were not telling them what to do, despair, and listlessness. Some students at the district's highly structured two high schools believed that Model was a "blow-off" school. They did not understand Model. Freedom to choose was the first step to disciplined growth, not the first and last steps to sloth. Model reminds me again of the Montessorian philosophy for children: provide rich resources, which Model did, to provoke students' choices that would reveal their interests and so potential growing edges.[3]

Writing for the faculty, Boughner identifies students' choices to be the first of the six most important contributors to students' growth.

> Choices were present in almost every facet of MHS experience. . . . choice increased the degree of ownership for and engagement in learning, the degree of persistence in pursuit of goals, the ability to weather periods of doubt and crisis, and the ability to recover from failure. The relationship between choice and intrinsic motivation can not be emphasized enough.

4. Everyone in the school is a learner to be held accountable for his or her own growth by *demonstrating* it.[4]

The faculty experimented with numerous ways to assess growth other than by quizzes, tests, and assigned papers. To encourage reflection about their growth, each student and faculty member kept a journal, portions of which they voluntarily read to assembled groups. I learned what safety and trust meant to them. I heard one student describe her lingering reactions to the suicide of a dear friend six years earlier. A boy described his feelings for another boy. Students kept logs about their courses documenting what they were learning as well as portfolios of their work. MHS relied on students' public demonstrations of their projects and results. Students assumed the responsibility for inviting community experts to evaluate their work.

One student designed her own ideal elementary school and presented it to 20 area educators and business people. Others created research experiments. A student-sailor studied the effects of zebra mussels on the Great Lakes. Others wrote books of short stories and poetry. A student team created an animated, interactive CD "book" for young children, testing its appeal on preschool children as they proceeded.

Boughner claims that reliance on authentic assessments was "one of the strongest and most satisfying areas" of Model's efforts. Such student demonstrations demanded risk-taking, responsibility, and competence that "far surpass[ed] . . . what adults thought the . . . [students] capable of doing."

5. Open the school to the community's resources and support, including securing parental involvement in their children's growth.

Model initiated innumerable efforts to involve its community and parents. It created a governing council of community people, parents, staff, and students, as well as parental advisory boards, parental focus group discussions, and business partnerships, among other steps. Such efforts "took up a lot of time and energy and tended to create more tasks than they eliminated for limited returns." A more discouraging result was what Boughner called "parental distance. It proved to be a tremendous amount of work to spark their interest and keep them actively involved in the program." Model may have unwittingly met its parents' need to feel that they and their advice were wanted; only a few rose to Model's invitation. Parents of elementary children would have been more responsive.

Model's vision and assumptions meant that its structure had to be fluid and flexible enough to serve, not constrain and impede, its students' growth. Structure must follow, not lead, goals and assumptions. What does the visible MHS look like?

Model's Structure and Program

Model accepts every student who chooses to apply. For 1990-91, a total of 161; 1991-92, a total of 171; and 1992-93, the last year of the Next Century Schools grant, a total of 214. By 1997, Model's teacher-student ratio was similar to that of the district's other high schools. Since the personalities of entering students affect their educability, Chapter 3 examines the type of student who applies for an experimental school like Model. Students commit themselves to one or two three-hour blocks of time each day; they may continue their other academic work as well as co-curricular activities in their home-high schools. They may re-enroll in Model in subsequent semesters.

The school's ever-changing "workforce" complicates sequential curricular planning—not to mention rigorous assessment of its effects. Students are not grouped by ages into grades. Instead, they move in and out of differently formed groups. Experienced students become models for and mentors to new students. Experienced and new students may work together on the same project. A tenth grader may teach a senior. "This teaching and collaboration on learning happens throughout our program, crosses all boundaries between notions of who ought to be teaching whom, and benefits everyone's academic progress"—including faculty less knowledgeable about the extensive computer-related technology that Model bought with its Nabisco grant.

The "curriculum" has two primary foci, each designed to achieve the school's goals.

Personalized Learning Plans

To encourage active responsibility for their education, students initiate a semester-long project, consult with faculty, and propose how their growth in competence will be demonstrated. The faculty expects students to show increased ability to be responsible for learning; to learn how to set goals; to plan and persevere; how to organize time and develop intrinsic motivation to learn. Students who succeeded in their independent work could not be predicted by their grades in their home schools. Boughner reflects that

> students, for perhaps the first time, . . . [began] to define themselves as independent learners, separate from how they responded to other-directed instruction. They had to grapple with all of the outcomes listed above. Many needed to fail . . . before they understood their importance. Procrastination, grandiose goals, or poorly laid plans at first led many students to sad results. Faculty . . . [learned] that one of . . . [their] most important tasks . . . was to become keenly

aware of students' failure . . . and to be there to see each one through it so that he or she could recover and try it again.

Group Shared Interdisciplinary Activities

The faculty believes its competencies apply across the entire curriculum. They are best learned in an interdisciplinary context that relies on group interaction to prod, question, clarify, and test out ideas. The faculty experimented with numerous configurations for organizing groups around interdisciplinary themes, such as gender issues. Group work provided the opportunity to assess students' developing interaction skills. The faculty, for example, reliably rated its students to be more cooperative and respectfully communicative than willing to assume leadership of their groups.[5]

In addition to their individualized and group projects, students may also continue other subject matter work, such as math and foreign language, at either Model or their home high schools.

Resources to Support Student Responsibility for Their Education

Model is a resource-rich school. Abandoning traditional age-graded classes and typical timed classes provided large blocks of time for the use of its resources. Except for foreign language and mathematics, textbooks were used only for quick over-views to be supplemented by technology-based information sources, parental experts, community lectures and interviews, field trips, in depth experiments, peer teaching, home-school libraries, and other student-sought sources.

The students' principal resource, however, was a faculty modeling, mentoring, and teaching them *how* to be responsible for their own continued growth. The faculty learned that an organization's structure may imprison or liberate growth and creativity. Boughner succinctly summarizes one of Model's five principal discoveries to be that teachers can handle the challenge of making a deep shift in their thinking about learning and their roles *if the structure of the school changes in a manner which supports these shifts.*

Pure Deming! A school's organization is a principal reason why schools fail to achieve excellence.

Formal Grade Evaluation

Much to the dismay of the faculty, students and parents demanded that they receive letter grades for their work at the end of the semester. The faculty wanted its students to develop passion for and enjoy learning, not to work for a grade. Acceding to their demands to assign grades at the end of the term sparked anger, resentment, and adversarial attitudes that undercut the trust and openness that the faculty worked to create. When given the opportunity to produce their own rationale for their grade, students' attitudes improved. They then began to say, "It's absurd to reduce everything I've done to a letter. The letter has no meaning."

Model's faculty knew how their students had grown much more intimately than most faculties have the opportunity to know. Their altered roles, close working relationships, diverse assessment procedures, and weekly faculty meetings to review each student's work confirmed their biases. Traditional test and grading procedures inadequately assess growth.

What advice does Model's faculty have for those who wish to create a healthy, growth-producing school? Its most important recommendations are to provide students with meaningful choices, an intellectually and emotionally safe school climate, adults who model the school's goals, peers teaching and collaborating with each other, weekly monitoring by the faculty of every student's progress, and deep technological literacy.

On a more personal note, pay careful attention to Boughner's advice:

> Get together as many people who are open to risking as you can find, build a collective vision, flatten hierarchy, empower downward, build a communication network with feedback loops, question everything, keep questioning, don't get defensive or self-protective, leave the complainers to complain and don't drain energy in their direction, tap collective creativity, listen carefully, talk a lot, build trust, keep your sense of humor, reflect, self-assess, be so honest it hurts, keep your eye on what's going on in the world around you, interact with anyone who is interested, forge partnerships, use technology to help if you can, dump

textbooks . . . look for and seize opportunity, let go, welcome chaos and learn to love it, stop tracking students,
clear away roadblocks to any good idea, enjoy metaphor,
discuss dreams, be prepared for anything, laugh a lot and
cry when you need to.

Such are Model's teachers' voices for whom Boughner speaks. I
do not doubt that they had created a healthy, growth-producing school
for themselves as Deming, Joyce, and other systemic theorists advocate. Their morale was not dampened by their first year's demands,
chaos, and failures; it was high. They were reliably more satisfied
than the district's high school teachers were with their relationships
with colleagues. MHS provided the opportunity to develop new
friends and interests. Its faculty members were very satisfied with
the social value of and recognition for their innovative work. Given
their uncertainties about how Model might fare, it was reliably less
satisfied than their district peers with the quality of their work at the
end of their first year.

Now it is time to listen to Model's students' voices. What do their
anonymous surveys and objective measures of their growth tell us
about the kind of students who opt for a Model, their satisfaction
with their growth at Model, and the school's culture that may have
contributed to their morale?

Chapter 3

---·•·---

ASSESSING MODEL HIGH SCHOOL:
ITS STUDENTS AND CULTURE

To understand and then hold a school honestly accountable requires a three step process: First, assess its students' morale and the culture of their learning environment. Second, determine how well a school achieves its school-wide or mission goals. And third, evaluate how well its departments achieve their purposes. How to take the first two steps, this book's focus, has not been as systematically explored and understood as the third step which shapes the national educational agenda.

Thirty years ago a year-long study of Proctor Academy of Andover, New Hampshire, taught me how an ideal assessment should proceed, the questions to ask of a school, and the type of methods most appropriate to answer them. *Assessing Schools of Hope* (ASH) summarizes what I learned then and since about how an ideal assessment should proceed. [ASH 1: Ideal Assessment Guidelines]. For example, one of eight ideal guidelines or standards is, "Use multiple measures of an outcome to check the consistency and possible validity of each against the other." If two measures of self-esteem, for example, don't correlate highly with each other, then one must go back to the drawing boards to clarify what self-esteem means.

It would be dishonest to claim that Model's three-year assessment met most of the standards that an ideal accountability study requires. Why it failed to do so can forewarn you of typical school-related "facts on the ground" that can limit the worth of any assessment, especially of novel alternatives to traditional test-defined ones.

Trying to assess rigorously Model's effects on its students was like trying to grasp a ball of mercury, for three principal reasons.

1. Assessments of innovative programs after only three years, as Model was required to do by its granting agency, are doomed to show few significant effects. Charter schools should resist a sponsoring agency's demands to "show results" for their first four or five years.

Several years of *preparatory* efforts are necessary to conduct an excellent study. It takes months to design and then preliminarily try out one's innovative assessment methods for their feasibility, reliability, and predictability. That is, if you use or design a measure of self-esteem then you should determine if it in fact predicts other indices of self-esteem, as Chapter 5 will illustrate.

Model was still creating itself when it first opened its doors; it continued to re-create itself throughout the three-year period. Any researcher committed to impeccable assessment standards would have had a three-year nightmare trying to get a "fix" on Model. Its goals, processes, students, and even staff ceaselessly changed from one semester to the next. Three examples will suffice.

a. The press of creating a school delayed securing some baseline measures until the school's second year.

b. As Chapter 2 described, the staff had not clarified its competencies to make their measurement possible. It had little time to develop and implement the instructional programs that might encourage their acquisition.

c. Model's yearly re-creation optimized the well-known Hawthorne motivational effect[1] and weakened the power of its assessment to detect change. Also, some survey forms and administration procedures were so altered from one year to the next as to preclude using their previous year's results as baseline data.

2. Traditional assessment models and control groups were not feasible when assessing Model's *innovative* educational programs.

Unexpectedly, comparable results could not be secured from the district's two other high schools for practical and political reasons. Lacking such information meant that changes noted could not be rigorously attributed to Model. They might be due more to adolescent growth that would have occurred anyway regardless of Model's programs. Most unfortunately, home faculty judgments about how responsibly Model's students took charge of their own learning *after* their Model experience could not be secured. Boughner secured limited anecdotal evidence of Model's effects from interviews with a few alumni who returned to visit the school, but no dependable evidence exists about what Model's enduring effects may have been.

Furthermore, Model's structure foreclosed a "pure" test of its potential effects. Most students simultaneously participated in academic and co-curricular activities at their home-based high schools. Model's effects therefore could more likely be frustrated and diluted than facilitated, so obscuring its potential effects. Only an exact concurrent assessment of a sample of the two high school's non-participating students could tell if such contamination occurred.

3. Model's small size limited interpretations of the sources of its effects. Research has compellingly demonstrated that students grow more healthily in small- rather than large-sized and impersonal schools.[2] The districts' larger sized home-schools could not hope to create Model's interpersonal environment without extraordinarily dedicated adult leadership. Whatever differences Model's students showed might not be due to its programs per se but primarily to its size, which altered students' interpersonal environment.

Model's small size also meant that it was impossible to secure large enough homogeneous subsamples to determine what aspects of Model contributed most to students' changes. A critical unknowable fact, for example, is how many semesters at Model are necessary for students to permanently become their own self-educating teachers.

On the other hand, Model's small size made it possible to secure information impossible to secure in large schools. Reliable judgments from its teachers about its students' growth, such as improvement in their interpersonal collaborative skills, could provide powerful confirmatory evidence of other measures.

A major failing of the assessment was that such judgments were not secured for promising measures, such as some designed to measure the core competencies, which had to be discarded. Why? Several possible informative reasons. Creating an evolving organization is so consuming, even exciting and fulfilling, that tediously rating students pales in comparison. Also, not all teachers are temperamentally simpatico with "scientific" or objective efforts to describe students. Some may feel the effort required would not produce information of immediate value to them or the school. Or an assessment might produce evidence that Model's efforts are fruitless. Or it may not be emotionally owned by other faculty members who view the assessment as an imposed mandate by a remote granting agency, as most such assessments are.

Though falling short of an ideal study, the assessment was fruitful. It provided provocative insights about Model's students, culture, effects, and most revealingly, the nature of healthy growth in adolescents in what turned out to be a growth-producing school.

The Assessment's Principal Findings

I first examine the similarity of Model's students to those at their home schools and to comparable students nationally. Not to do so might mean that Model's results could more simply be explained by the type of student attracted to its programs rather than by the school's vision and culture. I next search for reasons why students chose Model and whether Model fulfilled their hopes. Did Model increase their satisfaction with being students—a defining standard for TQM advocates? I postpone to the next chapter other questions: Did Model succeed in achieving its principal hopes? Did students grow healthily? What do the students tell us about what growing healthily means—the gold standard of a self-renewing school.

Method to Understand Students' Views

Bloomfield Hills' two high schools sought information *only* about their students' perceptions of their typical peers—their interpersonal learning environment—and their schools. Students described their typical peer by checking any of an inventory's 150 attributes and circling those that they wished would apply. Chapter 7 describes the inventory. [ASH 11: Description of Measure of Culture] For example, 20% of Model's entering students believed that their peers in their home schools were helpful but 44% of Model's other entering students wished that they had been more helpful. The remaining 36% apparently didn't feel being helpful was either salient or important enough to either check or circle.

Model's and Their Home-Based Students' Views of Their Typical Peer

Model's and their two home-based peers agreed in rating the district's typical student on 84% of the 150 personality traits. They believed that the typical student was competitive, academic, talkative, and social. Majorities of Model's and their peers also agreed that the typical student was self-centered, inconsiderate, defensive, critical of each other, sarcastic, and likely to put each other down—traits that students in other similar schools report hinder their own growth. A subsequent University of Michigan study of the district's high school students used a different method of appraisal, which confirmed my findings. An average of only 27% of the high school students viewed their peers positively; 37% of one school's students viewed their peers negatively. Such findings about students' peer learning environment are not atypical; they are, however, exaggerated in highly competitive academic high schools in all parts of the country.

Model's and their home-school peers agreed in wishing that the typical student were honest, accepting, genuine, and empathic. However, more Model's students were dissatisfied with their two home high schools' peer learning environment. About 45% of them, compared to about 30% of their home-based peers, wished that their peers were more considerate, self-motivated, flexible, and helpful.

How were Model's students viewed by their home-based peers in the school's first years? Model's faculty needed to know what its image was. Such views can quickly affect the type of person who goes to Model. It doesn't take long for a Model "type" to begin to filter out those who feel they won't fit in. Model has not done follow-up studies to determine if it is attracting a more homogeneous "type" than in its first years. The University's report found that Model's students were viewed to be "bright. . . talented. . . smart, very deep thinkers, artsy, different, interesting, individualistic; some viewed them to be "troubled . . . weird . . . strange."

Model's and Other Students' Views of
Their Home High Schools

To understand MHS's effects it was necessary to know how its students diverged from their home-based peers in their view of the district's high schools. If MHS attracted primarily the district's frustrated malcontents, then the worth of its programs and their effects might not be more generally useful.

Model's and their home-based peers agreed on 75% of the 150 attributes that described their home-based schools' cultures. Actually the pattern of the 25% of attributes on which Model and their home-based peers differed suggests that Model's students consistently viewed their home-based schools more positively. [ASH 2: Organizing and Interpreting Results]. Twenty-five to 33% more Model than their home-based peers believed that their home schools were capable, fair, cheerful, accepting, adaptable, caring, and proud. Noticeably more than their peers, students applying to Model also felt that their home-based schools were considerate, ethical, empathic, friendly, and happy. Clearly, entering Model students are better adjusted to and liked their home-based schools more than students not drawn to Model. These results disprove the widely held view that students who seek alternative educational routes are necessarily disaffected and reject their schools.

Then why did students opt for Model? They felt that their home-based schools were too conventional and unexciting. They were stifling the healthy growth of their individuality. In declining order, 39 to 21% more than their home-based peers believed that their schools were conforming, apathetic, lonely, traditional, conservative, and inflexible.

Given these views, it is understandable why 64% of Model's entering students compared to 51% of their home-based peers believed their home-based schools to be boring. "Boring" was the most frequently spontaneously cited word that entering Model's students used in essays to describe their previous year at their home-based schools. As we will see later, these views are similar to those of students from other of our country's most elite public schools.

Finally, does Model's students' ideal school differ from their home-based peers' ideal? Yes. Table 3-1 tells Model's faculty the kind of school culture its students hoped to discover at Model.

Table 3-1   Students' Wishes for their Home-Based Schools

Attributes	Home-Based % Students	Model % Students	% Model More than Other Peers
Flexible	20	59	39
Creative	16	55	39
Changeable	18	50	32
Adventurous	29	59	30
Cooperative	21	50	29
Self-educating	19	45	26
Open	33	50	17

What can we now say about Model's students?

1. They are recognizable American adolescents, especially the Bloomfield Hill students. They agree far more with their home-based peers than they disagree about what their peers and schools are like. Their agreement is probably much greater than even the 84% and 75% that I found. Because of the small number of Model students, I could not compare them to the peers in their own two home schools which do, in fact, differ in their students and culture.

2. They are positively affirming but frustrated, idealistic students. Compared to students who don't apply to Model, they view their peers and schools more favorably but are also more frustrated by both.

3. Model's students are lively, actively engaged, interesting, healthy, adaptable, and educable students who have not given up, even though bored. When compared to their peers, entering Model students are not rebellious malcontents. The tenor of their differences from their peers in their wishes is one of hope. The same interpretations can be made of faculties. Faculties who identify few positive attributes about their schools and are not frustrated enough to share many wishes for it are either dying or dead. Resurrecting such tenured faculties may not be possible unless radical systemic changes are made. Shared frustrations and expectations are sources of hope.

4. Model's students are more homogeneous than their peers in their views of and wishes for their peers and schools. Model attracted a sizable core group of students who should feel congenial with each other.

5. They may feel marginal to their home-based students' conforming culture and quality of peer relationships. Model attracts students educable for its vision, culture, and program.

Did Model's faculty succeed in creating the healthy, growth-producing culture its entering students sought?

Model's Students' Morale

System theorists agree that a sign of an organization's success is the satisfaction of those whom it serves. Chapter 5 describes in more detail a generic method that can be used to assess satisfaction of any age group (except prepubertal children) and any occupation, including being a student. The questionnaire measures satisfaction about one's role in the organization and with the organization itself. It essentially measures an individual's morale, which, when combined with the morale of others in an organization, portrays how well it serves the healthy growth of its members. [ASH 7: Introduction to the Morale Surveys].

The results were clear. With the exception of one of Model's three entering years' students, Model students' morale did not differ from the morale of their home-based peers. The exception's morale was reliably lower.

With no exception, however, students in every *departing* Model class had reliably higher morale than when they entered. The odds that these increases were due to chance are less than one out of at least 10,000. That is, if we repeated the study 10,000 times, we could expect one class's increase in morale to be due to chance.

From what you now know about the principles of assessment, can we firmly assert that Model caused the increase? Why?

No, not unequivocally. Perhaps morale increases as one approaches graduation. Since the home-based schools did not resurvey their students, we cannot eliminate increasing age and other district-wide uplifting events that could explain Model's students' increased morale. However, relying on other information I have about the course of morale in comparable students in other schools, I confidently believe Model did contribute to its students' morale. Morale precipitously declines from 5th to 8th grade in independent school students and then levels off through high school. I have never found any predictable increase in morale due to aging in high school students. Furthermore, no notable events occurred at the two Bloomfield high schools that might have increased their students' morale.

Furthermore, students' satisfaction reliably increased for the three different classes on an average 24 of the scale's 30 items. This widespread increase in satisfaction is exceptionally large. It suggests two hopeful ideas about students and Model. First, students' satisfaction with their schools is not fixed. Given schools' appropriate systemic reorganization, changes in students' morale can noticeably increase (also decrease) within fairly short time periods. Like a coal miner's canary, changes in students' morale can be a sign of changes in a school's health. Chapter 5 provides both faculty and student examples of this potential.

Second, some of the increases suggest that Model succeeded in fundamentally altering some of its students' identities as students. Some developed a calling to enjoy and love learning. They no longer viewed school as a job to go to every day, dislike, and work at only for the grade. Table 3-2 lists in declining order students' 10 greatest increases in satisfaction about their work at Model.

Table 3-2   Model's Students' Ten Greatest Increases in Satisfaction, Ordered Most to Least

Opportunity to create and try new things
Amount of freedom-independence I have
Way of life being a student in Model
Amount of personal growth experienced at Model
Model provides opportunity to achieve at level of potentials
Degree of self-fulfillment I secure from my work
Moral-ethical standards and practices of Model
Amount of recognition I receive other than grades
Model helps me live up to my best potentials
Model provides the responsibility that I want

Now test your intuition. We have no objective evidence that Model's effects persist once a student leaves Model. Does Table 3-2 provide clues that they may or may not persist? Again why? My answer is "Yes, they will persist for some of Model's students." Learning had become a calling, not just a job. What is the next logical question to ask about Model? For me, what is it about the culture of the school that undergirds and contributes to the increases in its students' morale?

Model's Culture

Five ways are open for us to understand Model's culture—its pattern of values, expectations, aspirations, and interactions. Two of the more illuminating ways are students' and faculty's views of the school. The third is Model's parents' views. The fourth provides a perspective about Model's uniqueness—the comparison of Model's culture to that of independent schools which attract students like Model's. And another more important one is Model's peers' learning environment.

Model's students' views of and wishes for their school

Recall that a premier attribute of a school of hope is that widespread agreement exists about its core values. When 2/3 of the students agree about a large number of values, it has a distinctive culture. At least 67% of all three of MHS's first classes agreed among themselves about 16 values describing Model's culture—an exceptionally high number of consensual values. Model's 1993's class may be the best harbinger of its future direction. It takes several shake-down years to discover which dreams are illusions to shed and which are realistic to prize. At least 80% of 1993's students believed that Model was, in declining order of agreement, friendly, creative, adventurous, imaginative, accepting, artistic, caring, and self-educating. Large percentages also agreed it was an intellectually exciting and empathic school with a deep ethical sense.

I concluded from the students' views [ASH 2: Organizing and Interpreting Results] that:

1. Model is a distinctive school whose core values were set in its first year. Despite the school's experimentation and ceaseless change, its character seems to grow only stronger over time.

2. Despite the two home-based faculty's skepticism and students who distrusted Model's "freedom" and loose "structure," Model's consensual values and expectations are its most formative strength. Model is not its visible programs and "rules," it is its shared values.

3. Like its students, Model is a lively, exciting school open to change. Its energetic dynamism is healthily integrated with a non-defensive interpersonal climate that can facilitate corporate learning as well as individual growth.

4. The school provides just the learning environment that its students wished their home-schools had. The 1993 students describing Model used every one of entering 1991's students' wishes to now describe Model's culture.

5. That the percentage of students' wishes declined each year suggests that the faculty had listened deeply to its students and took appropriate action. For example, whereas 34% of 1991's students wanted the school to be more intellectually exciting, only 3% of 1993's students wished that were the case, and a remarkable 70% believed it was already so. Students do not find MHS boring. TQM advocates would cite this progressive decline as exemplifying closely monitoring quality and making continuous efforts to improve it.

6. Model has a rich resource in its interpersonal relationships to rely on for developing peer group collaboration, cross-age mentoring and coaching.

Faculty and parental views of Model

Faculty and parents agree with the students that Model is an accepting, caring, empathic, casual and friendly school to cite just their five most frequently agreed upon traits. The 1991 faculty, more than parents, were aware of Model's initial Achilles heel. It wished that Model had a tougher mettle characterized by intellectual rigor (64%), clarity of thought (43%), thoroughness (43%), and excellence (43%).

Comparison of Model to independent schools (NAIS)

By 1993, however, Model had begun to overcome those weaknesses when compared to our country's elite private schools—members of the National Association of Independent Schools (NAIS). Table 3-3 compares MHS's 1993's students to NAIS's normative percentages for attributes about which at least 70% of *either* group agreed.[3]

Model's singular strength is that it maintained its intellectual integrity while creating a learning environment most conducive to the development of character's interpersonal and ethical values. Model disproves the dichotomous thinking of many educators who believe that a school cannot simultaneously educate for academic and character excellence.

Table 3-3   Model's 1993's Compared to NAIS Students' View of and Wishes for Their Schools

Attribute	View of School % NAIS	% Model	Attribute	Wishes for Their School % NAIS	% Model
Academic	92	68	Flexible	32	8
Competitive	73	22	Casual	30	5
Demanding	73	30	Adventurous	29	5
Hardworking	70	76	Changeable	29	8
Dedicated	62	70	Fun	29	5
Ambitious	60	73			
Friendly	60	86			
Cooperative	44	70			
Optimistic	36	73			
Self-motivating	35	78			
Intellectually exciting	33	70			
Deep ethical sense	29	70			

Model's Peer Learning Environment.

Model's fluid structure and accepting, cooperative interpersonal values make its peer culture a potentially powerful contributor to students' growth, certainly much more so than occurs in most other schools I have studied. The exiting students' views of their peers closely paralleled their views of Model for each of the three classes. Model becomes its students to its students.

Compared to NAIS students' views of their peers, Model's students view their peers consistently more favorably. They believe that their

peers exemplify the interpersonal strengths that Model's faculty hoped
would be educed.

Given the centrality of Model's students' peer learning environment to its success, the faculty should be sensitive to whatever singing canaries may be hidden in its students' relationships. From 1991
to 1993, progressively fewer exiting students had expressed favorable views about their peers. Forty-four percent of 1993's students
viewed their peers to be critical of others and sarcastic; 53% believed
that they were defensive. Model dare not unreflectively rely on its
Full Value Contract's laurels. Changing students' personalities demands continuous self-conscious monitoring of one of Model's greatest strengths. Model has not assessed its students or school since the
end of its Next Century Schools grant. Deming would say, "At its
peril." I agree.

Given Model's very favorable learning environment, did it succeed in achieving its primary goals, especially empowering its students to become more self-educating, socially competent, and mature?
Chapter 4 illustrates how a school can be held accountable for what
it advertises are its school-wide goals.

Chapter 4

HOLDING MODEL HIGH SCHOOL ACCOUNTABLE

FOR FULFILLING ITS VISION

The second step when fully assessing a school is to ask whether it achieves its hopes for its students. The goals of the schools with which I have worked are universally laudatory, even noble. In addition to specific academic goals they typically include ethical (honesty), interpersonal (compassion), and/or self-attitudinal ones (confidence) Except for assessing a limited number of departmental goals, few have ever tried to discover how their students may have grown, for example, in their character.

This chapter illustrates how Model held itself accountable for achieving its principal school-wide goals of producing self-educating and responsible community citizens and healthily growing students—goals widely shared by most schools nowadays. ASH describes in more technical detail how to go about identifying a school's priority goals to assess and create reliable measures of them, for instance, Model's specific competencies—goals less widely shared by other schools. After reflecting what Model teaches us about how to *realistically* hold a school accountable, the chapter concludes by evaluating how well Model fulfilled the standards that define a school of hope.

Assessing the Fulfillment of Model's Vision

Students Becoming More Responsible, Self-Educating Persons

The faculty believed that Model taught the majority of its 1993 students to be self-educating. They identified 63% to have fully empowered themselves, 26% still in transition to becoming more responsible self-teachers, and 11% to have shown little or no growth. The students' increased morale scores reflected their growing satisfaction with their role as students and their enjoyment in learning. More than a few had begun to develop an identity as lifelong learners. Appendix B reports some of their spontaneous written descriptions of their principal growths at Model. [ASH 29: Manual for Scoring Student Essays].

MHS's teachers had rejected academic grades and achievement tests; they were not appropriate indices of the school's goals and the students' academic growth. They distorted the meaning of healthy growth and gave students just the wrong message of what education should be all about. The faculty would also argue that easy-to-administer and precisely scorable tests of information on which such grades are most frequently based tell us what students only *temporarily* acquire.

Despite such strongly held faculty views, might not students' grades tell us if MHS had really empowered its students to be more responsible for their academic growth? I argued, should they not do at least as well as their home-based peers? Should they not also improve their academic grades upon returning to their home schools full-time?

Academic Grades as an Index of MHS Achievement

MHS's 1994 graduating students did not reliably differ in their grades from students in one of the district's two high schools (3.08 vs. 3.07). The students in the district's reputedly most academic school averaged 3.24. A reassuring conclusion is merited. Participation in Model's adventure at least did not adversely affect most students' academic achievement—a fear expressed by some students and parents worried about colleges' acceptance of Model's experience. Participation in Model's program actually improved some students' chances for acceptance by prestigious colleges looking for students who had done something distinctive with their lives.

Academic Grade Improvement. Comparing the students' home-school pre- and post-Model academic grades confirmed that Model's boys, but not its girls, reliably improved their grade averages. Can we now claim that Model contributed to their improvement? Not dogmatically. Why? Because no comparable home-based students' changes in academic grades for the same period of time were secured to determine if they also had improved. If they had, then some event other than Model's programs may have caused the boys' improvement.

Why did not MHS's returning girls reliably improve? Of the 31% of MHS's students whose grade averages declined fractionally, though not reliably, 75% were its girls'. From what you know of adolescent gender differences, can you suggest some reasons why only boys improved their grades? Why did three times more girls' than boys' grades decline, once they returned to their traditional high schools? Intuitive diagnosticians are alert to such clues. Though a few clues may not be statistically reliable in themselves, when combined with other clues, they may generate new insights about Model's differing effects on its boys and girls. Other clues will emerge later to provide some probable reasons for the gender differences.

Competency Goals

Model's competency goals defined the strengths that a self-educating student needed to develop. While specific to its curricular focus, I describe the assessment of only one goal which is more widely shared by most schools. [ASH 5: Creating and Interpreting Model's Competencies describes how it assessed its more particular goals.]

School and community citizenship responsibility. Model attracted engaged and responsible school citizens. Its students reliably participated more in socially responsible activities, such as athletic, co-curricular, and community groups and service activities than their home-based peers *prior* to entering Model. Confirming numerous other studies, Model's students who actively participated in their school and community activities were more psychologically mature. Both self- and faculty ratings confirmed this consistent finding. The faculty judged them to be energetic, purposeful, self-acceptant, ambitious, and flexible among other positive traits.

To develop your intuition, pay close attention to patterns that clues from different types of measures may weave. Both academic grades and school citizenship are associated with purposefulness, self-acceptance, and other traits of maturity. School citizenship reliably predicts various objective measures of maturity. Studies of other schools show that academic grades directly co-vary with frequency of participation in school and community activities. What might this pattern suggest about ways to encourage students' healthy growth or maturing? Encourage them to participate in varied co-curricular activities?

But only minimal reliable evidence suggests that Model' students increased their participation in their home-school's and community service activities. Yet I know of significant contributions that some Model students made to their schools and communities. The index of social responsibility may have been flawed. It might not have fairly assessed the competence. Don't let an obsessive commitment to objective measures, valuable as they may be, usurp your judgment or common sense. Find ways to check the accuracy of your judgments if they contradict survey or test results.

Understanding and Assessing MHS Students' Healthy Growth

Undergirding Model's goals of responsible self-education and its competency goal of citizenship was a more embracing personality goal. Commitment to being a self-renewing school assumes that it should further the healthy growth of its faculty and students. Once this basic value choice is made—one also made, for example, by John Dewey and Maria Montessori—then the psychological maturation of its students becomes another primary value.

Fortunately, objective standards and measures were available to evaluate how mature Model's students had become at MHS. Chapter 8 illustrates how such standards may be used to assess whether a school has created the kind of learning environment likely to further students' maturing.

Understanding a person's healthy growth or psychological maturity has been empirically found to be the most important touchstone for predicting many important adult outcomes. Like what? Marital happiness. Sexual fulfillment. Parental satisfaction and competence. Vocational satisfaction. Quality of intimate friendships. Virtue. Physical and mental health. Happiness. But not income.[1]

Model's assessment wove a similar pattern. More psychologically mature than immature Model students, whether self- or judge-assessed, received better grades, had higher morale, acted more ethically, participated more actively in school and community activities, and felt more comfortable in close relationships with people who differed from them. They also correctly believed that others would rate them as mature, were more empathic, independent, adventurous, and self-acceptant. They also made more mature value choices.

I now briefly describe the model of maturing and several methods for objectively assessing MHS's students' maturity. The students' own spontaneous voices tell us how they viewed MHS's effects on their growth. For me, their perceptive and frequently eloquent words provide the most persuasive evidence of Model's effects. They draw together the more fragmented objective assessment results into a compelling picture of Model as a self-renewing school of hope. They tell us what they believe schools should really be held accountable for. Let's see if you will agree by the chapter's end.

Psychological Maturity and Its Assessment

I assume that the course of *healthy* growth is transculturally universal,[2] marked by five interdependent generic dimensions: increasing capacity to symbolize and become aware of one's experience, other-centeredness, integration, stabilization, and autonomy. As persons, our minds and characters (including our relationships and values) organized by our selves mature on these dimensions. As we mature, for example, our minds or cognitive competencies become more reflective, analytic, synthetically organized, resistant to stress's disruption, and so autonomitized that they can be readily transferred and used in other settings. The complete model, its systemic assumptions, relation to developmental stages, educational philosophers' views, and supporting research have been described elsewhere.[3] Appendix A provides a simplified map of the model that identifies the twenty principal attributes of a mature person.

Survey Measure of Students' Maturity. MHS's students' psychological maturity was objectively assessed by the Perceived Self Questionnaire II (PSQII). [ASH 6: History of Measure of Psychological Maturity; 27: Perceived Self Questionnaire II and Scoring Procedure]. It is a 40-item, self-rating questionnaire which includes statements measuring each of the model's 20 categories. For example, an item that assesses Cognitive Skill Integration is, "I like to put ideas together from several courses and other sources." Students were given the PSQII twice: once upon entering MHS to establish a baseline in order to evaluate change in their maturity and again upon leaving MHS.

Comparing the first and second PSQII's maturity scores showed that Model's students reliably matured. They became more other-centered persons, improving their ability to understand, for example, why they fought with their friends or what their friends thought of them; they became more reflective, able to better understand why they had difficulties with their courses. They also developed more mature self-concepts and became more autonomous generally.

By now you know the answer to the question, "Did Model produce such changes?" Possibly. We do not have information about how comparable groups of their home-based students matured. We therefore cannot know with unquestioned confidence whether such changes were due to aging, Model, or other events. Students, however, believed that Model encouraged their maturing in these and many other ways.

Students' Descriptions of Their Maturing. To date the assessment of Model's effects has confined itself to objectively structured measures, such as the PSQII. What might students report about their growth if given freedom to describe in their own words what the Model experience meant to them? As Chapter 3 reported, an ideal assessment must rely on different types of methods. Studies of how Haverford College's students matured from freshman to senior year taught me that they changed in ways for which no objective measures were available.[4] Furthermore, neither I nor the faculty were aware of the complex kinds of growth students experienced which our examinations and papers did not assess.

Students entering Model spontaneously wrote brief essays describing how they had *changed* (not "matured") the previous year at their home school and then again upon leaving Model. Appendix B samples their comments that illustrate the model of maturity's twenty categories. [ASH 28: Preparation, Administration, and Scoring of Students' Essays about How They Had Changed in School].

What does this free-form assessment of healthy growth tell us?

1. Students invariably described maturing changes; few wrote about becoming less mature at Model or their home-based high schools.

2. Every statement about a change could be scored by one or more of maturing's 20 categories. This result confirmed earlier studies with college students and adults that the map of maturing comprehends most if not all of the changes that adolescents and adults frequently report.

3. Students who matured the most, as scored by their essays, had reliably higher academic grades and morale; they also were more responsible and tended to act more ethically, among other traits. The results agree with those of the PSQII.

4. The pattern of growth of Model's students while at MHS was reliably similar to the pattern of their growth at their home-based schools. This result suggests that the pattern of adolescent growth within a school district may be stable over time. If so, then a normative picture of student growth could be developed to which a school's pattern of growths could be compared and monitored for any changes due to major curricular, programmatic, or interpersonal changes.

5. Not one student, either at Model, the two high schools, or other schools where I've challenged students to report orally how they have changed (not what they have "learned" or "matured"), has ever cited a specific subject matter content for which we grade them. Reflect upon this startling report. Does it not tell us how huge is the gulf between what students value as important and what our society and schools tell and judge them on?

I had learned from earlier studies of schools that they greatly vary not only in how powerfully they affect their students' maturation but also in the pattern of their effects. Exiting Model's students described some growths more than they described had occurred the previous year at their home-based schools. Table 4-1 summarizes Model's distinctive effects. A rank of one means it was the most frequently cited change. I list only the five most and five least frequently cited maturing effects of the 20 possible effects. The table illustrates how a school can assess its relative impacts as its student believe them to be.

Table 4-1   Comparing Students' Entering and Exiting
Descriptions of Personality Change

Maturing Effect	Average Rank Entering Students about Home-Based Schools	Average Rank Exiting Students in Model
Five Most Frequently Reported Effects		
Developed more other-centered caring, tolerant, and understanding relationships	1	1
Became more in control of selves to make talents work for them	12	2
Developed more autonomous values, such as forming their own values and becoming self-motivated	9	3
Increased reflectiveness and communication skills	8	4.5
Became more aware of their own values, beliefs, and assumptions	4	4.5
Five Least Frequently Reported Effects		
Formed more stable and enduring friendships	12	20
Learned how to be alone, though not lonely	20	19
Increased ability to transfer learnings to other classes or situations	15.5	18
Developed reciprocal intimacy, mutuality, and more cooperative relations	15.5	17
Developed more stable cognitive skills more resistant to disruption by stress	17	16

Model's students are a most appropriate group to tell us how they have grown. Few other schools offer their students as many opportunities to reflect about their own development. Recall that students kept daily journals, shared them with others, and reflected on their own work at Model and its program as well. To make Table 4-1's rather abstractly phrased growths more accessible I quote verbatim examples from the students that succinctly illustrate Model's five most prominent effects. See Appendix B for examples of students' quotations about each of the 20 maturing outcomes.

Model's most frequently mentioned effect was to encourage its students to be more accepting, respectful, and trusting of other students. The Full-Value Contract established this ethic as Model's interpersonal norm. A tenth grade boy wrote that he was "much more accepting of others' little quirks." Though technically more appropriately scored for growth in other-centered values, two boys' words concern the quality of their relationships. A senior boy wrote, I have "come to an understanding of how different people come to be and therefore gained a greater compassion for all people." A junior boy wrote similarly. Model "showed me you can still be powerful but yet loving and to have open arms toward people."

The second most distinctive growth—to secure command of one's own talents— was simply described by a ninth grade boy as "Using [my] mind as a tool to do what I want to do; using it to see viewpoints other than my own."

The third growth was to form one's own values, follow one's own inner drummer, and become more self-motivated. A graduating girl said, "I think I've come to realize that my strengths and limitations may be different than somebody else's and it's mine that matter." Another senior girl wrote, "I am an individual and my feelings and actions are mine; I know I am special." Commenting about her motivation, a junior girl wrote, "I am learning more than I have in my entire life. I seem to learn better when working for myself; I am more motivated and generally self-directed."

Growth in mind's symbolizing ability and in awareness of one's values were Model's next two prominent effects. A tenth grade girl succinctly wrote, "My eyes have opened to what is around us." Another wrote, "I think about my actions and what I am about to do before I do it whereas before I would just go ahead and do it without thinking of how it would affect me and others."

Two students' comments explain Model's reflective effects on their values and what they wanted for their lives. A ninth grade girl wrote that I "realized school work is not the most important aspect of school—but that I enjoy myself while learning." I am partial to the comment of an eleventh grade boy who wrote, "I think how or why it is we live this way—becoming very philosophical with the way I see everything. Now I ask why we love to dance when dancing." Model forced such reflective growth by insisting its students make choices by discovering their own interests and creating their own projects.

Dewey claims the development of this capacity for reflection should be a primary goal of schooling. Public and independent teachers' and students' beliefs about the typical student as well as students' views of themselves reveal that few believe students are reflective; few students believe that their peers are; few believe that they themselves are. [ASH 37: Public and Independent School Teacher and Student Norms]. Model's deeply reflective learning environment apparently "took."

Four other quotations capture a central developmental task of adolescents: creating a firm sense of self that is the source of self-confidence which enables one to risk. A ninth grade girl wrote, "Now I have so much more confidence about myself. I realize that I can do absolutely anything I want if I put my mind to it." A junior girl affirmed her stronger sense of self when she wrote, I "feel special, supported and celebrated; I feel confident about myself and my actions." A graduating girl wrote, "I no longer get so worried I might fail because I have realized where the safety nets are [and so] where it is OK to jump." A senior boy simply wrote, "I have become a stronger person."

The girls' comments suggest hunches about why some of their grade averages slipped. Had they begun to abandon their identity as dutiful students who should work hard to please their parents and teachers? Had their growing self-confidence and firmer sense of themselves empowered them to listen to their own inner drummer to go *their* way, perhaps even to resist being told what they should do and be?

MHS's students also tell us how potentially powerful a school could be. It can contribute to their healthy growth. Holding a school fully accountable may illuminate strengths unknown to and therefore not valued by its faculties—nor by legislators and professional reformers who value only what they believe can be precisely measured. Holding a school only partially accountable is dishonest and betrays its integrity.

Model's assessment also alerts me to the steps that an honest but realistic assessment can take.

Steps to Hold a School Honestly and
Realistically Accountable

The "real world" of a school probably makes assessment's ideal requirements unrealizable though not unapproachable. Sustained administrative commitment, personnel continuity, moderate sophistication about assessment's principles, and cooperative faculty and students must be present to honestly assess a school. Charter schools proposed as novel alternatives to public schools should take special note of the following steps to hold themselves honestly accountable.

Step One: Make every effort to clarify your priority goals in ways that can lead to their implementation. Too frequently the creation of a school's mission statement is a haphazard exercise. Not guided by a deep understanding of a school's full potential to further students' maturing, its mission statement is left dangling, leading nowhere. I have used the Essay's scoring manual to assist schools in clarifying their values about what they want their priority goals to be. I have asked teachers to take the following steps:

1. In preparation for a workshop, read the Manual's 117 statements about how students had grown at Model. [ASH 29: Manual for Scoring Student Essays].
2. Then circle only the five growths of the 117 that you value most highly.
3. Get together with two other teachers from other departments to compare your priority values. Keep open to the others' views. Arrive at a consensus about the five most important outcomes, then rank order them.
4. Poll all of the groups of three for their priorities and map them into the model of maturing to determine which of the model's categories are most valued by the entire faculty.
5. Ask the teachers to reflect about the gaps between their priorities, about what and how they teach, and what the grades given tell students about what they believe the faculty's priority goals are.
6. Ask the teachers what their reflections tell them about their integrity; how divided are their and the faculty's collective souls?
7. Finally, ask if their school dares to hold itself accountable for the students' healthy growth? Following Model's procedures, determine what their students believe are their principal growths. Com-

pare them to the faculty's priority values to assess the magnitude of the gap between students' beliefs and faculty's goals.

Step Two: Given the resource and time constraints of most schools, teachers should use financially economical, easy-to-administer measures to assess their faculty's and students' morale and culture. Staff turn-over, changing students' personalities, and program innovations require adequate base line information to evaluate schools' effects. The next five chapters describe two of Model's surveys and how they can be used to understand, monitor, and improve a school's quality.

Step Three: Realistically appraise the conditions that must be present for a meaningful assessment to occur. Uncertain parental participation, student resistance to "another survey" or repetitive tests, and over-burdened faculty not emotionally committed to assessment must be considered when framing an assessment that spans several years. Model's faculty did not participate in the third year of its assessment, which then had to rely solely on students' self-evaluations. If faculties in small schools like Model are unable or unwilling to judge their students' growth in human interaction and group activities, for example, then such outcomes may not be practically assessable.

In a society that demands accountability, the ultimate result, therefore, could be the abandonment of character outcomes as legitimate educational goals. This would be an ironic disaster. Students tell us such outcomes are some of their most important growths. Research tells us they contribute to students' lifelong learning and adult success.

Step Four: Assessable outcomes should be selected that can be reasonably expected to be achievable for the resources available. For example, Model faced a daunting challenge to achieve its ethical competence. It shared its students with the two high schools whose cultures did not support its efforts. An assessable competency-based curriculum requires that a faculty more thoughtfully design systematic teaching and program strategies to achieve its outcomes. Model had not reached that point in its development. *Schools of Hope* illustrates how such self-conscious creation of teaching strategies to develop a competence can be done.

Step Five: Assessment should be a more intrinsic, on-going process— not an end-of-the-semester externally-imposed process. For example, Boughner created a survey identifying the principal components of

Model's Human Interaction competence, e.g., willingness to assume group leadership. It was subsequently abandoned due to students' resistance and lack of faculty commitment. If it had been incorporated as an integral component of the group's daily work, it might have encouraged greater growth in students' cooperative learning skills. Faculty may need "training" in how to incorporate monitoring surveys that go beyond daily quizzes and occasional papers. Failure to heed Deming's admonitions about this recommendation means little meaningful improvement in quality will be likely to occur.

Step Six: Assessments need to be simplified, severely focussed on only a few outcomes, and planned more deliberately in view of the realistic resources available. Model's inability to secure its home-based high schools' cooperation, while not fatal, limited identifying its effects.

Step Seven: Not just Model but all schools need to learn how to assess the autonomization of their effects and their transfer to other settings. Traditional, impeccable, objective test scores do not predict much for later life. Might this not suggest that continuing on this route to accountability may not be the most productive way to go? Methods such as the students' essays about how they had grown may provide more understanding of what schools are doing well. They could also tell us how a school needs to improve to become a school of hope. But until students' growth after school is assessed, no firm conclusions can be made about what school-related activities had an enduring effect.

A school that has assessed its members' morale, culture, and primary mission goals has the type of information necessary for an evaluation of how well it approaches the eight standards that define a school of hope.

Determining if Model is a School of Hope

What does Model's assessment tell us about how to evaluate it as a school of hope? I playfully and intuitively explored whether numerical ratings could be meaningfully assigned to show how closely Model approached each of the eight standards defining an effective school. One means disaster, ten means perfection. I arbitrarily define a school of hope as one scoring 70 or above. [ASH 47 describes a similar evaluation of Delaware's St. Andrew's school].

Standard 1: A widely shared distinctive vision of its goals.

Three classes of students and their parents uncommonly agree about Model's purpose, as their perceptions of the school have shown us. They agree about a large number of values that define its expectations of how students are to grow. The faculty labored countless hours to agree about the meaning of its competencies. One faculty member eventually disagreed with Model's direction and left the school. Because no objective evidence was secured about the number of MHS's faculty who shared similar values, I rate Model 9.

Standard 2: Adults committed to the maturation of students' character as well as minds.

Though the academic was Model's playing field, so to speak, the faculty's expectations that students develop their character was embedded in its competencies. The faculty relied on the Full-Value Contract, modeled a facilitative cooperative role, and closely monitored and worked with its students. It thereby created a humane learning environment likely to favor the development of its students' minds and characters. Model deserves a 10.

Standard 3: A leader who is a steward of and articulator of Model's values.

Model originated as a three-person team that resisted district advice to develop a leadership hierarchy. The diffusion of responsibility and potential instability of tripartite leadership may have adversely affected the projection of Model into more public view. Gary Doyle says that Cindy Boghner was the "philosophic steward from the start." She was an articulate spokesperson for Model when the other two originators departed for other positions. Based more on intuition than fact, I rate the effectiveness of the three-year leadership ambiguity to be about 8.

Standard 4: Faculty empathically understand students' interpersonal world.

Model originated out of the district's awareness that its distinguished schools were not meeting many students' needs for a different learning environment. The assessment's results are clear: The faculty deeply understood its students' needs and created a learning environment that met their ideal. I rate Model 10 on this standard.

Standard 5: Adults and students whose growth-inducing relationships are trusting, caring, adventurous, and intellectually exciting.

The assessment's results are unequivocal. The students exiting in 1994 viewed Model to be trusting (54%), caring (81%) adventurous (84%) and intellectually exciting (70%). These are exceptionally high percentages compared to those in comparable schools. It was not rare for students to write in their anonymous essays, "I never had much luck in maintaining good relationships with teachers until I realized they were on my side. . . . Model has shown me that a teacher can truly be your best friend." Only informal observations suggest faculty felt similarly about each other. I give Model a 10.

Standard 6: Teachers and students view their work as a calling and have high morale.

The students' morale was not only high but their pattern of satis-factions suggested that many felt the birth of a calling to learn for its own enjoyment. An eleventh grade girl said she was not "happy about going [back] to traditional high school all day. . . [but] leaving Model gives me the opportunity to prove to myself that I can truly become a lifelong learner." Some parents complained that their children stayed after school too long to work on their projects. The faculty's morale did not appreciably differ from that of other faculty but no objective information exists about its morale the remaining two years. The teach-ers' continuing dedication could only be fueled by a deep commit-ment to their work. I rate Model 9 rather than 10 on this criterion, primarily because of the lack of information about the faculty.

Standard 7: Faculty and students emotionally own the goals of the school and their implementation in their work.

The faculty's creation and continuing re-creation of Model's cur-riculum testifies to its commitment. Students attracted to Model shared Model's values and were educable for its programs. Their essays described personality changes that could only have occurred because of a strong commitment to Model's vision. I rate Model 10 here.

Standard 8: Adults and students value risking together to create ways to achieve their goals, are willing to hold themselves account-able, and reflect about their school and its effectiveness.

Model attracted risk-taking people. More than most schools, it created means for continuous reflection about its processes. Its reliance on a variety of ways to hold itself accountable was excep-tional. Faculty and some student resistance to more objective ways of assessing their work was understandable. They realistically felt overburdened by tedious assessment procedures whose immediate benefits seemed remote. However, failure of the faculty to participate in the third year's procedures meant their judgments were not available. The promising potential of the measures designed by Boughner to assess their work remained unrealized. I rate Model a 7 on this standard.

Just as Model's faculty shuddered at grading its students to two decimal points, so it will feel betrayed to be graded 73 or an average 9.13 (!) for its three-year effort, even when playfully done by a sympathetic, tough-minded assessor with his tongue in his cheek. But if it had scored a perfect average score of 10, what would it work on in future years to be a self-renewing school? Model's A- makes it a school of hope for me.

Model made three significant contributions to education. It showed that a school can successfully educate for character without violating its academic integrity. It created a growth-producing school culture that furthered adolescent maturing in ways that confirmed for the first time that a model of maturing is applicable to adolescents. And it experimented with a demanding, multifaceted assessment process that accomplished two things. It illustrated how a school can be more fully held accountable, and it taught us the theoretical potentials for and practical limitations of assessing a self-renewing school.

Though receiving only an average 9.13 as a school of hope, its contribution to education merits at least a 9.85.

The next five chapters examine how to assess and interpret the two most important attributes of a social system: its members' satisfaction or morale and its culture.

SECTION III

Assessing Morale

Chapter 5

MEASURING MORALE: AN INDEX OF ORGANIZATIONAL HEALTH

How quickly we forget what a school is not! It is not what a proud principal insisted on showing me when I arrived at his sprawling high school. He ushered me onto a golf-like cart parked outside his office to show me the school's 2.3 miles (sic) of corridors and two (sic) Olympic-sized swimming pools. I indelicately asked how long a passing time did students have to get to their next classes with a bathroom stop in between.

A school is also not what an ecstatic principal told me about a just-approved, Texas-size bond issue of $36,000,000 (in mid-1980 dollars) to consolidate the community's two competing high schools. The district's 3000 high school students would now feel a real sense of unity! Shortly thereafter he let slip that the community would finally be able to have a champion football team. I tactlessly asked how he was going to handle the bus congestion at 7:30 in the morning.

Neither principal nor one single student greeted each other during our interminable tour of the schools. Few students were talking with each other.

No, schools are social systems and

> are about people and about the way people behave and interact with each other in groups. They are about the attitudes, the aspirations and the motivation of people in work situations.[1]

TQM advocates are right to claim that the satisfaction of those we serve is one but, as MHS's assessment revealed and subsequent research shows,[2] not the only index of quality or organizational effectiveness. People's morale tells us about their attitudes, aspirations, and motivations. Their morale tells us (though not always) whether they feel their school is a healthy, growth-producing place in which to work.

Accurately understanding the morale of others (as well as our own) and its implications can be a key to creating healthier schools. Neufield's seditious teachers have been well-behaved, almost tractable, since they sandbagged its study of the district's schools. Why? Could they have learned from the high morale of the rest of the faculty that they were a rather small, unhappy, marginal group which other teachers were not going to follow? The St. Ignatius faculty learned that its allegedly "low" morale was typical of that of other college faculties. The low morale itself was not the problem. Its bitter dispute was due more to the lay faculty's failure to understand the special meaning of being called to the priesthood.

I first define morale and how you can reliably measure your students' and teachers' collective morale (including your own). Next, I summarize what we know about the personality of people with high morale and what I have learned about different groups' morale. Finally, I answer some questions about morale that have bedeviled the popular press and confused our understanding of gender differences. Building on this chapter, the next illustrates how to intuitively interpret morale scores. It also introduces you in some depth to four schools whose morale raised questions about their growth-producing potential.

Understanding and Measuring Morale

The Meaning of Vocational Morale

Morale has two sources: first, our satisfaction with how well our role fulfills our needs and provides us the opportunity to develop our talents; and. second, our satisfaction with the availability of resources, such as salary or the opportunity to be innovative. When our work fits and integrates our needs, values, talents, and personality we have a vocation to which we feel called. We feel very satisfied and fulfilled as an airplane pilot or teacher or parent. Model's students showed us that even teenagers have the potential to be called to their vocation as self-teaching learners. We so enjoy our work we cannot imagine being or doing anything different; the clock, status, even pay recede in importance. Van Gogh sold only one painting during his lifetime. Yet he continued to paint until his suicide. I know well an author (hmm) whose books never appear on the *New York Times* weekly best seller list but who continues to write, probably until he too dies. To paint or to write is **us.**

Or we may have a cushy high status job that pays well but does not fulfill us. We resist going to work in the morning; we begin to daydream about leaving to play golf or be with the children by mid afternoon. We have a job in that case. *Schools of Hope* lists 25 specific signs of when teaching, for example, begins to become a job, no longer a calling. Washington's principal learned what she didn't want to know and which her perceptive students had told me: Most of her teachers had a job, not a calling.

People who have high morale rate themselves as very satisfied with 30 attributes of their work on five-point scales. [ASH 7: Introduction to Morale Surveys]. The attributes are generic. They are universally applicable regardless of gender, age, type of role, status, or nationality. Some of the attributes of the role that define a calling are its fulfillment of one's stronger needs, utilization of one's best potentials, and opportunities to continue growing most of one's working life. [ASH 8: The Generic Nature of Morale]. Attributes that define a job are preoccupation with salary, status, and the amount of time and energy it requires. Teachers distinguish between the two sets of attributes by words like "intrinsic" versus "extrinsic", "inner" versus "outer." The attributes of the calling, not the job, best predict one's overall morale. They describe the satisfactions that Joyce would claim are what faculty and students in a self-renewing school should be most satisfied with.

Satisfaction's generic attributes can be revised to be appropriate for different roles and organizations. [ASH 9: Revision of Morale Items]. Forms are available for assessing the morale of adults [ASH 31A: Vocational Adaptation Scale-VAS], adolescent and adult students [ASH 31B: Student Role Satisfaction-SRS], and bright fifth to seventh grade students [ASH 31C: Student Satisfaction—SS). Most fourth graders are not developmentally ready for the surveys' vocabulary and conceptual level as well as their demand for abstract reflection. The VAS and SRS have also been used to assess teachers' and students' morale on every major continent. Harriet Heath translated the generic items to create a survey assessing parental morale, the Parental Adaptation Scale. Its results have been reported elsewhere.[3]

What Do Morale Surveys Predict?

For Adults

The adult survey, VAS, predicts a host of attributes for men but not many for women. For both, high morale is reliably associated with greater happiness, maturity, and androgyny. High morale men and women share stereotypic traits of both males and females. Colleagues rating the men and women on the VAS confirm that persons with high morale are more mature, androgynous, and ethical.

For a variety of reasons discussed at length in *Fulfilling Lives* and *Lives of Hope* men who have high morale share a large number of successes and personality traits. Women with similar high morale do not—at least middle-aged women brought up to be housewives and mothers who work outside of the home. Younger women with high morale may well be developing more similar personality strengths now; more are being raised to have a vocational calling in addition to or in place of their marital and maternal ones.

Men who are very satisfied with their vocation—which means in effect having a calling—are more happily married, sexually fulfilled, parentally fulfilled, and generally more competent in their other adult roles. Why? Because their maturity means they have the coping skills to adapt successfully to their other adult roles. If they feel dissatisfied with their vocation, they find ways to make it more satisfying or risk leaving to find other work.

Vocationally fulfilled men also share many personality strengths in common, *regardless of their type of vocation.* They are judged by knowledgeable others to be self-confident, energetic, assertive, independent, ambitious, decisive men willing to take risks and able to function well under stress. This consistent, stereotypic masculine portrait is mellowed, however, by their colleagues. The men they rate to have made a satisfying vocational adaptation also rate themselves to have high morale. Their colleagues view them to be more androgynous than the men view themselves to be. They have many of the warmer interpersonal strengths which are stereotypical of women. This portrait is more striking for male and female teachers. Both are more compassionate, understanding, and sensitive to others' needs than teachers who have low morale.

What is dramatically clear is that neither men nor women who have high morale share *in common* more stereotypic "macho" traits. Individual persons can have such traits and high morale; but competitiveness, forcefulness, and aggressiveness are not essential to have high morale. Their colleagues find such persons too difficult to work with.[4]

What we learn from these intensive studies of adults is that our morale is inextricably entwined with our personalities. Our morale provides a quick snapshot of our health and maturity. High faculty and student morale is a cardinal attribute of a school of hope; it suggests that a school's culture promotes healthiness and continued growth.

For Adolescents

Researchers have begun to identify school-related attributes that contribute to students' achievement. They are not objective ones like the size of a school's budget or number of library books, swimming pools, and teachers' Ph.D.s. No. Subjective attributes contribute more. In Coleman's words, a student must "feel he has some control over his own destiny."[5]   Others have identified other student traits such as enjoyment in learning and looking forward to going to school.

Most teachers are not aware of their students' collective morale. They do not listen to their students with the same care and persistence that Model's faculty learned to do. Most faculties I know have never systematically sought to measure their students' morale and then alter their "system" to increase students' satisfaction with their schools and courses. I am *not* talking about pandering. Today's perceptive students would know and not respect that. I have read numerous accreditation reports; only a few had assessed their students' (and faculty's) morale—or their school's culture, the topic of Chapters 7 and 8.

If researchers are right, then students' morale (SRS) should predict a variety of their successes as well as personality traits. It does. The results parallel those for adult morale. In contrast to those of low morale, and with few exceptions, students who are very satisfied are good students. They reliably get better grades and persist in school to graduate. Chapter 12 examines in depth the inner world of psychic dropouts—students who have low morale but who physically remain in school. It may move you, as it does me, to empathically feel how cruelly schools have ignored such students by not listening to how they feel about their schools, faculties, peers, and themselves.

Students who have high morale are also good school citizens. They reliably participate more frequently in co-curricular activities as well as in their community's service and youth activities. They devote more hours to their homework and work for money less frequently during the week. They also drink alcohol and take drugs less frequently.[6]

Confirming the tenor of the adult personality results, students who enjoy school and have high morale act more ethically. I have found this to be true for every school whose students' ethical behavior I have studied. More than students with low morale, they reliably believe that their parents expect and support their acting ethically. Model's students who had high morale also acted more responsibly. They also cited many more examples of maturing at MHS than students with low morale did. Their faculty reliably rated them to be more flexible, trustful, and understanding of others, among numerous other strengths.

Might not students' morale provide a window into how healthy and growth-producing their schools are? Adolescents only verge on forming a stable identity and pathway into adulthood. In contrast to adults whose vocational identities and morale are quite stable, adolescents' are not. More dependent upon external sources of satisfaction and affirmations of their worth, their morale may be more readily affected by changes in their environment. Their maturity and personality are more malleable. It is rare for adults to show as much change in their morale as Model's students did after one year. Model's hope for us is to show us adolescents' potential educability when in a friendly, growth-producing, learning environment.

Do you now have an intuitive answer to my question about whether Model's students' stirrings of a calling to be lifelong learners will persist into their adult years? Model may have wrought some profound maturing changes in some students that support their emerging calling. A senior boy said, "I have no problem motivating myself now to do something, even if its tedious." He had begun to secure command of himself.

High morale is, therefore, one of the eight standards defining a school of hope.

About Different Groups' Morale

A generic measure of morale enables us to compare different groups' morale in ways not possible before. The norms for the National Association of Independent Schools and elite public high schools are reasonably stable. They no longer change much when I add similar schools to my samples. Norms for elementary and middle schools, American schools abroad, and liberal arts colleges are more provisional. I have not had the resources to do representative or extended studies to determine how stable their norms are. So I cannot provide more reliable precise yardsticks against which to compare these latter schools. Their tentative norms, however, have proved suggestive. [ASH 33: Norms for the Morale Surveys].

Table 5-1 provides an overview of the average morale differences between teachers and students in public, private, American international schools and liberal arts colleges.[7]

Table 5-1   Public, Independent (NAIS), American International, Liberal Arts Schools' Faculty and Student Average Morale

Mean Total Morale*	Faculty		Students		
	Public	NAIS#	Public	NAIS	International
Elementary	109.4	117.3	115.4	119.5	121.8
Middle Schools	108.3	113.1	103.1	109.0	111.0
High Schools	105.1	111.6	97.8	105.2	103.3
College		110.8		104.8	

* 30 items x 5 points for very satisfied give total possible score of 150.
# The 25 international schools' faculties averaged 114.0.[8]

The first questions to ask of such a table are, "Are the differences between the various means due to chance? If we surveyed many other similar schools, would we find the same patterns of differences or would they show no similar patterns?" The *pattern* of differences is consistent and clear. For example, independent school teachers and students for every division are more satisfied with their schools and own fulfillment than public school teachers and students are with theirs. The odds are practically nil, though not for the specific mean scores, that repetitions of the study would produce a different pattern.

The odds are also remote that the NAIS middle and high school students' and teachers' higher morale are due to chance. I compared statistically each public school's division to its NAIS counterpart's morale as well as each division's with its following division's morale. With only two exceptions, i.e., public elementary versus public middle school faculty and NAIS middle school versus NAIS high school faculty, every comparison produced highly reliable differences. Though reliable, I have much less confidence that the public elementary school differences may be replicable. Its results come from only about 1,000 students. The American international students' morale scores, however, replicated the same pattern.[9]

Given the similarities in the different types of schools' patterns, let's push our analysis further: "How similar are the specific contributors to their highest and lowest morale? Are students in American and international schools most and least satisfied about the same attributes of their schools?" If so, then this additional evidence would substantiate further the generality of morale's meaning. We could then ask what school attributes account for differences in their students' morale.

Comparison of Specific Sources of Morale

Table 5-2 highlights the sources of public, international, and independent students' morale. It distills out of the SRS's 30 sources of morale the four most and eight least satisfying attributes about which public school students agree.[10] The table compares the international and independent students' most and least satisfying sources to the public students'. The international schools at the time had many more diverse types of students. Some schools had many local parents' children who wanted their children to have an American-style education. The table illustrates that the SRS can be productively used with internationally diverse students.

**Table 5-2   Comparison of International and NAIS Students'
to Public Students' Morale**

SRS Attribute	Public	International	NAIS
Most Satisfying Sources of Morale			
Ability to take courses	3.7*	3.7	3.8
Personal relations with students	3.7	3.8	3.8
School as source of new friends	3.6	3.7	3.6
Amount growth experienced here	3.5	3.8	4.0
Least Satisfying Sources of Morale			
Amount freedom-independence	2.6	3.1	3.2
Recognition other than grades	2.9	3.2	3.2
Opportunity to create in school	3.0	3.3	3.3
School meets strongest needs	3.0	3.1	3.3#
Moral-ethical standards, practices	3.0	3.2	3.3
School helps live up to potential	3.0	3.3	3.4#
Amount time spend on courses	3.0	3.3	3.2
Amount energy courses require	3.1	3.2	3.3

* 5 = Very satisfied to 1 = Very dissatisfied

\# Only items in table which were not one of the eight least satisfying for the three types of schools. NAIS students were least satisfied with their grades and the opportunity to achieve at their potential level of capability.

Table 5-2's pattern of satisfactions and dissatisfactions persuasively confirms the generic nature of morale. With only two exceptions, students from the three types of schools share identical most and least satisfying sources of morale. Though its pattern of satisfactions is the same, public school students have reliably lower morale than the other students. I explain the intermediate position of the international students' morale by their schools' mixture of attributes of private and public schools. Though drawing from the same professional and business population, the international schools are less selective, larger, and more urban than most NAIS schools. Chapter 13 examines the cultures of the public and NAIS schools for reasons that might account for their students' differences in morale.

Researchable Questions about Morale

Until the pattern of and differences in morale are also found by other researchers, let us provisionally accept them as reliable for illustrative purposes. What questions do the morale surveys permit us to raise and answer, even if only tentatively?

- Do teachers have as low morale as the media periodically report?
- Do male and female students and teachers differ in their morale?
- What may cause the consistent decline in morale across the school years?
- What could an intensive study of the transitional middle school years in other cultures suggest about the developmental course of morale?

Do Teachers Have Low Morale?

The availability of a validated generic morale survey permits us to now answer, with more sophistication, important current work-related issues. The question of vocational morale now looms prominently for different professional groups. The revolution in medical payment policies reputedly is damaging physicians', especially specialists', morale. I don't know of any objective evidence that compares their morale with that of other groups, such as lawyers. However, a 1981 American Bar study reported that large numbers of lawyers were dissatisfied with their profession.[11] Nor do I know of any objective evidence comparing the morale of and its changes in different down-sized blue- and white-collar workers. The extraordinarily rapid, even radical, changes in contemporary occupations, I believe, demand considered study of their psychic effects. What are the trade-offs between increased corporate bottom-lines and their workers' well-being and vocational calling?

Table 5-1 shows us that such questions are much too broad. We must ask of teachers' alleged low morale, "Low morale compared to whose morale?" I first ask, "Do NAIS teachers have low morale?" My immediate answer is "no." Not when compared to their public school divisional colleagues, or when compared to the varied professionals and executives I have studied for decades.[12] My answer is "maybe" when I compare NAIS' intra-divisional morale scores. Its elementary school teachers' morale differs reliably from that of its middle school teachers, whose morale does not differ from its upper school teachers'. But my answer is "yes" when I compare teachers' morale of any division to different types of more homogeneous groups of executives: the executives of the local clubs of a national youth organization or to the heads of mid-eastern and Asian American international schools. The latter are as happy about their work as fifth-graders! Why? Might not they have a greater opportunity to grow as more whole persons? The NAIS comparisons can readily model how to make similar comparisons for Table 5-1's public schools.

I am most troubled by the magnitude of the differences in satisfaction between NAIS and public high school teachers and students.[13] I have yet to study a public high school whose faculty and student morale is reliably higher than the corresponding NAIS averages. The "morale" problem of the teaching profession is concentrated within the public high school faculty and especially among students. The students' precipitous decline in morale from middle to high school is a disaster.

Why such a severe judgment? Because my studies of adult development identify youths' optimism (not their SAT scores and grades) to be one of the most powerful predictors of their future success and well-being.[14] Students' morale scores reflect their optimism, as Chapter 12 will show us. Students' morale of even some of the conventionally recognized "excellent" public schools in my sample is dreadful. If TQM advocates are correct that satisfaction is *the* only or best index of an organization's health, without question some high schools are not just schools of despair, they are **sick** schools. You might turn to Chapter 12, which explores the inner world of psychic dropouts, defined by low morale, to discover what such schools' immediate effects may be on vulnerable youths. Their long-term sleeper effects (ones that do not show up until later) could be pathological. Is anyone following such youth into their adult years to learn what un-healthy schools' effects may be on their dissatisfied students' future well-being and success?

Despite recent public concern about schools' adverse effects on girls, my accumulating evidence suggests it is boys more than girls who are most vulnerable to developing low morale.

Do Males and Females Differ in Their Morale?

The American Association of University Women (AAUW) sponsored a widely publicized and influential study of the changing self-esteem of 3,000 fourth-to-tenth grade children. It titled its report, *Shortchanging Girls, Shortchanging America.* I examined its results in some detail, not just because some of our results and conclusions differ, but be-cause our studies should alert us to the methodological and interpre-tive pitfalls in making such comparisons.

AAUW's study illustrates what such comparative studies should be like. It had the resources to survey nationally randomly sampled fourth-to-tenth graders in each of 12 regional locations in the same two-month period. How specific students were selected to survey in specific schools is not mentioned in its principal public report. On its general method-ological strengths alone the study merits serious study, however. Its representative sample permits generalizable conclusions.

The study's key conclusion is that

> both [boys and girls] experience a significant loss of self-esteem in a variety of areas; however, the loss is most dramatic and has the most long-lasting effect for girls . . . Girls, aged eight and nine, are confident, assertive, and feel authoritative about themselves. They emerge from adolescence with a poor self-image, constrained views of their future and their place in society, and much less con-fidence about themselves and their abilities.[15]

The survey's principal weakness is its theoretical understanding and measure of "self-esteem" for which it provides no independent, validating, objective information. It defined self-esteem by five questions: "I like the way I look," "I like most things about myself," "I'm happy the way I am," "Sometimes I don't like myself that much," and "I wish I were somebody else." No other information, such as other types of self-assessed personality attributes, morale, teacher ratings, or behavioral indices such as co-curricular or other activities, was reported to check out just what the five questions predicted.[16]

While not necessarily disagreeing with the study's conclusion, based on my studies of middle-aged women's development, I remain uncertain about how the authors reached their conclusion based on their five survey items. Furthermore, not knowing what the items predict, I also am uncertain about how to interpret their percentage differences between boys and girls. What about girl's greater verbal discrimination ability? Or girls' dependence on and sensitivity to other's opinions about their appearance? Or boys' greater expressive self-containment? Are differences due to schooling, societal, and/or genetic influences?

My studies were *not* of randomly sampled schools *nor* of randomly-sampled students matched to approximate the number of students in their region or of their age-group. Instead, my schools initiated their surveys. They typically surveyed their entire student body or representative samples of it. My norms draw their data from many more schools of many different types from all parts of the country and abroad for more than 20 years. My studies do not possess the AAUW's methodological strengths; I don't know how generalizable my findings are. What compensates for their potential selection bias is the consistency of the patterns across different schools, ages, genders, regions, and countries.

The interpretive challenge I and those of you who wish to be institutional diagnosticians now face is how to understand and reconcile, if possible, seemingly contradictory results from different types of studies.

Few researchers have studied systematically the inner world of boys and girls moving from elementary to senior high school. The AAUW study and mine begin to fill that subjective gap about their feelings and beliefs. To track down the sources of Table 5-1's grade differences, Table 5-3 summarizes in more detail than Table 5-1 the course of morale grade-by-grade for NAIS and public school boys and girls. To confirm the generality of the trends I include American international school students from the Middle East, southeast Asia, and the Far East. The 5th to 9th grade morale scores come primarily from all the students in Saudi Arabian international schools.[17] Note how sharply the course of morale differs from the AAUW's reported results in every type of school here and abroad.

Table 5-3   Course of Morale for Boys and Girls Through the School Years

			Total Morale Score			
School Grade	Public		NAIS		International	
	Boy	Girl	Boy	Girl	Boy	Girl
5	116.8	119.2	118.1	123.5	119.9	126.1
6	107.9	114.6	116.9	119.9	119.5	121.4
7	109.2	110.5	106.3	112.7	112.0	114.0
8	101.0	105.2	108.8	111.1	107.5	111.8
9-12	97.0	98.6	104.4	105.9	102.1	104.5
College			104.8	105.5		

Two of the table's patterns demand considered interpretation: the remarkably consistent gender differences in morale and the progressive decline in morale from one grade to the next. Their implications should disturb everyone concerned about creating healthy learning environments for every youth.

For every grade level, school, and region, girls are more satisfied with their schools and their own fulfillment and growth. How reliable are these extraordinarily consistent differences? Exceptionally so. Except for overseas schools' sixth and seventh and public school seventh graders, the odds range between only two out of 100 and one out of at least 10,000 that the differences may be accidental or due to chance. Louis Harris's 1997 national poll of students and teachers confirms the tenor of my findings. Girls enjoy school more, have higher expectations for themselves, are more confident, receive more encouragement from their teachers whom they believe are good role models from whom to learn, and are equally as competitive as boys.[18] Should not the title of these studies be *Shortchanging Boys?*

My normative information about gender differences among teachers is less trustworthy. A state-wide study of one state's NAIS teachers in the 1970s produced highly reliable differences between the females' higher and the males' lower morale. Since that time, I have found no consistently reliable differences between the genders' morale. More often than not, NAIS female teachers have higher morale than male teachers, though not always reliably so from one school to the next. Public school male and female teachers do not differ in their morale in my samples. So the long-term, more pressing question that Table 5-3 provokes is how to understand and respond to the consistently declining morale from fifth grade through the pubertal years.

What May Account for Students' Progressive Decline in Morale?

With only some minor exceptions, the pattern of declining morale across all schools and for both genders is indisputable. To reconfirm the finding with another group, I compared statistically the international school's combined boys' and girls' morale for each grade against the next grade's morale. The differences in morale for every comparison from fifth to ninth grade are highly unlikely to be due to chance. By ninth grade students' morale apparently stabilizes; I have found no consistent progressive change from ninth to twelfth grade and possibly through the college years, at least in small liberal arts colleges.

How shall we interpret this progressive decline in satisfaction from the ages of 10 to 14? This pattern of marked transitional change indicates a period of heightened vulnerability—hence educability—that can affect all subsequent growth. Why the decline? I illustrate how assessment can lead to new knowledge and disciplined hunches about how to organize schools to be more effective.

One hunch is that the decline is due to qualitative cognitive changes that occur during early adolescence. Children's minds become freed from the immediate here and now. They begin to imagine alternative and future possibilities against which to compare their past and present. Gaps between what is and what could be can fuel dissatisfaction and prepare the ground for developing critical thought. My lovable ten-year-old grandson is becoming an itch; he is hyper alert to my hypocritical inconsistencies. Tact is not yet part of his emotional vocabulary.

A second related hunch is that the expanding compass of a child's mental world and physical activities open schooling to more entertaining and enjoyable *competitive* activities. Schools' sameness becomes dreadfully boring to hormonally high-energy, pubertal children.[19] Its sameness has become even more acute in our television-dominated, high-intensity, fast-paced lives.

Another hunch is that schools become even more demanding that children accommodate to *their* structure and academic curricular requirements—even more so in a day that demands more academic work earlier, at the expense of fun-full activities like band and sports. Words like individuation, child-centeredness, the whole child, playfulness, curiosity, and expressiveness recede in priority. Does the declining pattern of satisfaction signal that middle schools are increasingly out of phase with children's healthy development, at least for marginal academic students, like schools' potential drop-outs? Chapter 12's analysis of their inner world traces their growing alienation back into the middle school years.

How might we discipline our speculations by empirically searching for answers? A study of every fifth to ninth grader in Saudi Arabia American schools provides an unexampled opportunity to tease out some probable answers.

What are the Sources of the Developmental Course of Morale?

A Case Study of Saudi Arabian American International Fifth-to-Ninth-Graders' Morale

I first briefly describe the Saudi Arabian cultural context within which American schools must operate. Then I compare their and comparable State-side students' specific sources of satisfaction for clues. Saudi Arabia throws up a stern bulwark against most adolescent temptations. It forbids competitive and disruptive societal excitements and seductions, therefore accentuating schooling's boredom and students' declining morale. No western violent TV programs, drugs, alcohol, sexual materials and other enticements are permitted in the country's moralistic society—except for wild car racing for older Saudis. Children are aware of how it severely punishes those who stray from its Muslim ethical code. Those who steal can lose their hands; others their heads.

Without the incessant intrusion into their lives by America's advertisers', TV's, and rock stars' entertaining temptations, the international students depend more upon each other for their entertainment. Thirty-three percent more than the State-side students view their peers to be joyful, for example. More see them to be natural, playful, relaxed, talkative; fewer view their peers to be academic, conscientious, hard-working individualists.

The American international schools and their curricula are modeled after the State-side schools to which most of their ninth graders will go for their high school years.

In spite of the country's stringent and suppressive cultural climate, its schools' teachers have reliably higher morale than their comparable USA NAIS teachers. Perhaps due to a spillover of the culture's suppressive moralistic tone, the teachers view their schools to be more conforming than NAIS elementary and middle school teachers view theirs to be. More of the latter believe that their schools are creative, adventurous, expressive, independent, individualistic and intellectually exciting than the international teachers believe their schools to be.

I compared the morale of the American schools' middle school children in Saudi Arabia with their NAIS counterparts in the states. They did not differ reliably in their overall morale. Socio-cultural differences apparently in and of themselves do not account for the decline.

I next sought clues from the comparisons of one grade to the next to determine at what point in the middle school experience the biggest declines occurred. The two largest and most reliable declines for the Saudi Arabian American and NAIS schools were between sixth and seventh and eighth and ninth grades for both boys and girls. The transitional year from elementary to middle school is such a vulnerable time that it even overwhelms the pervasive gender differences of the earlier and subsequent grades. In Saudi Arabia, the ninth grade can also be a tumultuously upsetting year. The Saudis do not permit foreign children to remain in the Kingdom after ninth grade. Either the parents return to the states or they must send their children back alone. The evidence suggests that much more care needs to be devoted to the transitional years when students' expectations and patterns of behavior are most vulnerable to new challenges.[19]

Since the morale scales contain 30 sources of potential dissatis-faction, I identified those items which showed a *consistent* year-to-year decline in satisfaction from fifth to ninth grade. The only source for both boys and girls that did *not* decline was their satisfaction with their personal relationships with other students. In order of *consistently* grade-by-grade declines in satisfaction were the sources

School not meeting strongest needs
Degree of involvement in their courses
Being a student as a source of identity
Quality of teaching and growth of teachers
School providing the skills believed needed

The sources of the *greatest* decline in satisfaction from seventh to ninth grade were

Amount of freedom and independence
Opportunity to create in school
School meeting their deepest needs
School providing the skills believed needed

The pattern suggests students become increasingly emotionally distant from school and their teachers. Are teachers failing to accom-modate themselves to their students' developmental changes as they perceive them? Is school beginning to lose its credibility as a growth-producing environment?[20]

How might an assessment and its methods pursue further the hypothesis that the growing mismatch between a school's structure and expectations is a cause of declining morale? As Chapters 7 to 9 will illustrate, we can now map the changing values and attitudes of fifth to ninth graders about numerous attributes of their schools and teachers. We can then discover the percentages of students who consistently use positive attributes less frequently from grade-to-grade. We can also identify a school's unfavorable attributes which increasing percentages of students use to describe their schools and teachers from grade-to-grade. In other words, we can search out con-sistent patterns in students' perceptions of their schools and teachers if we wish to pinpoint more specifically the schools' sources of their declining morale.[21]

To return to the AAUW study of gender differences, can you now understand my uncertainty about how to interpret its principal conclusions? Let us assume that the measure of morale is allied with and may tap into children's generalized feelings about themselves. We could test this assumption by using more valid measures of self-esteem. Or students could describe themselves on 150 traits, many of which reflect favorable attitudes about their selves. We could then create an independent index of self-esteem to correlate with the AAUW's measure and my measure of morale. My hunch is that the students' attitudes about themselves on only five generalized feeling-toned statements may vary from day-to-day. Self-descriptions of specific personality traits may not vary as much and of their morale much less so. So I predict the latter two measures would be much more highly related than the AAUW measure with either.

Do you also now understand that comparing boys' and girl's self-esteem is much more complicated and must be approached more contextually and thoroughly?

I agree that students' satisfaction with themselves declines in the pubertal years. I disagree that the evidence is clear that girls' self-esteem declines more than boys'. I disagree with the implication that girls are "worse-off" than boys in terms of their long-term future adjustment.[22] The sources of the different rates of decline are much more complicated than have been assumed. Schools increasingly shortchange both boys and girls. Much deeper and thoughtful studies of transitional developmental years, such as the pubertal ones, are essential to create healthier, growing-up school environments.

The next chapter provides examples of how measures of morale can provide illuminating information about a variety of problems that schools face. I recommend you use the examples to test your growing intuitive and judgment skills for understanding the morale of your organization more systemically.

Chapter 6

————•◦•————

INTERPRETING FOUR CASE STUDIES

Understanding any social system as complex as a school requires intuition. We never have enough information about the way its members "behave and interact with each other in groups . . . [Schools] are about the attitudes, the aspirations and the motivation of people. . . ."[1] Intuition helps us identify the critical information we need about a school's members and their relationships; it may even fill in information's gaps. It is a preconscious process of drawing hunches from clues of which we may be unaware or cannot readily identify. People say it is like listening with our third ear; or like the ability to see around corners; or like the diagnostic acumen of famed clinicians or court lawyers sensitive to nuances and barely perceptible changes whether of a patient's skin color or a jury's demeanor. Intuition requires openness to reflected upon past experiences and their lessons. Rich and varied experiences provide the matrix out of which hunches emerge—sometimes miraculously at just the right moment. If you wish to develop the intuition needed by an institutional diagnostician, pause, absorb, and actively reflect about the four different examples I now describe. They may sensitize you to clues you may need to better understand your own organization in the future. To change the metaphor, enjoy learning how to become a psychological detective.

Marathan—a Private Pre-K to Sixth Grade School with a Morale "Problem"

Marathon illustrates that a faculty's morale may not be what it seems and that intuition and judgment are required to make sense of seemingly contradictory information. Marathon's board president asked for help. Two years earlier the board had hired a new 35-year-old principal. It had since been deluged by complaints from a few older teachers. They said that she was destroying the faculty's morale with her demands and by asking some older teachers to leave. They also claimed that some parents were going to pull their children out of the school.

The board planned to meet to consider dismissing the principal; it sought assistance about its course of action. Fortunately, I had data about the faculty's morale prior to the new head's arrival. The school had participated in a regional workshop on assessment the year before she arrived. I recommended a more complete study of the school to learn the "facts" about the faculty's current morale.

Marathon's principal—brisk, decisive, well organized, masculine— told me she was the first full-time head. Previously, a faculty-parent had run the school part-time; the business manager had made most of the decisions. Board members were parents who contributed their services, including janitorial. The school had been formed 15 years earlier by a group of parents who had run the school until it had become too large for them. She said,

> When I came I discovered there had been no curricular coordination. The second and third grade teachers taught the same social science unit. I had to let some faculty go. Last year was chaos. The third grade teacher did not pull her weight. The "old guard" resisted suggestions to take on more responsibility, such as supervising the lunch hour; they refused to get more professional training which the school would pay for. Some teachers have very wealthy husbands.

She said that parental complaints had mounted; she recognized that some threatened to pull their children out of the school.

While other classes were eating lunch, I visited the third grade. Suddenly six other teachers appeared to circle the class' teacher to comfort her. Her car had been bumped by another car on the way to work, which they had just heard about.

During the afternoon's workshop I reviewed the faculty's morale which was similar to that of other elementary school faculties. To the obvious displeasure of several teachers, it had not declined from three years earlier. It actually had improved—though not reliably. They were most satisfied with their relationships with each other, the social value of their work, freedom and independence, and opportunity to be creative.

I was puzzled why the statistical analysis showed that the best predictors of their morale were, in declining order of their contribution, their satisfaction with

- the quality of their relationships with their students
- amount of energy their work demanded
- effects of the job on their marriages and children
- school's working conditions
- the status and prestige of their occupation [1]

Note that not one single "calling" item is in the list. So I asked the faculty for examples of behavior that distinguished a calling from a job. Few could cite any. Why? Fifteen minutes before the end of the workshop, six women got up to leave—one of many signs of a "job," which no one had cited as an example.

Later I asked the two male teachers how they felt working in a female-run school. Some of the "old guard" had criticized them for not being "feminine" enough. They spoke too loudly. They also touched the children too roughly.

Now pause a few minutes to test your intuition. What hypotheses make sense of the observations and survey findings? What would you have advised the board that evening?

The incredulous board searched for every possible reason it could think of to explain away the fact that the faculty's morale had not declined: Faculty wanted to please the board, protect themselves from demands to change, or were consciously manipulating its results. But the board could not then explain why the earlier and current statistically-determined pattern of predictors as well as the level of morale were so similar.

I suggested that the faculty, especially older ones, may view their work as a job, not a calling. They are closely bonded together as friends; the school may fulfill their needs for community recognition and status in their small but very wealthy community. The faculty's alleged morale was an illusionary result of "group-think," fostered by two charismatic "old guard" women who had very low morale, I subsequently learned. They had led the campaign to convince the board—and their friends—of the entire faculty's allegedly low morale. They viewed their school (themselves?) to be enthusiastic, friendly, creative, accepting and caring, a view shared by only 40% of the children—an unusually low percentage for elementary children, who typically are most generous in their praise of their teachers.

The advent of a professional educator temperamentally dissimilar to the "old guard" threatened to disrupt their cozy and comfortable relationships. Her style wasn't "feminine." Satisfied with their freedom and independence to do what they wanted, they resented the young head's assertive intrusion into their classes. She became the shared scapegoat to protect their relationships as well as self-esteem. That the school's younger teachers supported the more professional head's actions made matters worse.

If the hypotheses have merit, what would you suggest?

Marathon reminds us again how important it is for a self-renewing school to have baselevel information against which to check either actual or illusionary change. It also illustrates why anecdotes, impressions, and gossip must always be tested for their validity. The collective self-image of a faculty can unknowingly affect the healthy growth of a school's teachers.

Rosemont—Sources of Potential for Faculty-Student Misunderstanding

Chapter 1's Rosemont junior high school illustrates another basic interpretive guideline. Every singular strength, as its faculty morale was, should be evaluated cautiously; it could be a liability, depending upon the morale of others in the school. Recall what I labeled as the Rosemont paradox: exceptional faculty morale, much lower student morale, and faculty hyper-criticism of its pubertal children. Rosemont's high faculty morale, so envied by the district's other faculties, was the school's premier strength. But it blinded everyone, except its students, to the school's potential liability: the effect of the faculty-student discrepancy upon its students' healthy growth.

The paradox is important to pursue because it has much broader implications for assessing organizational healthiness. Consider, for example, the possible effects of too-large discrepancies between the incomes of managers and workers. Megamillion dollar salaries can dull one's empathy for and understanding of how "the other 99% live." Such discrepancies can create staff tensions and feelings of being unappreciated or devalued. (Some American businesses make it an annual ritual to antagonize their workers by their inordinate executive salary increases. Their executives should visit the homes of some of their workers for dinner to begin to develop the empathy that their high incomes may snuff out.)

The discrepancy in morale between Rosemont's faculty and its students is a case in point. Its students were not favorably disposed toward their faculty as we have seen. So they might not be as educable as they could be for their teachers' efforts to make them into high school students. How might we analyze their morale to understand how the students might be feeling?

Since the adult and student morale forms are generically identical and parallel in their order, the greatest discrepancies between their satisfactions can be directly compared and ordered. Table 6-1 lists the faculty's sources of potential misunderstandings of its students in declining order.

Table 6-1   Rosemont Faculty's and Students' Greatest Differences in Satisfaction

Satisfaction with	Faculty Satisfaction More than Students'
Amount of freedom-independence I have	1.8*
Degree of responsibility I want	1.2
Ethical standards and practices of school	1.2
My type of vocation [Role as student]	1.0
Quality of work-growth of my students [of my teachers]	1.0
School meets my strongest needs	.9
Amount of recognition I receive	.9
Opportunity to innovate and create	.9
Relation with those in authority	.9

* Out of a perfect score of 5, Rosemont's faculty rated its satisfaction 4.6 and its students rated theirs 2.8, almost two full points less, and reliably lower than other junior high school students in comparable schools.

Clearly Rosemont's faculty is securing satisfactions from its work that its students are not. What might be some implications and consequences of these differences? Consider the most egregious difference— their satisfaction with their freedom and independence. Draw on your intuition for a hypothesis about the school from these facts: The faculty scores reliably higher in its satisfaction than other comparable faculties not only with its freedom but also with its opportunity to create, the amount of responsibility that it wants, and its relationship with the principal.

Why? Might one implication be that the principal has given her teachers full rein to do what they individually wish? So of course faculty will be more satisfied than students that their needs are being fulfilled. Might this lead to the creation over time of a teacher- rather than student-centered school? Possibly at the expense of students' developmental needs to grow healthily? If a correct hypothesis, the telling question then becomes this: Has such a laissez faire administrative style created a growth-producing environment for both students and faculty?

What may be the consequences of a lax administrative style? Teachers most satisfied with their freedom and students most dissatisfied with their freedom and independence, 68% of whom are bored with their teachers whom the students believe are not growing themselves? Might one predict that the faculty may have continuous discipline problems, especially with potentially rebellious eighth-grade boys testing their independence? Or if squelched, how will their urge for independence be manifested? In passive negativism, stubbornness, and apathy toward their faculty? In self-derogation or self-destructive activity like drugs and drinking? Absent crucial information about their views of their peers and especially of themselves we can not check the judiciousness of our hypotheses.

Rosemont teaches us, when interpreting single scores, to be alert for large discrepancies from internal patterns or external norms. They may signal strength; they may instead signal weaknesses. Rosemont also teaches us to test hypotheses against all of the evidence and recognize when crucial evidence is missing.

Discrepancies between administrators' and teachers' perceptions can also be most telling and should be carefully analyzed for their sources and implications as Anthony College now tells us.

Anthony College—Founded by
a Male Religious Order

Anthony reminds us not only how administrators' high morale can blind them to their teachers' realities but also that a calling is not enough to create a healthy school.

Anthony's president called to say that an accrediting team had reported several years earlier that the faculty's low morale was a serious problem. The administration had sought to understand its sources without success. Could I help?

A midwest male religious order had created within a miraculously short period of time a liberal arts college that attracted increasing numbers of students. The administrators had secured adequate financial support. They had decisively moved to meet all of the suggestions of a searching accreditation report that had approved the college. I was not just impressed but moved by the administrators' dedication and commitment to produce a flourishing college during the troubled late 60s and early 70s. Was the accrediting committee's report about low morale true?

Yes. Although the all-male administrative staff's morale was high, the faculty's morale was indeed low, due in large measure to the reliably lower morale of its female faculty.

The administrators and students agreed with the faculty's views of the college.

Table 6-2   Anthony Faculty's View of College

Conservative	73%	Dedicated	58%
Authoritarian	71	Defensive	58
Friendly	69	Plans ahead	58
Hardworking	67	Conventional	56
Can say no	64	Can make decisions	51
Religious	60	Cautious	51

However, the faculty and administrators differed so markedly on 16 additional values as to suggest that they were working in two different colleges. The administrators viewed the college more favorably on every one of the 16 values: caring, cheerful, conscientious, considerate, feeling for others, fun, and so on. None of the faculty but half of the administrators described the college as *not* afraid to complain. Fifty-five percent of the faculty but only 8% of the administration described the college as emotionally cold. The students agreed with the administration that the college was caring, cheerful, considerate, and felt for others. They agreed with the faculty that the college was not accepting, fun, or possessing a deep ethical sense.

So why the low morale? I have provided you with enough clues to test your intuition. What hunches come to you that might explain the faculty's low morale? [ASH 10: Interpreting Morale Scores describes steps to learn faculty's ideas about how to improve morale.)

My hunch was that a decisive, driving, efficient administration had shaped a college that a significant number of faculty members did not feel belonged to them. For them, their teaching was a job, not a calling. For the administrators, their work was a calling. Those who have a calling find it difficult to understand those who don't. The administrators' genuine effort to understand and be empathic may have been viewed by some faculty as manipulative, self-serving, and paternalistic. An adversarial relationship had been created.

The decade was marked by the growing anti-Vietnam, anti-authority, and some women's anti-male attitudes and hyper-sensitivity to any signs of disrespect. No woman filled a departmental chair. Stereotypic authoritarian masculine but unempathic males were just not psychologically attuned to women's emerging autonomous self-hood. A symbolic clue to the administrators' blindness to their women's low morale was their catalogue statement about the college's purpose: to educate its students to become "Christian men"! The college had been coed from its founding!

Marshall's District Leaders' Conflicts— Real or Imagined?

Marshall illustrates how understanding different staffs' morale and perceptions of their schools can be a healing experience. It is a moderately-sized southern city with a district staff of about 160 for its 60 schools. The district had been under a court's desegregation order for years. Twenty-five percent of its students had left for private schools. Most schools remained effectively segregated because of residential patterns.

The state had recently mandated additional administrative supervision and evaluation of teachers and required burdensome reports. Marshall's staff felt under great time pressure. Its already fragmented and conflictual relationships had become even more aggravated. The superintendent's staff, central office personnel, and local principals were themselves internally divided. They were suspicious that their colleagues and the other two staffs were not carrying their share of the load. Words such as "indifference," "insensitive," "unappreciated," and "enormous frustration" described the feelings of the different staffs about each other. Gender and racial conflicts initiated by some alleged red-necks further aggravated the staffs' relationships.

To prepare for a two-and-a-half day retreat, the staffs completed an altered form of the VAS. I asked them to also rate how satisfied they were with their relations with each of the three district staffs as well as their views of the district.

The retreat sought to create a climate of trust that would encourage open and honest communication in numerous, varying, task-oriented groups. The changing groups were composed of persons of different status, gender, and racial backgrounds. The surveys provided the information necessary to identify their shared and conflicting problems, morale, and views of the school system. The retreat ended with exercises to implement the staffs' deepening understanding of each other.

Analysis of the three staffs' morale revealed two unifying themes. First, the prolonged desegregation and recent legislative mandates had not undermined the morale of any one staff more than that of the other staffs. Their collective total morale was high, especially in their satisfaction with their competence, type of occupation, quality of relations with their colleagues, and personal devotion to their work. Their overall satisfaction with their work and relations with the other two staffs did not differ reliably. Only the principals were reliably less satisfied than the superintendent's and central office staffs' on two of the specific sources of satisfaction: the effect of their work on their families and as a source of friends.

The similarity of the three staffs' level of satisfaction and principal sources of satisfaction surprised everyone. People became aware that they were more unified in their satisfactions than they had believed. They became freer to speak more openly about their concerns for themselves and each other.

The second unifying theme emerged from the statistical analysis identifying the most and least contributory items to the total morale. The staffs shared the same pattern of items that contributed most to work being a calling and the same items that contributed least to their total morale score. The implication of the results was obvious. In spite of the daily frustrations, conflicts, and suspicions, the three staffs were fundamentally united by their morale and calling to their work.

By this time, the staffs were emotionally ready to face the sensitive issues of their gender and ethnic differences in morale. Though the women and Afro-American administrators tended to have higher morale, the differences in their total scores from those of the remaining staffs were not reliable. However, reliable differences emerged for a few specific types of satisfactions. Male administrators were reliably less satisfied than their female counterparts in only two ways: the ethical standards and practices of their work as well as their relation with those in authority. Black administrators were reliably more satisfied than white ones with the quality of their work, amount of responsibility, and the time and energy that they spent on their work. Since the varying discussion groups always included different staff, gender, and ethnic members, each explained to the others their reasons for these reliable differences in morale.

The similarities among the three staffs emerged in more concrete ways when their views of and wishes for the district and their emotional commitment to the district's system-wide goals were assessed. Remarkably, they agreed in using the same values to describe their district: academic, capable, adaptable, hard-working, and caring. Only the superintendent's staff differed most from the other two staffs. It believed that the district was not as capable, empathic, and friendly as the other two staffs believed. The same pattern held for their wishes for the district. Furthermore, the majority of each staff was not emotionally committed to the district's goals of developing reflective, independent, self-educating, and self-disciplining students. They did feel committed to the district's remaining goals.

Finally, the males and females and Afro-Americans and whites shared remarkably similar views of and wishes for their schools.

By the evening of the second day, the staffs were emotionally ready to plan how to implement their understandings. As other school and college faculties have taught me, experiencing and

understanding how others really feel can dissolve doubts and
suspicions and release spirited energy. I have also learned how healing playfully working with others on critical issues can be. Playfulness encourages trust as well as vulnerability to change. Finally,
surveys of hundreds of schools and colleges have told me that few
students and faculties, even elementary ones, believe that their
schools are playful places in which to grow. Only 11% of public high
school faculties, for example, view their schools as playful. Marathon's
leaders' views were similar. No staff believed that the district was
playful. Playfulness makes taking risks and so change much easier.

I alerted the staffs on the second day's afternoon to come that
evening to be playful and have fun with each other. That evening I
randomly assigned the staffs to one of seven groups. Each was to
create in 25 minutes a spontaneous 20-minute skit to provide a
"solution" or resolution for one of the retreat's themes. By this time,
status, gender, and ethnic differences had become so blurred we were
just human beings having a playful but serious time together. The
skits revealed some extraordinary hidden dramatic talents, especially
among the blacks, whose souls were irrepressible. Everyone expressed
amazement at the transformation of their rather stuffy and reserved,
perhaps shy, superintendent. No one had guessed how spontaneous
and hilarious he could be. He would have won Marshall's Academy
Award if it had one to give.

The last group of the evening returned with a song—yes,
incredibly created, memorized, and practiced in 25 minutes so they
claimed. Titled *Side by Side,* it began "Oh, we ain't always been so
open" and closed with "We're together like never we have been . . .
SIDE BY SIDE!!" They had discovered they could be "honest" with
as well as "share" and "care" for each other Everyone joined in as
we sang the song together twice more.

I had never laughed with so much abandon and had so much
respect for the creative talent and hilarity of a group of educators
before. How our systems and structures and attitudes suppress our
humanness and healthy growth as Deming told us! Their playfulness
was a genuine sign of their healing. Only mature people can objectify and laugh at themselves so humorously.

Though this chapter has focussed on understanding the dynamics
of morale, it has been impossible to avoid mentioning a school's

culture that affects it. Chapter 7 more formally analyzes an organization's culture, ways to measure it, and illustrates how to interpret it. It describes another less objective survey that requires even greater judgment, synthesizing, and intuitive skills. Its interpretation is not a cut-and-dried exercise; no interpretive cookbook or computer program will help us make sense of its numbers. Schools' profiles may be similar, but not accurately reflect their uniqueness. Only intuition and its disciplined testing are the routes to understanding a school's complexity and uniqueness.

SECTION IV

———•———

Understanding Culture

Chapter 7

———•·•·•———

ASSESSING A SCHOOL'S CULTURE[1]

Recognition that institutions are social systems organized by patterns of values, expectations, motivations, and relationships is widespread. IBM, the Senate, Harvard, Public Broadcasting System, Hollywood, a Catholic parish church, and, yes, MHS each has its own distinctive culture. Researchers of organizational cultures use words like climate, character, ethos, and saga to refer to a system's uniquely unifying values. An institution's collective morale and culture are a social system's two more important attributes to which to attend, nourish, and preserve.[2]

Why? An organization's culture, subjective, hard-to-measure, and invisible as it is, can decisively affect its effectiveness. Corporate managers know this truth. Their organizational mergers flourish or flounder for many reasons, one of the more important being the extent of their shared cultures. After decades of study, researchers also know this truth. The most sophisticated international study of the determinants of research groups' productivity found no traditional material inputs like equipment or number of support staff to account for their productivity. It was their climate of cooperativeness, dedication, and innovativeness that contributed to their success.[3] British researchers of 12 London schools found that not students' intellectual aptitude or objective school attributes but their subjective ethos or climate to be the most powerful predictor of student outcomes, like dropout rates and academic achievement.[4] Hardy, examining the undergraduate origins of highly productive adults like creative scientists and scholars, claimed the most productive schools were those sponsored by the Society of Friends. He concluded that "it seems probable that a specific Quaker influence is at work."[5] Tinto, summarizing more recent research on the effects of classrooms' cultures, reports that the quality of their interpersonal climates contribute not only to increased achievement but also to persistence in college.[6] A prominent educational researcher, Mayhew, claims that clarity about one's distinctive character and purpose is "possibly the most significant long-run administration problem for an institution."[7]

As subjective and slippery a concept as "culture" or "ethos" may seem, several objective methods are available to classify educational cultures, for example, as academic or social egalitarian. Colleges' cultures rather than elementary, middle, and high schools' cultures have been most frequently studied using these methods.[8] When consulting with schools and colleges I have found such objective methods too constricting and relatively insensitive to schools' (defining colleges as schools) systemic uniqueness. Much more powerfully illuminating is a less structured method, called Word Check List (WCL), that maps teachers' and students collective perceptions of their schools and its attributes.

The Word Check List Measure of Culture

Structure of the WCL

The WCL consists of 150 words identified by educators to describe their schools' salient attributes and outcomes. [ASH 11: Description of Measure of Culture-WCL] The list includes words describing academic, interpersonal, lifelong learning, and ethical behavior, among other attributes. About 80 of its 150 words describe positive attributes such as intellectually exciting and caring; the remainder are negatively-toned words such as boring and emotionally cold. Schools occasionally add other words relevant to their goals.

The WCL's structure and generic list can be used to describe any target of interest to a school or researcher. The targets most frequently described are the School, Typical Student, Typical Faculty Member, and Oneself. Other targets can be described, such as the Athletic Department, the School's Head, English Faculty, a Fraternity, a specific Class.

The WCL's instructions have been designed so that even fifth graders can complete the task. "As rapidly as you can, check every word in the list you believe describes . . . [target being described] If you believe the word doesn't describe the target but you wish that it did, then circle the word. Work rapidly. Don't pause. If you hesitate, skip the word and go to the next." [ASH 34: Description of Word Check List for Different Aged Groups].

WCL's free-form has both strengths and limitations. Its foremost strength is that it can map a person's self-concept as well as an organization's members' collective view of their reality. When working with faculties or students, I playfully provoke them in order to make this strength experientially clear. I hold up a yellow pencil and ask volunteers to share what they see.

What might you report?

What might an art teacher see?

And a seventh grade boy say?

Who is right?

What is the most profound and important principle this simple example illustrates about how to understand a social system as complex as a school?

For me, and most others, the principle is that the reality to which we adapt and which governs us is the reality we subjectively perceive—not what may objectively exist, however that is to be determined. If I, as a playful seventh grade boy, believe the pencil is a missile or a prod to poke a girl with, then that is the pencil's potential reality at the time. Our perceptions can determine our behavior and so become self-fulfilling prophecies. If I believe that my students are dull, unmotivated, and hostile, then I will most likely react accordingly. Today's perceptive students will sense my belief about them and may begin to react accordingly. If I learn from my colleagues' WCL descriptions of their typical student that they believe their students to be otherwise, my view may change. We begin to know reality or the truth more fully when we empathically understand other peoples' views about students, our school, even ourselves.[9]

Other advantages of the WCL are its generic nature and target flexibility which make it useful for any institution. It also provides indices of a school of hope's eight defining criteria, as I will demonstrate shortly, and of its healthiness, as the next chapter will explore.

The WCL also shares the limitations of free-form measures. It maps perceived but not always actual reality. Even teachers and students can be collectively deluded! To understand their behavior we need to enter empathically into their views of reality; but, from other perspectives, their views may indeed be delusions. Just remind yourself of those who have "seen" invading Martians or who believe the apocalypse will occur at 12:01 a.m. 2000 A.D.

A more manageable limitation of the WCL is that its administration is liable to numerous errors that may distort its reliability. I will alert you to most of them.

Another limitation is that the WCL's format, offering a respondent only three choices (for example, check, circle, or ignore), does not provide the opportunity to assess *degree* of agreement. To refine the survey to measure it would require more time and concentrated effort. To sustain students' concentration, the WCL would probably have to be shortened 50%. I opted for the richness of the tints and shadings that the WCL's 150-word pictures make available. [ASH 12: Limitations of Word Check List].

I now turn to the WCL's most severe potential limitation: its interpretive challenge. Given the WCL's unstructured form, its results can be organized in a variety of ways for interpretive purposes, depending upon the questions asked of it. This chapter illustrates how the WCL provides information to assess if a school fulfills the standards of a school of hope. The next chapter illustrates how the WCL can be used to assess a school's systemic health. Chapter 9 enters into the inside of three urban minority schools currently schools of despair; it seeks to understand how the WCL may help us understand why and their potential sources of hope.

Astute intuitive diagnosticians, even detectives, have access to memories of rich and varied experiences. These memories are sources of hunches about similarities, deviant patterns, or the significances of seemingly irrelevant clues. The WCL norms [ASH 37-39: Stable, Provisional, and Illustrative Norms] are an inadequate substitute for securing the first-hand experiences out of which hunches can arise. However, the norms do provide vicariously rich patterns of collective teachers' and students' perceptions for different targets. If you are using ASH as a supplement while reading this book, why not now reflect about what ASH's norms tell you about what thousands of students and teachers believe about their exemplary schools. Pay close attention to their beliefs that disagree with yours. What findings especially shock or surprise you? Wise psychological detectives are aware of how their own personal biases can blind or oversensitize them to some clues rather than to others.

One warning. Some confuse norms with the "ideal" or what should be. They are not. Norms describe what teachers and students believe and wish. I use the norms as information by which to make disciplined hunches about whether a school approaches other types of standards drawn from other research.

Another warning. Studies as complete as of Reagan's academic high school produce a massive amount of information that overwhelms most faculty in an academic workday. To not overwhelm you also, I abbreviate some tables which ASH completes. They can provide the vicarious experience necessary to hone your diagnostic skills.

Assessing Standards that Identify a School of Hope

Schools of Hope Have Distinctive Cultures

Distinctively shared or communal values is a cardinal attribute of a school likely to produce enduring effects on its members. What Word Check List criteria define "distinctive?" Two-thirds agreement about 15 or more of WCL's values by the constituents. While arbitrary, I have found that criterion identifies strong schools whose values are palpable when visiting and talking with their members. Adelphi is one such school. Remember, every constituency, including its board and parents, agreed about its academic excellence. They collectively selected every academically related value on the WCL to describe the school. It is rare, and presents a diagnostic problem, when faculty have a distinctive view of a school and the students don't, or vice versa.

A school whose faculty and students do not agree about its character or culture drifts from one contentious argument, program, or "improvement" to the next. It does not have the shared core values necessary to provide direction, guidance, and expectations about how faculty and students should behave or grow.

Table 7-1 compares how distinctive are the cultures of some of America's most prestigious schools. The independent schools are members of the National Association of Independent Schools (NAIS). Many of the suburban public high schools are their region's lighthouse or nationally known schools. I single out Reagan high school because of its exemplary reputation as a public school that fulfills conventionally accepted criteria of academic excellence.

Table 7-1 includes all values that at least two-thirds of at least one of the three types of faculties and/or students agreed described their school. All of the chapter's tables order their values in terms of declining agreement by public schools' teachers' views.

Table 7-1   The Culture of Suburban Public, Reagan, and Independent (NAIS) High Schools

Value	% Public		% Reagan		% NAIS	
	Faculty	Students	Faculty	Students	Faculty	Students
Academic	77	83	92	94	84	92
Athletic	67	79	54	88	63	68
Capable	65	47	62	52	70	60
Caring	64	34	54	45	73	54
Dedicated	64	45	68	58	73	60
Hard-working	58	54	70	64	67	70
Competitive	55	73	56	83	64	73
Friendly	53	41	34	44	68	60
Demanding	45	59	26	62	62	73
Excellence	42	33	70	66	47	45
Artistic	37	48	36	70	40	47
Total # 66%	2	3	4	5	6	5
Average % agreement	57.0	54.2	56.5	66.0	64.6	63.8

Table 7-1 leaves little room for equivocation. Independent schools generally have more distinctive cultures than Reagan and other affluent suburban public high schools. Both public school faculties and students agree that the premier values of their schools are academic and athletic; NAIS faculties and students view their schools to be academic and hard-working. Reagan's faculty and students almost universally agree about their school's academic culture, which probably contributes to their shared belief in its excellence.

Table 7-1 points to one of public schools' greatest collective weaknesses: the lack of coherent communally shared values which could unite a faculty. Individual NAIS upper school faculties or students share at my 2/3 criterion level between 5 and 15, rarely more than 18, values that describe their schools. Not one of the table's favored 19 public high school faculties or student bodies agrees about more than Reagan's five faculty or student communal values. Might not this reflect the constriction of their vision of departmental academic excellence that excludes character development?

Does not Table 7-1 point to another collective weakness of our schools? Research suggests that genuine academic excellence and adult success and well-being depend upon the healthy growth of the person, not just of his or her mind. Elementary school faculties, more than middle school faculties, more than high school ones typically agree about many of their schools' values. Why? They share a common developmental understanding of students that includes character values. Table 7-1 clearly tells us that the principal, even singular, value of affluent suburban public high schools and many NAIS ones is educating the mind.

Schools of Hope Educate Character as well as Mind

Americans are, in my judgment, obsessed in unhealthy ways by numerical measures of their students' minds. Do we not believe that intelligence accounts for all of the good things in life? It seemingly is our highest value, the key to adult and national success—a collective delusion about what really contributes to future adult success. Why do books with titles like *Endangered Minds* or about black's lower IQ scores, "multiple intelligences" (really competencies technically), "emotional intelligence" (really character attributes), and "moral intelligence" (really conscience and ethical sense) capture public attention and best-seller status? Given our other national obsession, how soon will another enterprising author publish a book titled *Sexual Intelligence*?

Schools of hope value mind but also the character strengths now known to contribute more to youths' future success and fulfillment.[10]

Character refers to interpersonal strengths which are the soil out of which ethical values grow. Chapter 15 will compare in more depth public and independent high school differences in their moral climates. Until then, I focus on schools' interpersonal learning environment that may contribute to their students' ethical development.

Always examine the values about which faculty and students agree for clues about the tone or character of a school. Table 7-1 tells me that faculties more than students and independent more than public school students view their schools to be caring and dedicated places. Few faculties and students ever agree at my strict two-thirds criterion that their schools are personal, sympathetic, understanding, and trusting places. When interpreting WCL figures, keep in mind that adolescents, especially, are learning how to be critical, even hypercritical.

Table 7-2 lists six of the more important WCL values that describe schools' interpersonal cultures. [ASH 13: Interpreting Schools' Interpersonal Culture].

Table 7-2 Suburban Public, Reagan, and Independent (NAIS) Faculties' and Students' Views of Their Schools' Interpersonal Cultures

Traits	% Public Faculty	Students	% Reagan Faculty	Students	% NAIS Faculty	Students
Helpful	47	41	36	43	55	57
Feels for others	33	21	26	24	49	33
Understanding	32	22	24	32	44	36
Open	30	26	20	35	33	37
Personal	22	16	22	15	39	30
Trusting	22	17	12	22	34	30
Average %	31.0	23.8	23.3	28.5	42.3	37.1

To interpret wisely such objectively based tables we must draw upon not just our common sense and experience but knowledge of relevant research. For example, do not hastily believe that a high average trusting, personal, and understanding (what I label as "warm") interpersonal environment necessarily guarantees more mature students. Leaders of marine boot camp and some military academies might claim otherwise. It may, but it may not, even for girls. A study sought to compare two boys, two girls, and two coed independent schools; one of each pair would have a favorable personal and trusting culture and the other not. Unfortunately, the researchers could not find an accessible warm boy's school. They found that girls matured most in emotionally cold girls' schools.[11] Given widespread concerns about learning environments appropriate for each gender, the study should be redone. But its implication tells me that we should not incautiously jump to conclusions based either on our biases or just WCL's findings.

What hunches does the table suggest to you? To remind us once more that our hunches are only that, not conclusions of high certitude, I phrase my hunches as queries.

Do the majority of independent and public-Reagan faculties and students believe that their schools provide them a friendly interpersonal environment?

Who believes their schools' culture is more interpersonally friendly? Who believes it is the least?

Which faculty—independent, public, or Reagan—may understand its students' beliefs about their school's interpersonal relationships least accurately? What interpersonal attribute present in their schools do faculties and students disagree most about?

If you were on a school improvement committee, what finding would trouble you most about the committee's likely success?

Whose results raise questions about their reliability and/or deviate most from the pattern of the other groups?

Two implications especially trouble me.

Why do independent school faculty and students consistently view their schools to be more interpersonally friendly places than public-Reagan school faculties and students believe their schools to be?[12]

Have our country's academically competitive schools, like Reagan, created the learning environment or culture that might further character's interpersonal maturation? Chapter 15 returns to answer this query with respect to character's core ethical values.

Given how hypercritical today's teachers and students are and how stringent my criterion is for identifying a shared cultural value, I pay close attention to the positive or health-related values that faculties and students definitely do not attribute to their schools. When 20% or fewer of the faculty or student body describe their schools with such words, then the attribute is *not* salient enough in the school's culture to have an impact on its members. Recall Rosemont's junior high school students. Fewer than 20% of them believed that the school was empathic, loving, personal, sensitive, sympathetic, or warm. Table 7-2 suggests that suburban public school students do not believe that their schools are either personal or trusting. If you were a teacher, member of a school improvement committee, or parent, how might you feel about your school if these attributes are not salient?

Schools of Hope Have Leaders Who are Stewards of the School's Culture

Schools of hope need leaders, not just administrators. As they are held more accountable for their school's success, we need normative information that describes how their faculties and students view them. The WCL could provide that information. I don't have that data. Only one head of the several hundred schools I have studied in depth ever requested his faculty to describe him on the WCL. His courage was not foolhardiness. His faculty saw him as a leader and steward.

Bloomfield Hills district has been blessed by two leaders-stewards in my judgment. Each has taken numerous steps, including TV and radio interviews, to communicate his vision for the district to the community. After speaking to the district's parents one super-intendent rose to affirm for five minutes his agreement with my message. He hoped that the district's schools would become more caring places. I was dumbfounded by his affirmation. It was the only time a leader had seized the opportunity to interpret and extend my message to the school's community.

Faculties of Schools of Hope Empathically Understand Their Students' Interpersonal World

As aging teachers continue to teach the same aged but changing generations of youth, they risk becoming less understanding of and empathic for the inner turmoil, motivations, and hopes of their

students. Rosemont's faculty-centered school shows us some consequences of such psychic shearing. Faculties vary greatly in their
collective understanding of their students' views of their peers.

Table 7-3 illustrates the principal normative differences between
teachers' and their students' view of the typical student. The table
includes all of the differences larger than 20% between the
public-Reagan and the independent school teachers' and students'
views of the typical student. It orders them by the public schools'
teachers' differences. For example, 27% more public school teachers
than their students believe that the typical student is a conformist.
More critical for teachers to understand is how many more students
than they, i.e., 30%, believe that their peers are sarcastic.

What ideas can you draw from Table 7-3 about teachers' understanding of their students' views of their peers?

**Table 7-3   Comparison of Public-Reagan High School with
Independent (NAIS) Faculty's and Students'
Views of Students' Peers**

% More Faculty than Students' Beliefs about Typical Student				*% More Students than Faculty Beliefs about Typical Student*		
	Public	Reagan	NAIS		Public	Reagan	NAIS
Conforming	27	29	15	Show-off	35	30	15
Apathetic	26	27	-3	Sarcastic	30	38	24
Needs approval	21	18	30	Rebellious	29	32	18
Cooperative	20	33	23	Athletic	26	29	15
Conventional	20	25	14	Creative	26	23	8
				Courageous	25	23	10
				Humorous	23	40	6
				Moody	23	18	18
				Stubborn	22	19	15
				Adventurous	21	20	7
				Aggressive	21	17	4

When interpreting this and similar tables, keep in mind that
they do not report the *actual* percentages of faculty who believe

that their students have the trait. Note, for example, that 26% more public high school teachers than students believe that the typical student is apathetic. Actually, 40% of public high school teachers believe that; only 14% of their students believe that their peers are apathetic, hence the difference, 26%. [ASH 37C,E: Public and Independent School Norms].

What do you interpret to be teachers' most serious misunderstandings of their students which could limit the creation of a growth-producing learning environment?[13] Students' perceived conformity, cooperativeness, and apathy may block out of teachers' awareness their students' potential strengths, such as their humor, willingness to take risks, creativity, and courage.

Adults and Students of Schools of Hope are Adventurous, Caring, Intellectually Exciting, and Trusting

To understand schools as social systems we must empathically understand their members' perceptions and relationships, which are keys to their effectiveness. This view generates radically different questions about how to improve schools than legislators, reformers, and educators ask. The most critical is: What are the personality strengths of faculty members that contribute most to their and especially their colleagues' continued self-renewing efforts? Teachers from diverse schools in all parts of the country agree that they need colleagues who are trusting, caring, adventurous, and intellectually exciting. Few schools have had the courage to get the WCL information about their faculty's collective view of their colleagues' growth-producing strengths. So I do not have norms about how teachers view their colleagues. But is it not foolish to talk about becoming a self-renewing school if teachers do not believe that their colleagues are at least adventurous, caring, intellectually exciting, and trusting? Are not such teachers essential if students are to also grow as self-renewing people?

Only Sandia, a poor African American and Hispanic urban high school of my public school sample and a few NAIS schools have had the courage to ask about their teachers' personalities. Table 7-4 gives their answers supported by their students' beliefs.

**Table 7-4   Selected Sandia and Independent (NAIS) Faculty's
and Students' Views of Their Faculty's
Growth-Producing Character**

Growth-Producing Trait	% Sandia		% NAIS	
	Faculty	Students	Faculty	Students
Adventurous	18	22	29	23
Caring	51	22	86	67
Intellectually exciting	9	24	33	41
Trusting	16	18	35	45

The table tells us that only 9% of Sandia's teachers believes that their colleagues are intellectually exciting people to work with, and that only 18% believe their colleagues are willing to take risks. Does not Table 7-4's answers go a long way to explain why efforts to improve schools are so laborious, joyless, and seldom sustained? Does it not suggest that we must examine more thoughtfully what is it about the way schools are structured that blocks the emergence of such growth-producing strengths? Should we not more thoughtfully reconsider the goals of faculty development programs?

Teachers and Students of Schools of Hope Are Called to Their Work

Chapter 5 distinguished between work as a calling and as a job and its implications for a growth-producing school. I have noted that morale cannot be understood independently of other information about an organization. The level of teachers' and students' morale should be reflected, for example, in how favorably and unfavorably they view their school.

The WCL provides the opportunity, therefore, to check the reliability of the morale scores. Rosemont's failure to secure the faculty's view of its school gave me no clue about how trustworthy its exceptionally high morale score really was. Not having its views of its school also crippled interpreting what school attributes may have contributed to its high morale. Since Rosemont's students' only average morale was mirrored in their view of their school, I assumed that I could trust their morale scores. So I more confidently interpreted the unusually large differences between their and their faculty's morale to suggest a more teacher- than student-centered junior high school.

Teachers and Students of Schools of Hope Are Emotionally Committed to Their Goals

Experienced teachers have endured a succession of new heads, each of which has engaged them in another year-long debate about their school's mission. They also have participated in interminable improvement committee meetings. Many are cynical about the results of one more debate or committee. "Nothing will change in the long-run," they tell me. Why? Because too often the faculty does not emotionally own or is emotionally committed to the revised goals. Teachers play their principal's or legislator's games but continue to do their job as they have always done it. Implementation of a school-wide goal or improvement plan should begin with the goal or plan to which the largest number of teachers are emotionally committed.

How can a faculty's emotional commitment be assessed? You may disagree with my method; however, it often illuminates why schools fail to achieve their goals. Remember the instructions for completing the Word Check List? To complete it as quickly as you can and not to hesitate. The WCL assumes that decisions made under time pressure are likely to be more emotionally than thoughtfully and rationally based. If you completed ASH's WCL, why did you not check or circle some of the more favorable words you could have selected? I measure emotional commitment by the sum of a faculty's checked and circled percentages as Table 7-5 illustrates. A value not immediately in awareness and not an "alive option" is unlikely to motivate behavior.

Table 7-5 reconstructs Sandia's portion of Table 7-4. How ready is Sandia's faculty to take more adventurous steps to improve its school? How might Sandia's teachers' view of and hopes for their colleagues affect their readiness to renew themselves? Could we count on Sandia's students to support efforts to shake up the faculty to be more intellectually exciting?

**Table 7-5   Sandia Faculty's and Students' Emotional
Commitment to Faculty Growth**

| | % Faculty | | | | | | % Student | | |
| | About Colleagues | | | For Self | | | About Faculty | | |
	Check	+Wish	=Total	Check	+Wish	=Total	Check	+Wish	=Total
Adventurous	18	22	40	49	9	58	22	8	40
Caring	51	24	75	96	0	96	22	32	54
Intellectually exciting	9	29	38	25	19	44	24	12	36
Trusting	16	9	25	70	2	72	18	28	46

For comparison purposes, more NAIS than suburban public school students would emotionally support efforts to encourage their teachers continued growth: adventurous 56 vs. 54%; caring 81 vs. 69%; intellectually exciting 63 vs. 47%; and trusting 55 vs. 46%. As a relevant aside, 37% of NAIS but 64% of suburban public high school students believe that their teachers are boring. Are they self-renewing models to their students?

Do you, as a rational critic, find such results to be inconsistent? If two-thirds of Sandia's students believe that their teachers are boring, which is in fact the case, why are only 36% committed to their teachers becoming more intellectually exciting? But isn't this just Sandia's and most other schools' problem? As the Department of Education reports, large numbers of today's students do not have an ideal for themselves, their teachers, and their schools.[14] The discouraging reality is that only small proportions of adolescents think of themselves as idealistic: 32% for NAIS, 29% for public, and 12% for Sandia. Don't count on students to prod their teachers to become more adventurous, caring, intellectually exciting, and trusting people.

Schools of Hope Welcome Accountability

Most schools shy from being held accountable for their members' morale and culture. The consequence is that a school's systemic attributes are seldom assessed. The morale surveys, WCL, and other methods I describe later are semi-accountability measures of those attributes. When I visit a school I ask how open is it to change, how is it holding itself accountable for its school-wide goals, how educable will it be for interpreting its own data non-defensively, and who will be most resistant to the type of assessment that the morale and cultural methods provide? The WCL provides initial answers. I rely on about 20 traits, including adventurous, cautious, conventional, and traditional, to give me clues about an organization's educability. It is the pattern of traits, not a single or only a few traits, that is the most reliable indicator of a school's openness to renewing itself. [ASH 14: Clues to Readiness of a School for Self-Renewal].

This chapter has demonstrated how the WCL can assist us to answer a variety of significant questions. The next chapter examines a different type of question: Can the WCL provide clues about the health of an organization?

Chapter 8

Evaluating the Healthiness of
Schools and Colleges

Sick societies. Dysfunctional families. Paranoidal religious groups. Such evaluative terms imply a standard of health and wholeness.

Growth-producing cultures. Self-renewing schools. Healthy classrooms. Similarly, such terms must rest upon some evaluative standard for their assessment.

Chapter 4 proposed just such a standard for evaluating the healthy growth of individual students. Extensive empirical studies of adolescents from MHS and comparable independent schools, transcultural studies of mature and immature college men, and longitudinal studies of men and women throughout their adult years mapped similar maturing effects. Might not the confirmed dimensions that describe the healthy growth of individuals provide a standard, a template so to speak, with which to evaluate an institution's health?

In this chapter, I explore if and how the WCL's findings can be organized to provide clues about the healthiness of schools and colleges. Is it not reasonable to assume that if an organization is devoted to the healthy growth of its members it should provide a healthy learning environment? What then would be marks of a growth-producing culture and self-renewing school?

Schools of Hope assumed that schools that contributed to the growth of both its students' minds and its characters, resulting in a strong self, furthered the healthy growth of its members. Most schools of hope like MHS are growth-producing ones as well. However, I am now mindful that there might be exceptions. Ideologically organized schools, such as military academies and religious schools and colleges, may possess the attributes of a school of hope but not thereby encourage the healthy growth of their students. Their consensual values or mission may be to develop, as is the case for some military academies, honor, discipline, and obedience or of religious schools commitment to a theological orthodoxy that may limit healthy growth. Honor, discipline, obedience, and theological orthodoxy may be more important than healthy growth. But, as Chapter 4 proposed, if healthy growth or maturity is our principal value, then its course is now known with more certainty.

The formal model of healthy growth identifies five attributes of a healthy school which contribute to how well it adapts. Healthy schools

- reflectively and accurately understand themselves, and are
- empathically responsive,
- internally coherent,
- stably resilient, and
- autonomously distinctive.

As Appendix A summarizes, healthy schools' cope more effectively, have freed energy for creating cooperative relationships, and the objectivity to laugh at themselves.

Model was a hopeful school that produced healthy changes in its students. It was reflectively self-aware, empathic, coherent, resilient, and autonomously distinctive. Its healthiness enabled it to cope adaptively to subsequent financial stringencies with grace.

This chapter highlights the character of healthy organizations by describing schools and colleges that faced issues to which they were not adapting well. They lacked some of a healthy system's coping strengths which the WCL can identify.

Adaptive Strengths of a Healthy School

Healthy Schools Accurately and Reflectively Understand Themselves

More mature persons accurately reflect and understand themselves. Insight into one's strengths and weaknesses can assist adapting more effectively. Faculties similarly aware about their school's culture and classroom's dynamics should be able to take more effective actions. Chapter 1 described Countryside's Montessorian faculty and student differences in their views of their students. Only 8% of the faculty but 59% of its elementary school students believed, for example, that the typical student put each other down; none of the faculty but 43% of its middle school students believed that their peers were sarcastic. Not being aware of these facts meant that the faculty did not know it had to take steps to create a friendlier school culture.

Lack of faculty insight into their schools' culture is not confined to elementary or secondary school teachers. Focused on their departmental interests, many college faculties with which I have worked are singularly unaware of how their students' peer culture affects their classroom behavior.

Appalachia—a Rural Southern Coed College Losing Its Best Students

Appalachia attracted good students from its region but lost its better ones by the end of their freshman year. Its mountainous isolation accentuated its students' need for fraternities and sororities. During each fall's first six weeks, freshmen were heavily "rushed" by fraternities trying to "out-party" each other; they lavishly wined (more accurately, illegally liquored) their freshmen. The chosen fraternity became the students' home for their remaining years. Students said the peer pressure made it impossible to resist the rushing pressure and/or drop out of the frats.

How did the faculty view its typical student? Eighty-one percent agreed that their students were conforming and friendly, 73% that they were easy-going, and 69% that they were accepting, conventional, and needed approval. Scarcely an inspiring and exciting group to teach.

But what was the tenor of the students' beliefs? Happy and amusing friends who would make cheerful bar companions. At least two-thirds believed their peers were friendly, easy going, adaptable, fun, and humorous. Clearly a fun place to be with some prolonged "happy hours"! Perhaps because the faculty sees its students Monday morning, it does not believe they are as amusing, humorous, and happy.

What did this suffering faculty wish its students were like? Few other faculties have been so united by its frustrations and pains. For a faculty, a remarkable 75% wished its students thought more clearly. Perhaps a reaction to their students' Monday morning hang-overs— if they even showed up for class. Atypically large percentages (more than two-thirds) also wished that their students were creative, hardworking, intellectually exciting, and curious.

The students were quite content with their companions. Fewer than a third agreed about any ideal quality it wished for them.

By now you probably have the same hunch that I had. The pattern of growth that occurs in school during students' first six weeks tends to set the pattern of behavior for the remaining years. The faculty had unknowingly yielded the opportunity to alter its students' minds and characters to the dominant fraternity culture. What character attributes did students need to survive in that culture? Just the attributes students saw in their typical peer. Since academically oriented and involved students have been found to be less involved socially with their peers, did the better students soon come to feel out of synch with their peers?[1]

The faculty tested this hypothesis for the next two years. It worked with the fraternities to initiate rushing the second semester, established and enforced alcohol guidelines, and created alternative living arrangements and special educational supports for its honors students. Two years later a smiling dean told me the new programs were working; the dropout rate of good students had declined, student morale was higher, and the school's culture was healthier. Students were grateful for the faculty's sensitive but firm leadership to free them from peer pressure they couldn't resist by themselves.

Healthy Schools are Empathically Responsive

When we mature, we grow out of our narcissism or self-centeredness to more empathically understand, respect, and care for others. Similarly, a healthy school is student-centered; it empathically understands, respects, and cares for students' welfare. Model's students' descriptions of growth on this other-centered dimension reflects an empathic school. Recall the Rosemont paradox. What was the effect of its self-centered faculty upon its students' healthy growth?

Marlboro Boy's School—From Playing Football to Serving Minority Kids

Marlboro's head had participated in a national conference on assessing a school's morale and culture. He invited me to assess both and to work with the faculty on their findings. When I arrived, his first words were, "Doug, I don't understand our seniors. Two-thirds of them have spontaneously volunteered to work with a neighboring boy's club. You know, the school was founded to make men out of boys. That's why for more than 35 years we have required all boys to take tackle football among other things. More and more upper school boys resist that requirement. Why?" I knew. Their surveys had told me.

Despite the school's prestigious record for preparing its students for college, the faculty's and students' morale scores were too far below comparable schools' norms to suggest a healthy growing-up environment. Tables 8-1 and 8-2 provided me with the key to understand why. Can you find the key?

Table 8-1   Students' and Faculty's Views of and Wishes for Marlboro

% View of the School Ordered by Student Views		Faculty	% Wishes for the School Ordered by Student Wishes		Faculty
Demanding	84	69	Flexible	52	31*
Competitive	80	69	Changeable	50	8*
Authoritarian	69	54	Loving	39	0*
Helpful	69	54	Creative	36	62*
Dedicated	68	77	Fun	36	15*
Conservative	66	54			
Intellectually rigorous	66	31*			

* Indicates a large enough difference to which to pay special attention.

Fewer than 20% of the students checked words like "feels for others," "genuine", "loving," "open," and "sympathetic" to describe Marlboro—though not an atypical result for high-powered academic schools.

**Table 8-2   Students' and Faculty's Views of and Wishes for
Marlboro's Typical Student**

% View of the School Ordered by Student Views		Faculty	% Wishes for the School Ordered by Student Wishes		Faculty
Competitive	83	75	Logical	59	29*
Critical of others	72	29*	Loving	59	0*
Not afraid			Thinks of others	50	63
to complain	66	58	Feels for others	38	46

The boys also believed that their peers were defensive (60%), self-centered, sarcastic, and show-offs (at least 52%). They wished that their peers were also less critical and more caring—again not atypical views of and wishes for contemporary male students.

For me, one wish was *the* tell-tale clue about why so many of Marlboro's boys volunteered to work with black youngsters. Forty-four percent more Marlboro than private high school students wished that their peers were loving. Large discrepancies from norms, especially of those for stereotypic gender roles, can be the keys to understanding a school's uniqueness and health. I suggested that Marlboro's rigorous effort to create "men" unheathily stretched its boys too far out of shape. It activated unconscious compensatory efforts to regain a healthier equilibrium. Was volunteering to work playfully with emotionally needy and expressive black kids the boys' unconscious way of growing more fully, and so healthily? Was it also a way of telling an authoritarian and stubborn (checked by 55% of them) school it needed to change? Was its singular goal of "making men" in the 1920's model getting in the way of helping the boys learn how to adapt to the changing meaning of gender roles? I don't know. But years later, a teacher told me that my hypothesis had shaken up the school. It subsequently altered its emphases.

I still would ask the question today of most schools I have studied. How healthily is the school preparing its students to live in an egalitarian future? Won't it increasingly demand that they be sensitive to and empathically feel and care for others' needs to be future parents, professionals, and managers? Chapter 14 will tell us we still have a very long way to go, especially in preparing boys for such a future.

Healthy Schools are Internally Coherent

A healthy system's component sub-systems work harmoniously together to support each other and the welfare of the system as a whole. We now know that mature persons are well-integrated. Their values and actions are so consistent that they act with integrity; their relationships are cooperative and reciprocally mutual.

Bellewood-Wells—a Girl's and Boy's K-12 School Beginning Its First Merged Year

The female head of Bellewood, a girl's school, asked for help. It and Wells, a boys' school, wanted to know what issues might trip them up as they began their first year as one school. The Wells' middle and upper school faculty moved to Bellewood's campus; the elementary schools occupied Wells' campus. She said the predominantly male Wells' faculty was uneasy and apprehensive; it had resisted its board's mandated merger.

The study's results reassured both faculties. Neither school's culture would be compromised. In fact, the combined school would be stronger; the school would have a more distinctive culture than each school had had separately. Faculty morale would be normatively high. The Bellewood-Wells school could provide a healthier climate for both its boys and girls.

One large fly in the ointment was Wells' male faculty whose morale was lower than its female colleagues' and Bellewood's faculty's. Its views of and wishes for its school were also least congruent with the impending school's culture. The merger would upset Wells' male much more than it would its female faculty.

The ointment became less sticky when Wells' male faculty learned that Bellewood's male faculty tended to have lower morale also. The combined male faculty would be reliably less satisfied with about a third of the VAS 30 items, especially with several items indexing work as a calling. Recognizing that the morale differences were due more to gender uncertainty about the meaning of their vocation than to differences between the schools lessened the male faculty's apprehension about the merger.

The WCL results were fortuitously comforting. Simply averaging the two faculty's views of their individual schools showed that at least two-thirds of the combined faculty agreed about a remarkable 19 values describing Bellewood-Wells. Equally as reaffirming of its distinctiveness was that the two faculties disagreed noticeably on only four of the 19 values. Fewer Wells' than Bellewood's teachers believed that their school was friendly (61 versus 95%), considerate (57 versus 90%), giving (39 versus 83%), and feels for others (39 versus 83%%).

The Wells' male teachers were relieved. Bellewood's more typical feminine interpersonal strengths scarcely threatened their well-being.

Furthermore, both faculites agreed about the attributes that did *not* describe the combined school. Like normative faculty beliefs, neither faculty believed that their schools anticipated consequences well, planned ahead, completed their plans well, or were efficient and thorough.

Finally, both faculties did not differ by more than a few percentage points in their wishes for their schools. When their wishes were combined, they did not differ from my NAIS faculty norms.

So far so good for institutional integration. Male faculties inexperienced teaching girls tend to be apprehensive about teaching them; they express uncertainty about how to cope with girls' moodiness and tears. They find boys' coolness and stiff upper lips easier to deal with. Although the Wells and Bellewood faculties agreed in most of their views about their boys and girls, they did differ on primarily gender-related traits. Fewer Wells' teachers believed that their boys were cooperative, caring, social, empathic and fun; fewer Bellewood's teachers believed that their girls were academic and hard-working, a non-stereotypic difference.

Interestingly, and again very affirming, each faculty wished that its students would grow in just the ways that the other faculty had described its students to be.

The last index of the internal coherence of the two faculties' beliefs was the similarity of their emotional commitment to their goals for their students. With few exceptions they shared very similar commitments.

I predicted that the merged school would flourish; the merger would make two strong schools even stronger. Their differences were complementary, not divisive, and tolerable; their similarities were highly integrative. Like other schools, the combined school would continue to grapple with its gender differences. Its culture was supportive. I did not forsee other issues that could fracture its coherence, except one—faculty disagreement about the meaning of excellence. Too few teachers emotionally committed themselves to educating for both mind and character *at the level of excellence* I assumed its type of students could reach.

Would I include Bellewood-Wells on my list of schools of hope? No, not yet. I did not know its students' morale and views. The two faculties' similar pattern of emotional commitments was not enough. If I were head of the new school, I would challenge the faculty to raise its hopes for its students' growth. Its internal coherence is not enough to create a growth-producing learning environment for itself and its students. Its singular integrative strength could prove to be too great; it might produce too great contentment. Recall that too extended development on one attribute can inhibit or distort development on another.

Healthy Schools are Stably Resilient

Studies of mature persons confirm that they are more stably organized and resilient than less mature persons. But not rigidly so. They are open to new growth requiring new integrations. For example, mature American Protestant and Jewish, Italian Catholic, and Turkish Muslim males compared to less mature ones have more stable cognitive skills; they maintain their cognitive efficiency even under stress. If disorganized, they quickly recover their cognitive efficiency.[2] They also have stronger identities that provide them the self-confidence to take risks.

Analogously, healthy schools are stably resilient. They organize their identities around a core set of values that provides institutional self-confidence and sense of direction.

Broward illustrates how critical it is for a school's health that its culture be understood *and monitored* as changes are introduced by those in power.

Broward—a Girl's School Adjusting to an Authoritarian New Head

Broward, a girl's school, had a new head who in only three years converted a resiliently stable school into an unhealthily rigid one. Its assessment also illustrates how the WCL can be used to monitor the effects of changes on a school's culture and health.

A faculty committee asked me to resurvey the school eight years after my first study. It was worried about the health of the school and the beginning flight of some of its most competent teachers. It was too circumspect when replying to my question about the head's support for the survey. I sensed trouble. I sensed more trouble when the head refused to permit the morale of the faculty to be assessed.

An engaging but quite assertive female head took charge of me when I arrived. She reminded me of Marathon's head, whose board had been ready to fire. During her three years at the school she had had some acrimonious run-ins with some teachers she felt were not very professional. Though she did not place much faith in surveys, she wanted to know what I had learned. I gracefully tried to prepare her for the results' onslaught the next day.

The tenor of the workshop told me it was not going to be a fun day for me. The faculty was restless. Its tension was obvious. The surveys had suggested that it might be divided between academic traditionalists and what I couldn't quite name. Faculty identified with a more free-spirited culture? I was not sure what the handkerchiefs that some women wore on their heads meant. Were they protesting the workshop and my presence or defying the head?

I let the survey's results speak for themselves. What do they tell you?

Table 8-3   Comparison of 1980's and 1988's Faculty's View of and Wishes for Broward

View of School	% 1980	% 1988	Wishes for School	% 1980	% 1988
Academic	100	100	Adventurous	20	43*
Ambitious	84	80	Adaptable	16	40*
Demanding	84	87	Flexible	15	40*
Caring	80	77	Democratic	8	30*
Friendly	80	63	Happy	4	27*
Intellectual	80	77	Fun	0	20*
Competitive	76	97*	Open	0	20*
Energetic	76	70	Sensitive	0	20*
Hardworking	76	90	Warmth	0	20*

* Large enough difference unlikely to be due to chance

Table 8-3 told me that in spite of the signs of trouble, the school was not on a self-destructing course. The school's tough academic core and very distinctive identity had not softened during the eight years. Broward had purified its academic climate even more. It had become more competitive; twice as many faculty members viewed it to be intellectually rigorous than other comparable NAIS faculties viewed their schools to be. At what cost? Possibly a warmer more humane climate. About 20% more faculty than the 20% eight years ago now wished its severely masculine culture were leavened by more stereotypical feminine interpersonal strengths. Whether or not the purification created a healthier culture for Broward's girls could not be assessed. The faculty committee had not requested that I study the students.

How healthy has the purification process been for the faculty? Table 8-4 orders the faculty's largest positive and negative perceived changes from most to a 25% perceived change. It also lists each attribute's NAIS norm to highlight Broward's distinctiveness. Compare columns two and four as you study the table.

**Table 8-4   Largest Changes in Faculty's Perception
of Broward**

Increase in Faculty Perceptions	% 1980	% 1988	% Difference	% NAIS
Conventional	8	63	55	45
Defensive	8	53	45	28
Authoritarian	16	57	41	32
Perfectionistic	8	43	35	18
Rigid	12	47	35	20
Conservative	36	67	31	60
Conforming	24	50	26	35
Inflexible	4	30	26	16
Decrease in Faculty Perceptions				
Initiative	56	17	39	22
Expressive	8	20	28	30
Humorous	40	13	27	37
Deep ethical sense	45	20	25	37

What might be your reaction if you were a board member? The academic purification of Broward had paid a price. Would it have been too great for you? The school's strong core academic identity had not been diluted. But the systemic context that made its academic values acceptable to the previous faculty had been wrenched out of shape. Perhaps even the academic traditionalists would agree, given the large percentage increases in words like "defensiveness" and "authoritarian." So what has been the cost? Would you agree with my hunches?

1. Decreased faculty ownership of their school.

2. Closing down of opportunities for innovative, creative, and adventurous faculty initiatives.

3. Devaluation felt by more student-centered teachers of themselves and their values.

4. Increased stress and decreased faculty joy in teaching and possibly a beginning transformation for some people of their work as a calling into work as a job.

5. Faculty perception that the feminine interpersonal sensitivities that support and contribute to ethical development have diminished.

While not directly relevant to illustrating how healthy schools are resiliently stable, you might try inducing some possible effects of Broward's changes upon its girls.

What does Broward teach us? Institutions are sturdy systems and despite severe twisting can retain their core identities. Too purified and limited focus, whatever it be, risks becoming maladaptive. In the pursuit of excellence, again of whatever type, efforts can overshoot and activate compensatory resilient efforts to seek a more healthy equilibrium. Marlboro's boys also taught me that. Stability without the means to express and accommodate compensatory efforts becomes rigidity. When only 17% of Broward's faculty (representing a 23% decline) believe that it is not afraid to complain then tensions, apprehensions, and hurting voices are not heard. Was this why I was asked to resurvey the faculty? To give an authoritative voice to what the teachers felt they couldn't say directly for fear of losing their jobs?

I had to conclude that Broward had become an unhealthy though even stronger academic school.

Healthy Schools are Autonomously Distinctive

A strong distinctive identity is a mark of mature persons. They are their own persons. They feel in command of themselves and are able to maintain their individuality even when pressured not to. Broward's handkerchief-covered women apparently had no other way to assert their values. But their protest showed burgeoning signs of autonomy. Mature persons are not so autonomous that they are immune to others' influence and change; their empathic responsiveness moderates the dangers of excessive autonomy that breeds narcissism.

The WCL provides one way to assess schools' distinctiveness. Recall Table 7-1, which compared the cultural distinctiveness of suburban public, Reagan, and independent high schools. With the exception of Model and Reagan, the public high schools I have studied do not have as autonomously distinctive identities as independent schools do. Why? They must be everything to everyone—especially to their vocal taxpayers and legislators. They lack the special character necessary to win students' respect and desire to acquire their values. The charter school movement may be a compensatory or equilibrating response to the sufferings of such schools that feel so powerless to develop and defend their own identities.

Why are large urban schools so intractably difficult to turn around? For many complex reasons. But an important one is that some are not autonomously distinctive. They are too vulnerable to external changes that, paradoxically, make them too resistant to improvement. As was true for Washington, transitory administrators, lack of meaningful local control, here-today-and-gone-tomorrow faculty, central office assignment of personnel, and diverse students from unsettled homes do not make for strong identities and cultures—even agreement about a few values. Word Check List studies of three urban schools reveal how psychologically impoverished such schools can be; they do not have the cultures and strong identities to unite their faculties and students for communally initiated and sustained improvement. Is there no hope for them? No, the WCL identifies their leading hope.

Wentworth—a Transitional Low Middle Class White and Black High School[6]

Wentworth town borders a large metropolitan area from which blacks had been fleeing for about two decades, preferring to live in the town. Their resistant white blue-collar neighbors had also been moving but further away from Wentworth. The high school also had changed from a majority of white to a majority of black students. A dedicated core group of predominantly white teachers had remained. The high school had been formerly controlled for years by an authoritarian ex-naval commander. He had ordered new teachers not to smile at students their first months at the school! The district has had a superintendent revolving door history: For years, a new one has arrived, on average, every two years. Each has had his own policies and priorities.

The high school does not have a strong distinctive culture. The surveys confirmed a perceptive teacher's comment since the study that the faculty did not have a common language to be able to talk with each other; in her words, "the district has no bonding vision." Two-thirds of the high school faculty could not agree about *one* single value when describing its school. Fifty-seven percent could agree that it was defensive and conservative and 50% that it was authoritarian and conventional, but also accepting and caring, possibly because of the core faculty. The arrival the year before of a new principal had brought hope. He encouraged his faculty to smile.

What is it like to be a student in a school that is in transition? Altering the gender or ethnic composition of a school is risky. It may dilute its identity and autonomy unless it has strong stable leadership and a distinctive culture. Table 8-5 compares the views of Wentworth's white and black students about the high school. Because the students could not agree at my two-thirds criterion on more than three values describing the school, I include those at least 60% could agree on.

Like its faculty, other than boring, two-thirds of the white students could not agree about any value of the school. While physically integrated, Wentworth was not psychically integrated. Black and white students worked as if in different schools. Black students also saw the school as cautious and needing approval; whites did not. Whites saw the school as amusing and humorous; blacks definitely did not. Blacks wished the school were more reasonable, alert, and amusing; whites did not. Wentworth was moving to be a divided school with two weak cultures.

Table 8-5   Comparison of Wentworth's White to Its Black Students' View of and Wishes for Their School

View Ordered by Black %	White %	Wishes Ordered by Black %	White %
Boring	90	67*	Understanding	50	30*
Adaptable	70	44*	Joyful	45	41
Dull	70	55	Happy	40	30
Accepting	60	33*	Trusting	40	15*
Conservative	60	19*	Fun	40	48
Talkative	60	44*	Considerate	35	44

* Differences of 20% in view of school and 15% in wishes are large enough to merit special attention.

A principal source of hope was the faculty's shared frustration about the school. It was united in its wishes that the school were more academic, intellectually exciting, ambitious, and excellent, among a number of other wishes. Regretfully, I had to conclude that the odds that that hope would be realized were low. Like Washington's faculty's "loser" image, its faculty also had a miserable collective self-image that would scarcely sustain efforts to improve the school. Apparently the teachers described themselves when they described their peers. They believed that their peers were rigidly defensive, authoritarian, conservative, and conventional.

The promise that its new principal could bring apparently had not been fulfilled. Since I studied the school, its faculty worked three years without a contract. Forseeing no change, it desperately resorted to a lengthy bitter strike which split it further. I have not restudied the school but I suspect frustration's hope has been squashed for years to come.

Sandia—a Poor Black and Hispanic High School

Chapter 7 described Sandia whose students were overwhelmingly poor, Hispanic, and black. Like Wentworth, it too had no distinctive identity to its faculty. Recall that few members felt their colleagues were adventurous, intellectually exciting, or trusting, Few were emotionally committed to assist their peers develop such strengths.

Only 44% were committed to becoming more intellectually exciting teachers themselves. Two-thirds of its 74 faculty members could *not* agree on one value that would set the school on the path to a stronger more autonomous identity. Fifty percent of the faculty did agree, however, that the school was inconsistent and defensive.

Its students also agreed about few values, but scarcely ones of which the faculty could be proud. Like Wentworth's students, 68% (and 36% of the faculty!) agreed that their school was boring. An additional 62% believed that their school put them down, and 60% that it was dull and unfair. Again, like Wentworth, a principal source of hope was the extent of the faculty's shared frustration. More than a third of the teachers had 13 wishes for the school. It wished that the school were more academic (62%), intellectually exciting (44%), efficient, enthusiastic, and excellent (39%).

Washington— a "Loser" Public Junior-High School for Very Poor Students

Washington's WCL results are remarkably similar to those of Wentworth and Sandia. Do Washington's teachers teach in each other's school? No. Two-thirds of its faculty also did not agree about one value that its school stood for. When I lowered my criterion of distinctiveness to 55 from 66%, as I did for Wentworth and Sandia, Washington's faculty could agree about only three values. Sixty-three percent believed that their school was a friendly place and 61% as accepting and caring. Significantly, 52% viewed it as apathetic. Again, like Wentworth and Sandia, the faculty's wishes were similar. Forty-three percent wished the school were more academic and consistent. At least 37% also wished it were intellectually exciting, enthusiastic, and excellent.

Washington's students agreed on only three values. Seventy-one percent believed that their school was capable and 62% adaptable and friendly. However, at least 55% agreed about seven more primarily positive values. Still, lack of strongly-held values about the school's academic and character's interpersonal and ethical values made uniformed guards a necessity at each corridor's corner.

Do Washington's teachers teach in the school in which their students learn? No, definitely not. The faculty did not agree with its students on

53% of their descriptions about Washington. I noted earlier that lack of agreement was a sign of unhealthiness. Washington was not a "together" or psychically integrated school. It was a school of despair.

What is the hope for such urban minority schools? National standards? Computers in every classroom? Increased math requirements? Fine for the Adelphis, Edinas, and Models, but for Wentworth, Sandia, and Washington, scarcely. We must *first* deeply understand our schools as social systems whose morale and cultures are the growth-producing keys to sustained improvement. Not until we emotionally own these keys will standards, computers, and more math assist students and faculty to discover their potentials.

Healthy Schools Cope Adaptively

The model of maturity maps the core strengths needed to cope adaptively. The sign of the maturing mind's strengths is incresing mastery, competence and power. The signs of the maturing character's strengths are increased ability to create communal relationships and freed energy for new projects. The sign of the maturing self is its heightended capability for transcendence marked by objectivity and sense of humor and hope.

Prairie College's renewal efforts—one might even say rebirth—illustrate the more visible signs of increased institutional coping effectiveness.

Prairie College—a Dying College Seeking a More Vital Identity

Prairie is a small, midwestern, liberal arts college rooted in a 19th-century religious tradition that is no longer a source of inspiration or vitality. Its aging president, retaining control of its board, had publicly vowed to remain in office until his death. Because the college's student applicant pool had declined at an alarming rate, it admitted most students who applied. The faculty was divided, discouraged, and dispirited; its older teachers were marking time until retirement. In preparation for the college's first faculty workshop four days before June's academic grades were due, I asked myself, "Where was hope?" The faculty could agree about only two values when describing Prairie: conservative and accepting (70%); the students only conservative (67%). More revealing were the values that at least a majority of the faculty checked to describe Prairie: conventional, worrying, friendly, caring, cautious, defensive, lacks vitality, apathetic, and plays it safe.

I wondered if the faculty had at the periphery of its consciousness become collectively resigned to its demise. What hope did it have for the college? Almost none. The majority of the faculty could agree about only four wishes: intellectually exciting (68%), excellence (60%), anticipates consequences (55%), and intellectually rigorous (50%).

The students did not appear to be a source of revitalization. Both faculty and students agreed that the students were conventional, friendly, good-natured, conforming, conservative, and dependent on others' opinions. Nor did the students agree about their wishes for the college. Though 40% believed the faculty was boring, only 30% wished it were more intellectually exciting. No restless, dynamic energy here to count on.

The workshop's atmosphere was gloomy. Ten older faculty sat in the rear row grading papers. Others only reluctantly talked with each other in small groups. Clearly, my two-day plan had to be suspended. I confronted the faculty with my apprehension and urged them to try to work in small groups again. This time I asked them to identify every actual and potential strength of the college which we then listed in large print on newsprint. We left the list prominently displayed in front of the faculty for the two days. Individual members were surprised that their colleagues believed the college had so many strengths. The gloom slowly began to lift. By the end of the two days I sensed the emerging life and spirit of a caring and dedicated faculty which had begun to rediscover hope in itself.

A small group of faculty successfully sought foundation support to reshape the college's mission. An enterprising and perceptive younger faculty member emerged as a leader. He prodded, provoked, angered, and perceptively led the faculty to develop, with the help of a consultant, a long-range plan. In the meantime, one-third of the faculty retired or were replaced by younger ones. Two years later the faculty reached the point of making the commitment to implement its plan.

I was invited back to illustrate how the faculty might implement its goals. Again, in preparation for the workshop I asked myself if the faculty had been only playing the verbal games we faculty engage in? Or had it fundamentally begun to change its self-concept?

Through the months of wrangling, confrontations, and anger, the college had retained the core of its identity. In decreasing order of agreement, the faculty still felt the college was caring, cautious, conservative, friendly, and accepting. But it had shed the gloom and despair that its lack of vitality, worry, and apathy had created. To the faculty, the college had become more dedicated, hardworking, helpful, fair-minded, and capable. The faculty clearly had also increased its collective wishes for the college. At least a majority now also wished it were also creative, efficient, imaginative, and adventurous.

Prairie teaches us about the dynamics of hope. Fearful of its future, paralyzed by worry and defensiveness, the faculty had slipped into apathy and hopelessness. Identifying the college's strengths rather than focusing on its weaknesses opened its faculty to positive energies that could initiate hope. Also anger (so I was later told) by the confrontation with their collective WCL portrait of the college (actually of themselves) activated energy. The youthful faculty leader and his committee had successfully channeled it into sustained creative planning for two years. The faculty had learned to cope. As I discovered in my return visit, I felt its energy and pride in its collaborative work; we laughed a lot. It was a lively, alive faculty.

The faculty now had reached the point of committing itself. Did it wish to proceed to implement its plan? Or would it emotionally opt to take the known path of playing it safe and risk dying? Despite reservations, it subsquently voted unanimously to risk taking the unknown and uncertain path of creating a stronger identity.

An identity that integrates numerous and varied values is more stable and resilient. It enhances adaptability. The increased number of faculty who agreed about the values for which Prairie stood showed me it was on the way to becoming a stronger college.

Prairie taught me not to abandon hope lightly even in the midst of the most gloomy of prospects. It also taught me how much hope can be resident in anger aroused by confronting the truth about one's self.

A social system is a pattern of relationships. Chapter 9 asks how can we assess a schhool's relationships that may affect achieving its goals. My repetitive but, I believe, illuminating litany of despairs, especially about Wentworth, Sandia, and Washington, compels me to search them, in particular, for other sources of hope.

Chapter 9

———•◦•———

Understanding a School's Social

System: Three Minority Schools

". . . organizations are more than technical systems. Apart
from anything else, they are also social systems. They are
people and about the way people behave and interact with
each other in groups."[1]

The previous two chapters have shown how the WCL helps us understand a school's culture from its insiders' perspective—teachers and
students. This chapter focusses more specifically on the heart of a school
as a *social* system: the quality of its relationships between teachers and
teachers, teachers and students, and students and students.[2]

I explore three questions central for understanding schools as
social systems: Do teachers and students believe that their colleagues
and teachers have the strengths that describe ideal teachers? Do
teachers behave in ways that model their schools' goals? How can
we understand teachers' and students' views of the students and their
relationships? How may student relationships affect their educability?
I draw some tentative answers from my sample of urban minority
schools. Obviously, their plight is due to many complicated factors.
But their lack of shared values and the quality of their relationships
are two of the more critical but neglected ones by reformers. Other
researchers with greater resources may wish to explore WCL's
results with larger numbers of schools.

Teachers' personalities and the quality of their relationships
with other teachers and with their students have not been extensively

studied. I know of no reliable evidence about their effects on students'
growth and/or achievement, but teachers know. Two experienced
teachers have written,

> . . . who we are matters to our teaching every bit as much
> as what we teach and how we choose to teach it . . . our
> personalities determine the quality and effectiveness of
> our teaching . . . "Who you are," a student once remarked
> to a teacher, "speaks so loudly that I cannot hear a word
> you say."[3]

How we get along with others is affected in part by our ideas about
ourselves and about those with whom we work. Fortunately, the WCL
can provide some information about teachers' and students' collective self-images and their views of their colleagues and peers. Again,
unfortunately, I do not have reliable normative information about
teachers' collective self-images and views of their colleagues' personalities. The information has proved to be too sensitive for many schools
to secure. Fortunately, however, Sandia and some others courageously
sought such information from both their faculties and students. I
searched Sandia's findings to identify the critical questions we should
ask about our teachers' personalities and their relationships.

Teachers' Personalities: As Ideal Teachers

The Strengths of the Ideal Teacher—Sandia's Faculty

The *National Commission on Teaching & America's Future* has identified the attributes of the ideal teacher which it insists every student
should have, especially vulnerable children like Sandia's and
Washington's. John Goodlad describes the Commission's standards
for its ideal teacher to be competence, acceptance and understanding
of students, trust and belief in them, and care for them.[4]

Do Sandia's students have such teachers? Do public schools'
students, including Reagan's, believe that they have such teachers?
My information comes from teachers' descriptions of themselves and
of their typical colleagues and students. Information about students
comes from their descriptions of themselves, typical peers, and
typical teachers.

Most teachers believe they are competent. They are typically more satisfied with their competence than with any other attribute measured by the 30-item morale survey. Sandia's faculty was no exception. It also was most satisfied with its competence. Most teachers also describe themselves on the WCL as caring, empathic, and understanding. Again, Sandia's teachers were no exception.

What are the personalities and interpersonal worlds of Sandia's teachers and students like? Empathically take the role of a Sandia student as you read Table 9-1. How would you feel and how might your feelings affect your growth? How might Sandia realistically create a healthier interpersonal learning environment to enable its students to become more competent human beings?

Table 9-1 compares Sandia's teachers' self-image and views of their colleagues with their students' view of them as ideal teachers. Suburban public school and Reagan's students' views of their faculties are included to provide perspective.

Table 9-1   Sandia Faculty's Self-Image and View of Colleagues Compared to Sandia's and Public-Reagan Students' Views of their Ideal Teachers

Ideal attribute	% Sandia Faculty View of Self	Colleagues	Student View of Faculty	% Public Student View of Faculty	% Reagan Student View of Faculty
Caring	96	51	22	40	41
Accepting	87	36	26	40	53
Capable	87	62	28	58	38
Feels for others	81	42	20	25	21
Understanding	70	27	26	30	23
Trusting	60	16	18	24	27

Individually, the majority of Sandia's teachers, as other schools' teachers also, were quite content with themselves.

Collectively, Sandia's faculty believed it had the strengths of the ideal teacher. It did not agree about any single attribute it *wished* it had. Other faculties occasionally do. Typically, teachers and students consistently think more highly of themselves than they do of their colleagues or peers. The Sandia faculty is no exception.

The students definitely do not believe their teachers fulfill the National Commission's ideal of the faculty they should have. I questioned the trustworthiness of Sandia's students' replies at the time. The differences between the teachers' beliefs about themselves and the students' view of them was, in my experience, much too large. After constructing Table 9-1 years after my visit to Sandia, I now accept the students' views as reliable. Sandia's faculty's collective view of its colleagues is generally closer to its students' view of their teachers than to its own self-image. Its students' views are understandable when I compared them to favored suburban peers' views of their teachers. Sandia's teachers and students both view their faculty to be not trusting nor understanding. This latter finding fits what I have intuitively believed for years. Improvement of schools will only occur when teachers and students understand and trust each other.[5]

Remember that perceived reality is not necessarily actual reality, however that can be measured. The size of the discrepancies between Sandia's teachers' self-images and their students' views was dangerous to Sandia's health and efforts to improve itself. If I already believe that I am an ideal teacher, how predisposed will I be to improve *my* competence or change how *I* care or teach? Will I genuinely hear the 66% of my Sandia students who think I'm boring or 56% who say I'm dull. I'll probably say to myself, "The students describe the rest of the faculty. After all, I am highly competent and caring."

I urge those who wish to improve a school to find out the faculty's collective self-image and view of its colleagues. The answer may tell you how educable the faculty is for altering its relationships with other teachers or students.

The WCL can also tell you what percentage of the teachers believe their colleagues have strengths, such as adventurousness and intellectual excitement, to support their efforts to change. A faculty's collective image, such as Washington's "loser" one, can be a silent but formidable barrier to change. We too often believe that "Our students, colleagues, administrators, and especially the infamous 'system' need to change. Certainly I don't!"

My work with the Sandia administrators and faculty persuaded me that a sizable number did hope that some improvement was possible. If I had returned, I would have provoked them with at least three questions: Why do so few students believe you have the strengths that so many of you believe you have? What has prevented you from developing a healthy, growth-producing school not just for your students but for yourselves? You have little to lose so what practical steps could you take now to begin to create such a school? [ASH 15: Workshop to Aid Teachers Understand What Students Mean by Caring].

It is an educational truism that faculty modeling of its goals is necessary for students' growth—as Model's faculty discovered. I know of no evidence that demonstrates that commonsensical belief. We have not had measures to describe different types of faculty models to learn how students grow in their presence. The WCL may provide a way to do just that, but how?

Teachers as Models
of Their Goals

Researchers of colleges' cultures type them in terms of their salient attributes, as Chapter 7 suggested. The WCL's 150 words can be similarly grouped into sub-groups of attributes that go together to define a type. For example, schools committed to academic excellence, such as Adelphi, are described by large percentages of their constituents to be

Academic	Demanding	Intellectually rigorous
Ambitious	Clear thinking	Intellectually exciting
Dedicated	Well-informed	

A valid typology of different types of outcomes offers the opportunity to hold a faculty accountable for renewing itself in ways that model the school's goals. [ASH 41: Creating Cultural Typologies of Outcomes]. It would enable us to answer a variety of questions about how well a school has created a coherent culture that models its goals. Table 9-2, which compares Sandia's, Reagan's, and other public school students' views of their teachers, portrays how well their teachers model six common types of goals.

The table shows that 39% of Sandia's teachers believed that their colleagues possessed traits that describe good school citizenship.

Table 9-2   Comparison of Public School Students' Views of Their Faculties to Sandia Faculty's View of Its Colleagues

Type	% Sandia Faculty	Rank	% Reagan Student	Rank	% Other Public Student	Rank	Student	Rank
School citizenship	39.0	1	27.0	1	38.9	2	42.0	2
Strong moral character	36.6	2	20.5	5	34.0	3	35.9	3
Interpersonal maturity	34.3	3	23.0	2	26.9	4	30.9	4
Academic achievement	27.8	4	21.5	4	41.8	1	42.4	1
Creative contributors	24.9	5	22.0	3	23.5	5	26.3	5
Lifelong Learners	21.1	6	14.3	6	22.9	6	25.9	6

Please don't take my playful and preliminary attempt to establish ideal types and Table 9-2's figures too seriously. I am showing you how flexibly WCL's results can be organized to answer different questions about holding a school accountable. National leaders call schools to educate for citizenship. Though Table 9-2's results show that teachers model its strengths best (e.g., plan ahead, cooperate, responsible), faculties fail the majority of their students in modeling these traits. Only 27% of Sandia's students attributed such strengths to their teachers.

More distressing and puzzling is why do not more students, say at least a majority, attribute positive traits to their faculties? How have we organized our schools to obscure to so many students that their teachers are more ethical, interpersonally mature, and lifelong learners than they believe?[6]

What other insights might tables like 9-2 provide? I offer a few possible ones.

• Develop a faculty typology for different types of schools, such as high, middle, and elementary and/or liberal arts colleges to which to compare one's own school
• Identify the extent of different constituents' agreement about a faculty's character as an index of the organization's healthy integration
• Measure degree of and correspondence of students' readiness for achieving a school's goals
• Measure a school's distinctiveness and purity of type (for example, narrowly focussed, as for Adelphi, or broadly ranging, as for Countryside)

Table 9-2 cues us to one of a school's more crippling handicaps. Neither Sandia, one of our least achieving schools, nor Reagan, one of our most achieving schools, has teachers who model lifelong learning as judged by their students. Is not this result a serious indictment of how well schools now prepare today's youth? Their future will demand that all of us educate ourselves for the rest of our lives. Within the past decade every school I have studied in America and abroad has recognized that its teachers and students must learn how to become their own self-teachers. To create self-renewing schools like Model requires a faculty that seeks to learn continuously. Many, like Model, have elevated self-teaching or its variants—such as lifelong learning attitudes and skills, becoming an autonomous learner, or developing self-renewing attitudes and skills—to be a priority outcome for students.

The WCL enables us to specify the attributes of a lifelong learner that a faculty development plan should set as a priority. Table 9-3 compares Sandia's and suburban public school students' views of their teachers. (Table 1-1 described Reagan's teachers similarly.) Table 9-3 also includes Sandia's teachers' views of their colleagues to compare to their students' beliefs.

Table 9-3   Comparison of Sandia's and Suburban Public High School Teachers' and Students' Beliefs about Their Self-Educating Attributes

Self-Educating Attribute	% Sandia Faculty	% Sandia Student	% Suburban Student
Self-confident	31	20	28
Self-motivating	29	12	30
Enthusiastic	22	24	30
Self-disciplined	22	10	29
Self-educating	18	6	25
Self-reliant	18	6	22
Deep interests	16	22	26
Curious	13	14	17
Average	21.1	14.3	25.9

You may find Table 9-3's results too dismal to be believable. However, the relative similarity of the diverse groups' views about the eight attributes (that is, they don't vary by more than about 20% points), suggests too great agreement to doubt their validity. Collectively, teachers just don't come across as curious and self-educating persons to students or colleagues. You might argue that the table's students don't know what "self-reliant" means, for example. But surely Sandia's faculty knows.

What do Sandia's teachers think about themselves? Fifty-six percent describe themselves as self-educating persons. Twenty-six percent of Sandia's students also think of themselves as self-educating. Given such self-concepts how realistic is it to expect Sandia to pull itself up by its own bootstraps? How many will read about and implement legislative and educational theorists' ideas? Or read books like this? As I mentioned in Chapter 1, only a bare handful of faculties—four out of six were Montessori—of the several hundred about which I have data emotionally commit themselves to produce self-educating students. I now reluctantly must reassert that

1. Most teachers teach students to need them, not wean them to become their own self-teachers,

2. The majority of public school students view their teachers as boring, even 65% of Reagan's students, which suggests they are not continuously educating themselves,

3. Educational reform efforts will continue to fail badly until we more deeply understand that our schools as social systems do not now provide the growth-producing opportunities for their members that must be present for educational improvement to occur, and

4. Schools like Model show us that teachers and students can change to become more self-renewing and self-educating persons.

Because my studies of adult development show conclusively that more mature people continue to grow and become more successful, I advocate that teachers should be first selected for their maturity and then for their technical competence. Mature persons have the cognitive and motivational strengths necessary to continue to educate themselves; they have the interpersonal strengths necessary to create facilitative learning environments for themselves and others. Immature faculty, even though technically competent, most likely don't.

The Chapter's third question asks, How can the WCL help us understand students' relationships and their effects on students' educability?

Understanding Students' Peer Learning Environments

Crucial to the growth of students, especially adolescents, is the quality of their peer relationships. An adolescent's trade-mark is sensitivity to peers' expectations and values. A host of factors can heighten a youth's vulnerability to peer influence: uncertainty about one's own identity, intense needs for peers' approval, acceptance and respect, and loosened ties to familial and adult values, among others. If I believe, rightly or not, that all of my friends are scoring with girls, or ripping off a local music store, or getting drunk or stoned every weekend, or are bashing other boys for doing well in school, then unless I have strong values and a sense of myself I too may be swayed to do the same.

How can the measures of students' morale, perceptions, and wishes help us understand their peer-learning environment as a source of hope? I first return to Wentworth to compare its white and black students' views of and wishes for their peers. Though students in the same school, how similar are their peer learning environments? Are they sources of hope on which their teachers can rely? I then examine in depth Washington and its students' learning environment to identify if it is a resource for hope.

Wentworth's Black and White Students' Peer Cultures

In contrast to Washington's students, Wentworth's come from more stable lower middle class families who have made it out of the city's poorer violence- and drug-prone, run-down area. The black and white students have gone to school with each other for more than 20 years. Have they created a common or a separate peer culture? Recent reports describe ethnic resegregation in schools and colleges and a seeming rise in ethnic tensions. Mapping ethnic groups' perceptions of their peers might help each to better understand the other's interpersonal world. [ASH 16: Assessing Afro-American and White Students' Peer Cultures].

Wentworth's black students disagreed noticeably in their views on 30% of their peers' principal traits, i.e., more whites than blacks believed that their peers didn't care (81 versus 60%), were adventurous (76 versus 28%), and adaptable (71 versus 12%). Generally, however, they do not seem to have developed a polarized peer culture. Might their shared views provide the basis for more cross-ethnic *personal* relationships?

Their wishes for their peers provide a possible answer I had not anticipated. More black students felt more frustrated with or had higher hopes for their personal relationships. More than the white students, they wished that their peers empathically felt for others (52 versus 42%) or, more dramatically, were helpful (48 versus 14%), considerate (44 versus 29%), friendly (40 versus 10%) as well as caring and loving. If the school had mapped its students' views of themselves, would its blacks have felt more friendless, lonely, even estranged from the dominant peer values? Are their wishes poignantly hinting that the price of being a minority member is being an emotional outsider? I let my intuitions go beyond the available evidence to suggest the WCL's possibilities for more deeply understanding how those who differ from us may really feel.

Despite the high percentages of both groups who believed that their peers didn't care, Wentworth's students had not given up hope. In contrast to students in most other schools, both ethnic groups wished their peers were more academically involved, e.g., hardworking, dedicated, and helpful. Though as frustrated as their teachers with their school and other students, it is just the depth and extent of their shared frustration that is Wentworth's chief hope. It would take astute leadership to capitalize on that latent hope, given the school's history of mercurial and contentious administrator and faculty relationships.

Chapter 8 showed us that Sandia, Wentworth, and Washington were similar. Their WCL results revealed that they lacked a school of hope's most important quality: widely shared consensus about the values that could define a distinctive identity. Neither their faculties nor their students agreed about what their schools stood for.

I have shown you how the WCL can be used to compare Sandia's teachers to the proposed standards of an ideal teacher and to map how well they model different educational goals. Wentworth's WCL's results have shown us how to understand students' peer relationships.

Washington's WCL's complicated results provide a diagnostic challenge to understanding. They reveal sharp faculty and student disagreements in their views which provide clues about why it is a school of despair. *Assessing Schools of Hope* describes in detail how I pursued the students' puzzling results to determine whether they were trustworthy. It shows how I had to intuitively follow a faint trail of clues to understand a principal cause of the faculty's and students' disagreements. [ASH 17: Understanding the Morale of Washington's Students]. To what ideas about the school's core social problem and its potential sources of hope did the trail take me?

Washington's Interpersonal School and Peer Cultures

Adolescents not supported by strong families, drug- and violence-free schools, and cultures and futures of hope, are especially vulnerable. While a society cannot directly provide stronger families for its children, it can provide physically safe and emotionaly secure, caring, "family-type" schools for them. How did Washington's students feel about their role as students in the school's interpersonal culture? [ASH 18: Washington School's Interpersonal Culture]. As vulnerable as many of them were, Table 9-4 either reveals their resiliency or is a damning critique of our suburban public schools' interpersonal cultures. (See Table 7-2 to compare Washington's and Sandia's interpersonal culture with NAIS and Reagan students'.)

Table 9-4   Comparison of Washington, Sandia, and Suburban Public High School Students' Beliefs about Their Schools' Interpersonal Culture

Attribute	% Washington	% Sandia	% Suburban
Caring	51	22	34
Feels for others	37	20	21
Giving	37	10	21
Warmth	32	8	14
Personal	27	14	16
Trusting	17	12	17

Though far from an ideal interpersonal culture, Washington had created a marginally more interpersonally safe and friendly environment than my normative suburban schools. For all practical purposes, Sandia's students did not believe that their school had *any* health-related interpersonal strengths.

More than the students' and teachers' views of their school, however, student views of their peers were most diagnostic of Washington's core problem. Washington's poor, minority, and vulnerable students needed empathic teachers who understood their peer culture and learning environment. Perhaps because of the student-bashing that went on among the teachers in the lunch room, Washington's principal had asked them to visit their students' homes—which old-fashioned teachers used to do. "No way. Too dangerous." How well could the teachers reach such children when they knew so little about their homes: Who did and did not have a quiet place at home to do homework, paper and pencils to work with, or at least one adult to assist them when stuck with a math problem?

Though the faculty could not agree at all about their school's values, they could agree about what their students were and were not. Of the 13 traits at least two-thirds of the faculty agreed about, they agreed that their students had only *one* unalloyed positive one: friendly! Much higher percentages agreed about the weaknesses of their students: defensive (80%), distractible (79%), lack self-confidence (73%), and apathetic (70%). Like Appalachia College's faculty, their severe frustrations bound them together in their wishes for their students. Seventy percent and more of them wished that they were, for example, academic, self-disciplined, and conscientious.

As telling as the faculty's pervasive negative view of its students and its frustrations is the size of the gap between their and their students' views of their peers. Two-thirds of the faculty used only four of the students' 12 words to describe their typical student, i.e., distractible, defensive, talkative, and argumentative. Washington's teachers disagreed by at least 20% with 59% of their students' views of their peers. But surprise! It is the students' even greater negative view of their peers that accounts for the size of the gap. The students were as frustrated by their peers as was the faculty. Was it the devoted principal and her core group of caring faculty whom the students had in mind when they described Washington to be a caring, empathic, and giving school in Table 9-4?

My principal hypotheses drawn from ASH 17 and 18 are:

1. The teachers are more united in their views about their students than about their school. They overwhelmingly agree that their students are not educable. Their shared lexicon is that their students are apathetic and don't care. Such widely shared and monolithic beliefs can become self-fulfilling prophecies. Teachers may no longer demand excellence from their students. Only a third of the students believe that the school is demanding.

2. The faculty is not tuned in well to its students' interpersonal world. Two-thirds of the faculty use only one third of the words that students use to describe their peers. It may not empathically understand how much their students' share faculty frustration about other students.

3. Washington's faculty believes its students have 51% fewer positive character strengths than teachers in academically achieving public high schools believe about their students.[7]

4. Washington's faculty is more frustrated by its students than most other faculties I have studied, even more than Sandia's, whose views of its students were almost identical: distractible, defensive, lacking self-confidence, apathetic, not caring.

5. Such severe faculty frustration must make some resent their students. Less mature faculty may give up and withdraw their commitment to students, angrily explode, or possibly indulge in retaliatory punitive behavior. Even though a professional faculty may contain its anger, today's perceptive students will sense it. Interviews with the students' Steering Committee about their teachers produced this sampling of their themes:

   • Half of the students' Committee believed the faculty expected them to fail at some point during their school years.
   • Teachers expect respect from them when they don't give it to students.
   • Teachers put down students, (for example, "They call me dumb.")

- Teachers embarrass students by making examples of them in front of others.
- Most students "believe many teachers don't care," like not staying after school to help them to catch up or pass tests or, I would add, remain after their contracted hour to learn what the students' surveys said about them and the school.

6. Despite students' reports and beliefs about the faculty, their teachers have not given up on them. Though frustrated, they remained hopeful. Faculties that give up on their students believe that they have as many negative character attributes and as few positive character traits as Washington's. However, they no longer care enough to wish their students were different. Such faculties have died. It is probably wiser resource-wise to close the school and bury the teachers than to try to revive them. They will have shifted their energies elsewhere. Washington's administration and a core of the faculty still cared—greatly.

7. The students care similarly. More than the faculty, they believe that their peers are playful, demanding, and curious. They are as frustrated as the faculty that their wishes are not realized.

8. Like other faculty, Washington's teachers' wishes center on strengths needed to achieve academically; like other students, the students' wishes also include interpersonal traits, such as understanding, accepting, and sincerity.

A Tentative Interpretive Assessment of Washington

Washington was currently a school of despair with numerous potentials for hope. The most decisive sign of its despair was the faculty's complete absence of shared values about the school, which lacked any special character or culture. Faculty and students suffered from having been typed as "one of the worst" of the state's schools, which reinforced a collectively shared self-image as "losers." The image was so entrenched in the faculty's mind that it could not believe its morale did not differ from the morale of other public high school faculties who they believed were "winners." They rejected the evidence that their students also had high morale, perhaps due to the faculty's awareness that it had lowered its academic expectations to bolster its students' self-esteem. (An interpretation from ASH 17's analysis of the students' morale.)

Rather than assume responsibility to unite and create a strong school culture of expectations and values, the faculty may have protected its own self-image as competent by derogating and blaming its students. Believing them to be uneducable, it closed itself to the hope that its students did represent: their high morale, consensual positive view of the school, widely shared wishes for a more intellectually exciting, ambitious, and imaginative school of excellence, a balanced positive and negative view of their peers about whom there was widespread frustration and wishes that they were more interpersonally and academically mature, and, as I interpreted its test scores, more academic potential than the faculty was willing or knew how to educe.

Washington's trial tells me that there must be a better way to help schools than to type them as one of the "worst." To label a school that way can have the same effect as calling a student "dumb." It becomes a "loser" and blinds itself to its potential sources of hope. Who wants to attend, stay in, and work hard in a school called "one of the worst?"

Accountability at its best should prefigure steps to create more effective organizations. The remaining chapters illustrate how the surveys have been used in a variety of settings to understand and respond to important contemporary issues.

Applying Measures of Morale and Culture for Understanding Contemporary Educational Issues

Chapter 10

———•◆•———

IDENTIFYING THE COMMUNITY CULTURE
OF A UNIVERSITY'S DISRUPTIVE STUDENTS

The surveys of an organization's morale and culture have been most frequently used with public and independent schools and liberal arts colleges. They have also been used to understand a technical university's concern about its students' disruptive behavior, a national youth organization's concern about its executives' anxiety aroused by their boards' increased involvement, and a New England's consolidated high school's and two southern independent schools' psychic dropouts. Each survey provides insights about the impact of an organization's culture on issues of contemporary concern. Each survey also illustrates other ways of organizing the morale and cultural information to clarify a specific problem.

Tech is a moderately sized technical university whose publicized distinction is its purpose to integrate the development of professional competence with a liberal education. However, its engineering and business colleges overshadow its humanities-social science college. The university has sought to create a distinguished faculty of research scholars who, over the years, have created an academically excellent institution of high selectivity. Originally a male university it later opened its doors to women, about a thousand of whom were on campus at the time of the study.

The vice president for student affairs and chairman of a commission to study the "quality of community life" asked me to assess it. Disturbing student behaviors, including wide-spread fraternity drunkenness, fights between the frats, thefts, and arson had become more prevalent. Male harassment of women accompanied by several incidents of individual and group rapes were most troubling. The university had been sued by some women. Prior to my return visit to work with staff and students specifically on male-female relationships, a female student was murdered on campus.

The Culture of Tech

I had no norms for similar universities to which to compare Tech, so I focussed on comparing different groups' views of the university. Only its administrators agreed that Tech had a distinctive culture; at least two-thirds agreed about 10 values, beginning with conservative, competitive, cautious, and demanding. Tech's faculty united on only two values: conservative and conventional; however, at least 60% also described Tech as competitive, playing it safe, authoritarian, and conforming.

What did Tech mean to its students, the quality of whose community was at issue? I had expected that Tech's students, identified with one of three different colleges, would be more heterogeneous and would not agree as much about their university as students do in smaller schools. Table 10-1 tells us otherwise. I mark with an * when the faculty and administrators differed from the students by more than 20%.

Table 10-1 Comparison of Students' to Faculty's and Administrators' Views of Tech

Ordered by Views of	Students %	Faculty %	Administrator %
Competitive	87	63*	89
Conservative	77	79	100*
Demanding	77	37*	81
Intellectually rigorous	75	37*	46*
Hardworking	74	53*	73
Intense	71	16*	54
Difficult	65	15*	50
Ambitious	63	40*	62
Emotionally cold	61	47	35*
Authoritarian	59	61	58
Rigid	59	34*	23*
Aggressive	57	16*	27*
Apathetic	55	40	27*

Regardless of their collegial identification, Tech's students view the university as rigorously academic; the business students viewed the university as more aggressive and intense.

The table tells us that Tech's adults, especially faculty members, are not tuned in well to how their students' view the university. The potential for miscommunication and conflict with, even lack of empathic understanding for, their students is great. Such large discrepancies between the views of faculty and students about the academic quality of the institution signals severe faculty frustration and possibly unreasonable demands of its students.

Just as the three groups agreed about the university's core identity as competitive and conservative, they also agreed about most of their wishes for it. The faculty was most frustrated with the university, wishing it were more intellectually exciting, creative, enthusiastic, imaginative, and artistic. About a third of both faculty and students wished the university were more caring. Remarkably, the Engineering, Business, and Liberal Arts students agreed about all but one of their wishes for Tech. The Liberal Arts students wished it were more intellectually exciting.

Of 22 publicly stated university goals and descriptions of itself, the only character attribute mentioned was honesty. Perhaps because interpersonal and ethical values were not part of the community's lexicon, the commission did not seek information about its students' relationships with either their peers or the faculty. Since "quality of community life" surely involves relationships and ethical values, I compared the three groups' views of Tech for the WCL's 16 interpersonal and ethical attributes.

No group identified an attribute of character, i.e., interpersonal and ethical, to be a cardinal value of the university. The administrators agreed more than faculty and students but scarcely convincingly. Only 50% believed that the university was fair; only 48% agreed it was honest!

Tech's students, even more than its faculty, could not agree that the university had any interpersonal or ethical character. Twenty-six percent of the students could agree that it was helpful and honest; only 21% of the faculty could agree that it was fair.

Was anyone disturbed by the anarchical character of Tech? Basically no. Only 37% of the faculty and 38% of the students wished it were more caring. Thirty-one percent of the administrators and 29% of the faculty wished it had a deeper ethical sense; only 14% of the students wished the same.

To make clear what Tech was *not* to its students, I list the seven attributes least visible to them: understanding (0%), warm and sympathetic (2%), feeling for others and loving (4%), open and trusting (6%).

Conclusion? Tech did not have a community culture providing expectations or guidance to its students about how they should act, certainly not outside of the classroom.

This most revealing portrait of stereotypic feminine attributes not viewed to be visible or desired for Tech immediately provokes the question of whether Tech's female and male students differed in their views of and wishes for the university. Using my criterion of a 20% difference, the female and male students did not disagree in their views of Tech; however, 10 to 15% more females than males agreed about Tech's core identity: competitive, conservative, demanding, and hardworking. The women apparently were not too frustrated by Tech's predominant academic and masculine culture. Only 41% wished it were more caring.

Clearly the male and female students worked in the same university and were not seemingly frustrated by its lack of ethical and interpersonal values. As the Appalachia faculty learned, who controls freshmen's first six to eight week's socialization into a college shapes their growth and behavior for their remaining college years. The commission needed to know what its freshmen's views and wishes were. When I compared their views to those of the seniors, I found the same pattern I had found for male and female students. The views of both freshmen and seniors were similar. Seventy-eight percent of the freshmen and 93% of the seniors agreed Tech was competitive; 67% of the freshmen and 78% of the seniors believed Tech was hardworking. However, for every senior-identified attribute, fewer freshmen than seniors attributed it to Tech. Why? For the same type of reason that Appalachia lost its most capable students after their freshman year? I did not have the information about Tech's dropout rate or other background information to determine what kind of students may have fled from the demands of its severe culture.

How Trustworthy are Tech's Results?

Are Tech's survey results believable? The commission took its survey seriously. It secured representative samples of each category of its respondents and followed the instructions exactly. In retrospect, I cannot recall why I did not insist that it secure information about students' morale, their view of their peers, fraternity membership, and other background information, such as frequency of alcohol usage and partying as well as academic grade average. Ideally, I would want a random sampling of the men's and women's WCL self-concepts to discover, for example, how closely Tech's women's personality fit the school's monolithic masculine culture. Such information would have offered the opportunity to cross-check the results of different methods and information for empirical as well as theoretical consistency. By now you can probably infer the host of other questions one might ask so as to understand Tech's community life in more depth.

Fortunately, the limited data the Commission made available to me confirmed their own reliability. Regardless of how I analyzed the results, every group agreed much more than it disagreed about Tech's core identity and culture. Such inter-group consistency reassured me that I could trust the data.

However, interpretation of results drawn only from one survey might easily err—the absence of other types of information about student morale, for instance, meant interpretations could not be cross-checked for consistency and validity. My analysis will illustrate how necessary intuition, disciplined by experience and knowledge, becomes when seeking understanding about pressing real-life issues from only one limited survey. I also illustrate how the WCL can be used to reflect on issues that affect an institution's systemic health. You may believe my intuitive reflections jump too far ahead of the available information.

An Interpretive Analysis of Tech's Culture

The survey's results provided three principal foci for future discussion by the commission: the quality of Tech's community life; the university's response to its women; and Tech's educability for changing its culture.

Quality of Tech's Community Life

The commission was not charged to just describe Tech's community life but to assess its "quality," which to me meant assessing its healthiness.

Tech's great strength was proving, I felt, to be its greatest weakness. Tech had a very stable identity to 77% of its administrators but a rigid one to 67% of its seniors and 34% of its faculty. Tech was unique; no other school has been so described in such terms by so many of its members. High percentages of every group agreed that it was a conservative, conventional, and competitive school—traits which do define other comparable schools. Its administrators and students agree more with each other than either did with the faculty. The faculty did not believe that the university was as demanding, intellectually rigorous, difficult, hardworking, and intense as its students, and even the administrators, did.

The strengths of such a strong culture should not be minimized. Tech is an intellectual marine corps boot camp to its recruits. Tech was a tough male, even macho, school. Its survivors—its seniors—told us that. It was competitive, demanding, difficult, ambitious, emotionally cold, aggressive, and authoritarian. Tech pushed its students to discover their limits. Just as the marine corps is proud, so was Tech proud, according to 61% of its survivors.

Tech's tough, demanding culture—more typical of technical and professional schools, like law and medicine, than liberal arts schools—was so dominant that it set the tone for the traditional liberal arts. The university's culture integrated the three colleges, providing clear expectations of what a Tech student should act like as a student. One told me, "Here we work hard and we play hard." Given that such a culture is typical of academically excellent schools, why did only 45% of Tech's students, 24% of its faculty, and 58% of its administrators attribute excellence to Tech? What was missing?

Two clues suggested Tech's great strength may also have been a great weakness. Was its strength achieved at the expense of a dynamic intellectual vitality? Was its severe masculine character suppressing students' non-academic needs and contra-sexual energies? Students' troubling-intense partying and impulsive acting out suggests the answer is yes.

A liberally educating faculty kindles intellectual excitement and a calling to learn. It also educates for wholeness. At one level of integration, a faculty enables late adolescents to unify their psychic dichotomies—for Tech's males, their femaleness; for its females, their maleness.

Forty-seven percent of the faculty, though only 24% of the students agreed that the university lacked vitality. Confirmation of this belief came from the sparse numbers, i.e., 11 to 32% respectively, who believed that the university was energetic, enthusiastic, and intellectually exciting, and the 40 to 55% of faculty and students who labeled it apathetic.

Why this lack of vitality? My hunch is Tech's singularly focussed, intellectually rigorous culture. Tech's culture was so unambiguous that its reputation must be known to its applicants; it quickly becomes known to its freshmen, who might not have known. It probably attracts a "Techie" type: self-demanding, hardworking, intellectually competitive, intense, and vocationally focussed. Research has found that technically oriented adolescents tend to be conservative, conventional, and cerebrally inhibited.[1] Valuing a Tech degree, they work hard to meet the faculty's expectations. Some risk, however, being stretched out of shape by Tech's prematurely foreclosing the development of a healthy identity. By not valuing or modeling interpersonal and ethical strengths, the university leaves students without expectations of how they should act and become more mature.

"Not fair," some Techies might claim. "Tech's goal is to integrate the liberal arts with the technical."[2] The data suggest it has not developed the psychic culture for that integration to occur.

How healthy was Tech's community life? It may not have been as healthy as it should be for three reasons. First, the gulf between faculty's and students' expectations for and beliefs about Tech was too great. They disagreed about how demanding, difficult, intellectually rigorous, and intense Tech was. Might the result be that some faculty were very discontented with the quality of their students' preparation for the high quality academic work they demanded? Their discontent might produce frustration, resentment, or even withdrawal of personal investment in and involvement with students, particularly by Tech's research scholars.

The second reason Tech's culture may have been unhealthy is that it provided too narrow a channel for student growth. The lack of both faculty and student emotional commitment to 15 of the WCL's 16 character attributes impoverishes its students. With no university expectations, encouragement, and support to develop their character, Tech's students became prey to their impulses and immaturities. The intensity and frustrations of their demanding academic days provided little time for dreaming, reflectively exploring their interior selves and relationships. So why should we be surprised about their playing and drinking "hard?" The extreme discrepancy between everyone's views about what Tech is academically and is not interpersonally and ethically is unhealthy.

The third reason Tech's culture may have been unhealthy is, paradoxically, its strength. Its internal coherence and stability might be so strong that it was inflexible or rigid, as the majority of seniors claimed. Remember that any dimension of healthy growth may be overdeveloped and distort development on growth's other dimensions. A test of Tech's healthiness is how well it adapts to its women.

Tech's Response to its Women

More women than men believed that Tech's culture is as I have described it. When I compared the women's and men's views to all of the WCL words, more women than men believed Tech was masculine, friendly, intense, uptight, and lonely. Also more women than men wished that the school were caring. Typical of other male institutions which admit women, more female than male students felt the pressure to "measure up" much more than the males felt. Had Tech expected its female students to just accommodate to Tech's ethos? The women did not believe that the university had accepted and supported their strengths. I asked the women's student leaders what their principal sources of support were. They replied, "We must rely on ourselves." The university had made only minimal efforts to provide such support. Less then 10% of the faculty were women; only one female dean was available to 1,000 women. Only one "sorority-like" living residence had been made available to them. Their social life was confined to the fraternities on the men's psychological turf. They received no support from consensual university values that they should stand up to the fraternities' male values.

Tech's Educability for Change

What were the commission's prospect of initiating change in Tech's "quality of community life"? What strategies would you recommend?

The levers for altering Tech's community life were depressingly few. The majority of the administration were proud of Tech and comfortable with its achievements. Its three wishes for Tech were that it be more creative, intellectually exciting, and enthusiastic. It viewed the university more positively than did the faculty and students. However, more than a third believed Tech was defensive; only 27% believed Tech was an optimistic place.

Collectively the faculty was not likely to be the spark that might light and sustain enthusiasm for change. It did not agree about what Tech's strengths were. It did agree it was not an institution ready for change. Forty percent believed it was defensive, 60% and more that it played it safe, was authoritarian, and conforming. A meager 11% thought Tech was optimistic.

Nor were Tech's students a rebellious source of fire and sustained passion to alter a culture which reflected, I believe, their own character. They had no ideal or cause for which to marshal what leftover energy remained after their demanding academic work and partying. Besides, the institution guaranteed them a future meal ticket. Their fraternity parties met their other needs for raucous relaxation to release a variety of suppressed tensions.

The commission's dilemma was the school's unalloyed maleness—its authority and power—and the absence of any cohesive challenge to it. The most likely lever for change were the women students. But they too had little fire to initiate and passion to sustain change. Though 41% wished the school were more caring, they could unite around no other wish. They had not even organized a women's support group or social activities to provide them alternatives to the extended fraternity weekend parties.

The only hopeful lever was the commission itself. Could its survey results be used to heighten awareness of what Tech was and was not? The student newspaper interpretively reported some findings.

Task-forces began to work on some identified issues, like better living and socializing arrangements for the women. Deans initiated workshops on male-female relationships. I doubted these steps would be enough to alter Tech's culture.

Significant alteration or mellowing of Tech's identity probably had to wait for the 90s' generational changes in values and gender relationships and governmental and judicial regulations about equity and sexual harassment. How well Tech would adapt to these external pressures remains unsettled.

Chapter 11

EVALUATING CHANGING BOARD AND ADMINISTRATOR RELATIONSHIPS OF A NATIONAL YOUTH ORGANIZATION

Since the 1960s, generational and societal evolving changes in attitudes toward authority and work have been reported by researchers. The Puritan work ethic is still alive for those whose calling is their primary goal in life. Those who value more extrinsic reasons for working, such as salary and status, apparently work less hard.[1] Conflicts between boards, administrators, and teachers over working conditions are more widespread nowadays. They frequently are aggravated by the absence of the "facts on the ground", so to speak. Remember Marathon's problem? Its board believed the opinions of a few disgruntled teachers who had claimed that a new head had destroyed the faculty's morale. This chapter describes how the surveys of morale and organizational culture can be applied to a similar problem that a non-educational organization believed that it had.

A telephone call from the executive director of a National Youth Organization (NYO) gave me the opportunity to study executives' morale and their relationships to their boards. He began by saying, "We have a new breed and need a new program." I thought he referred to breeding heifers! But he continued, "Our local clubs report that their boards are more actively micromanaging them and causing a significant amount of executive anxiety. Would you speak to our annual meeting of the heads of our clubs about this change in leadership style?"

"What do they say?"

He read me a sampling of their comments.

"More competent people have joined the board recently. They want to operate more like a business than in the past."

"We have a few young adults that have grown up in the last 20 years who have the 'now' attitude for our present time."

"My staff nowadays will work its 40 hours but not more."

These and other comments sparked my empirical self's curiosity. I agreed to speak provided we could get objective answers to these questions: Is there really a morale "problem" among NYO's executives? Do older, more experienced executives, presumably in more conflict with the new breed of board member, have lower morale? Do executives with high and low morale differ in their perceptions of their boards? If so, how? Can we identify the characteristics of the ideal board member of the executives who have high morale?

The director readily accepted my conditions. His staff's computer randomly selected 20% of the executives. It mailed them some survey questions, the 28-item Vocational Adaptation Scale (two items about students were omitted), and the Word Check List modified to ask each executive to describe his board. (There were too few women executives to permit an analysis by gender.) An unusually large 76% completed the packet of coded surveys.

The typical executive was 40 years old. He had 20 years experience with the NYO, 12 of them as an executive. His full time staff averaged eight. Seventy-two percent of the representative sample agreed that their board had changed its style. Of this group, 3/4 claimed their morale and executive effectiveness had improved; only 6% claimed the change in board leadership had blunted if not destroyed their morale.

Does NYO Have a Morale Problem?

Did the more objective survey results confirm the unexpected executives' judgments that their morale had, in fact, improved as a result of their boards' greater involvement? How does their morale compare with that of other similar groups? What attributes of their work are NYO's executives most and least satisfied with? Is their pattern of satisfactions and dissatisfactions similar or dissimilar to that of other men?

I could not confirm whether the executives' morale had improved, since I did not have a measure of it five to ten years ago. But I could answer the question, "Did the NYO executives really have a morale problem?" The immediate question is, of course, what defines a "morale problem?" If we compare their morale to that of other comparable occupational groups, then the answer is unequivocal—definitely not. The NYO executives' total morale score of 109 was reliably higher than the 103.5 of independent school teachers also working with similarly aged youth. It was also higher than the 101.5 of my sample of similarly aged 45-year-old executive and professional men working in a wide variety of occupations.

But if we define a "morale problem" to mean a large departure from perfect contentment (a score of 140, i.e., twenty eight items each weighted five for great satisfaction), then the answer is unequivocal—definitely yes. However, of the thousands of persons whose morale has been studied only a handful ever have achieved that pinnacle of vocational fulfillment.

The more informative questions are two: What vocational attributes are NYO executives most and least satisfied about? How does their pattern of satisfactions compare to that of other comparable groups? [ASH 19: Comparing NYO's Executive Morale with that of Other Groups]. The executives are most satisfied with their type of occupation, its social value, and their degree of involvement in their work. They are most dissatisfied with their salaries, effect of their work on their personal lives, and the amount of time and energy their work demands of them.

With few exceptions, the pattern of the executives' satisfactions and dissatisfactions was similar to that of the independent school teachers and other executives. NYO's executives are noticeably more satisfied than other professionals with the social value of and involvement in their work and with their growth and self-fulfillment. As has been found in almost all groups which I have studied, salary, work's effects on other areas of life, and work's demands for time and energy were least satisfying.

The results tell board members that what satisfies and does not satisfy them about their work are the same as for their executives. My advice to board members is that when they make policy decisions they should make them in a way which they would like to have them made if they were the executive. What makes board members happy most likely makes their executives happy.

Confirming the generic structure of morale found with other types of groups, intrinsic satisfactions, such as self-fulfillment, contribute most to NYO executives' morale. Extrinsic sources such as working conditions and for professionals, including NYO executives, their relation with those in authority contribute much less.

Do Older and More Experienced Executives Have Lower Morale?

The answer to the second of my original questions is a resounding "No." Age was not a factor that affected morale, regardless of the board's style of leadership. Given the executives' calling to their work and their high satisfaction with their self-fulfillment, they probably are quite adaptable, regardless of their age. They are able to learn new ways to respond to their board's changed composition and leadership style.

Do Executives of High and Low Morale Differ in Their Views of Their Boards?

While not surprised by the answers to the first two questions, I was by WCL's answers to the remaining one about the quality of the boards of the executives with high and low morale. I had shortened the WCL so that the NYO's staff could add some items it believed to be more appropriate to boards, such as "out of touch with kids" and "strongly supportive." I then identified from the VAS 58% of the executives who were very (including quite) satisfied. Of the remaining sample, I identified 32% usable surveys which ranged from very to quite dissatisfied to satisfied. I call the first group "Very Satisfied" and the second "Satisfied," since the large majority of it were satisfied. Table 11-1 explains my surprise. Given that the two groups were not extremes, they differed markedly in their views of and wishes for their boards. I reported only those attributes identified by 70% or more executives. Until other organizations, such as businesses, do similar studies I do not know whether Table 11-1 may describe generic attributes of effective board members or not.

Table 11-1   Comparison of Very Satisfied to Satisfied Executives' Views of and Wishes for Their Boards

Very Satisfied Views %	Satisfied %		Very Satisfied Wishes %	Satisfied %
Caring	89	52*	Aggressive	42	57
Capable	87	61*	Creative	38	70*
Cooperative	85	57*			
Responsible	83	43*			
Can make decisions	81	81			
Honest	81	70			
Sincere	81	52*			
Accepting	76	70			
Considerate	76	43*			
Dedicated	76	35*			
Helpful	76	43*			
Knowledgeable	76	48*			
Can say no	73	65			
Hardworking	73	26*			

* A difference of 20% or more should be examined more carefully

The only additional trait that 70% or more of the Satisfied executives attributed to their boards was conservative (78 versus 69% for the Very Satisfied executives.) The executives with low morale sharply disagreed with the views of NYO's executives of high morale on 70% of their boards' attributes. Such a large gulf could lead to misunderstandings between NYO executives when discussing board relationships and policies.

The Very Satisfied executives were very content with their boards. They agreed on only two wishes for them. Also, fewer than 20% believed that their boards were curious, reflective, or took the initiative. These were the only positive traits the executives felt their boards lacked.

The wishes of the Satisfied group for its executives were most instructive. Whereas the Very Satisfied executives agreed on two wishes, the Satisfied executives agreed on 25 wishes for their boards, beginning with ambitious (74%), completes plans and creative (70%), imaginative (61%), and adaptable, dedicated, and does "homework"

(57%). The high percentages of their wishes are most unusual and suggest intense frustration with their boards. Twenty percent and fewer Satisfied executives failed to identify 19 positive traits to describe their boards, e.g., does "homework" and energetic.

The study's results were unequivocal;most NYO executives had excellent morale. They had adapted well to their changing boards, which they believed had many positive leadership traits. Ironically, NYO's headquarters staff had been too sensitive to its few executives complaining about their aggressively intrusive boards. Though 36% of its executives believed that their boards were "aggressive," an additional 42% of the Very satisfied but 57% of the Satisfied wished that they were *more* so!

I recommended that NYO use the attributes associated with high executive morale and wishes as its criteria for selecting board members. I also suggested not believing that its squeaking-wheel executives spoke for others than themselves. Develop an empirical scepticism, I advised. Go out into the field to discover just what NYO executives and boards are like and wish. Do a similar study of board members to discover their morale and their picture of the ideal executive. And provide targeted assistance to executives who felt beleaguered by or discouraged by their boards.

I next applied my prescription to a national concern: How to keep more students in school. What can the WCL tell us about psychic dropouts: those predisposed to drop out but who, for one reason or another, must remain in school.

Chapter 12

---·•·---

EXPLORING THE INNER WORLD OF

PSYCHIC DROPOUTS

Until recently, dropping out of school and college had always been a societally acceptable option for an adolescent. Technology's rising dominance of a country's economic life has made dropping out of school, even of college, an increasingly perilous option for one's future job prospects. Ironically, a leader accelerating technology's influence and its requirements for more education dropped out of Harvard to become the world's richest man. Reducing America's drop-out rate is a principal national educational goal to be achieved by the year 2000. It is even one criterion used to label Washington as one of a state's worst schools.

We know little about the inner world of dropouts: what they think of their schools, teachers, peers, and themselves. They disappear into anonymity before they can be so understood. Obviously many objective reasons, such as their family's need for additional income or the availability of a good job, "explain" why some drop out. But more subjective reasons, beginning with discouragement with school and its irrelevance to one's needs, provoke the boredom one researcher found to be the principal reason for dropping out of college.[1]

A preliminary study of a northwestern public high school's students had suggested that the students' morale survey (SRS) predicts who might drop out and why. Students were anonymously asked to rate how seriously they considered leaving school. Of the 18% who reported that they possibly, probably, or were certain that they would drop out, 69% were male and 31% female. Forty percent were juniors.

154

When compared to a sample of those who planned to graduate, the potential dropouts did not think of themselves as students nor share their school's values. Essentially they felt like friendless strangers in their school. The consequence of their estrangement was decreased motivational commitment to be part of the school's culture. This alienation resulted in reduced satisfaction with their academic achievement and how they had grown otherwise.

The SRS measure of morale identifies the students discontented with themselves and their schools who are most likely to drop or be pushed out. Urban minority kids like Washington's vote their low morale with their feet. Suburban white ones like Edina's vote their low morale by dropping out emotionally. Compelled by their parents, the law, lack of jobs, or fear of the unknown, psychic dropouts physically remain in school—and so are available for studying to understand their inner worlds. This chapter supplements Chapter 5, which first described the morale surveys; it further validates the SRS by identifying consistent, possibly generic, personality differences between high and low morale students.

How can we identify groups of the most emotionally uninvolved or psychic dropouts to compare to groups of the most emotionally involved or committed students? How do their similar objective school worlds differ from their dissimilar inner school worlds? To test how generally applicable our hunches may be, I compare several different types of schools' unemotionally and emotionally committed high schoolers. I then trace the roots of their differences back to eighth, sixth, and then at least fifth grade.

Comparing Three Different Schools' Psychic Dropouts

New England's Belmont's large, consolidated high school, highly regarded in its region, drew its heterogeneous students from the town and surrounding rural communities. It loses between 20 to 30% of its local students before they graduate, primarily sophomores and juniors. It is one of two public schools in my sample with a dropout "problem." I compare Belmont's larger high school's least and most satisfied students with similar ones from two smaller southern independent upper schools.

To compare fairly the three schools' high and low morale students required that I identify comparable sized samples of similar morale. So I combined the two smaller schools into one school I label Parkworth. Its combined student population of 750 is a bare minimum to identify large enough extreme groups for each of the WCL's four targets. One quarter of Belmont's and Parkworth's each rated one of the WCL's four targets. Combining two different schools to contrast to Belmont may dilute and so blur finding differences between Parkworth's low and high morale students' views of their schools. However, this more severe test might uncover a generic meaning to "psychic dropout." If so, then we may discover clues about changes other schools may wish to consider to involve students more fully.

Identifying Psychic Dropouts

Every school's students completed the SRS morale scale and one of the WCL's four targets. Potential psychic dropouts whose morale scores that were 85 or lower out of the SRS's total of 150 were compared to their opposites whose morale scores were 120 or higher. Each represents about 20 points below and above the average for students. To avoid misinterpreting the results, keep in mind every student described only *one* of the WCL's four targets. If the tone or theme of a school's four groups of low morale students is similar, we can be more assured that there may be an underlying generic meaning to being a psychic dropout. And if the same tone or theme holds up for different schools from different parts of the country, our reassurance will be strengthened.

Rather than anticipating similarities in percentage replies to specific WCL attributes, I will be searching for similarities in the *patterns* of replies. Intensive comparative studies of three schools produce more information than can be conveniently presented. So I resort to abbreviated tables organized in various ways to illustrate how flexibly the WCL can be used to answer different questions. Given the importance of understanding the inner world of potential dropouts, I will provide you with more tabled findings than usual.

High and Low Morale Students' Views of and
Wishes for Their Schools

Table 12-1 compares in simplified form the largest differences between the high and low morale students' views of their schools. It orders the declining differences using the more reliable Belmont's students' views. Compare Belmont's and Parkway's high and low differences to identify the similarities and dissimilarities in the *patterns* of attributes, not in their actual percentages.

Table 12-1 Comparison of Parkworth's to Belmont's High and Low Morale Students' Views of Their Schools

Attribute	% View of Belmont			% View of Parkworth		
	High	Low	Difference	High	Low	Difference
Friendly	80	19	+61	64	20	+44
Boring	18	78	-60	12	76	-64
Fun	63	6	+57	52	0	+52
Excellence	55	3	+52	92	52	+40
Helpful	75	28	+47	68	44	+24
Open	65	19	+46	16	0	+16
Understanding	55	9	+46	40	28	+12
Hard-working	73	28	+45	92	36	+56
Social	73	28	+45	52	40	+12
Emotionally cold	10	47	-37	32	48	-16
Proud	83	47	+36	76	24	+52
Self-centered	23	59	-36	28	52	-24
Doesn't care	3	38	-35	12	48	-36
Dedicated	78	47	+31	76	32	+44

The table tells us that large percentages of Belmont's and Parkworth's students who have high morale believe that their schools are friendly; their low morale students definitely don't.

The table also tells us that all of Belmont's largest 14 principal differences between high and low students are similar for Parkworth. Its psychic dropouts agreed that their schools were not only boring, emotionally cold, self-centered, and uncaring but also inconsiderate, authoritarian, uptight, strict, and stubborn. Given that Parkworth combined two independent schools, the similarity in the patterning of the high and low morale students' morale is convincing. Is the *pattern* of differences between high and low morale students' wishes similar? Table 12-2 tells us yes.

Table 12-2   Comparison of Parkworth's to Belmont's Low and High Morale Students' Wishes for Their Schools

	% Wishes of Belmont			% Wishes of Parkworth		
Attribute	High	Low	Difference	High	Low	Difference
Friendly	10	44	+34	12	40	+28
Fun	18	50	+32	36	48	+12
Caring	20	50	+30	28	44	+16
Accepting	30	59	+29	28	44	+16
Intellectually exciting	20	47	+27	9	20	+12
Adventurous	18	44	+26	28	36	+ 8
Easygoing	18	44	+26	32	36	+ 4

The consistently large differences between students with very low and high morale in their views of their schools as happy and productive places to be are not surprising. After all, they were selected because of their low and high satisfaction with their schools and their roles as students. I also was not surprised that low morale students wish their schools were more accepting, caring, as well as (for those remaining 9 wishes not included in the table) understanding, sensitive, trusting, considerate, fair, and feeling for others. Belmont's and Parkworth's low morale students agreed at my 1/3 criterion level on 64% of their wishes for their schools. Is there any doubt that the schools have failed as social systems? They have not created the interpersonal and ethical culture their more vulnerable students need.

High and Low Morale Students' Views of and Wishes for Their Teachers

Not unexpectedly, similar themes describe other high and low morale students' views of their teachers. Although Belmont's and Parkworth's emotionally committed students who had high morale used different attributes to describe their faculties, every one was favorable. Similarly the majority of every school's psychic dropouts attributed mostly unfavorable traits to their teachers. More than 70% of Belmont's dissatisfied students, confirmed by Parkworth's students, believed that their teachers were, for example, dull, boring, demanding, and stubborn.

Belmont's and Parkworth's satisfied and dissatisfied students view their teachers radically differently. Comparing their differences, 30 to 40% more of Belmont's (25 to 64% more of Parkworth's) high compared to its low morale students believe their teachers are capable, trusting, and helpful. But 23 to 40% of Belmont's low morale students (supported by Parkworth's) believe their teachers are not just dull and critical but Simon Legrees! They believe their teachers are aggressively argumentative, sarcastic, and unfairly put them down. [ASH 20: High and Low Morale Students' Views of and Wishes for Their Teachers].

Might their universally negative views of their teachers reflect their own relationships over the years with teachers? Dissatisfied students are more likely than satisfied students to create strained relations with their teachers. I examine shortly students' self-descriptions which suggest that teachers' reactions may be due to the contentious personalities of low morale students.

If I had tabled the greatest differences between the satisfied and dissatisifed students' wishes, the pattern of differences would be similar to those of Table 12-1. Belmont's most dissatisfied students, for example, reported three times more wishes for their teachers than its most satisfied students did. Both agreed, however, in wishing that their teachers were more adventurous, open, and amusing people to be around.

High and Low Morale Students' Views of and Wishes for Their Peers

If psychic dropouts do not find acceptance, affirmation, and support from their schools and teachers and are so pervasively turned off from them, why do they remain in school? Do they look to and find support from their peers? No. Belmont's and Parkworth's psychic dropouts are as socially alienated from their peers as their most emotionally committed students feel at home with theirs. More than

Parkworth's students, the majority of Belmont's potential dropouts do not identify even one positive trait about a typical peer. Instead they expect their peers to be uncaring, critical, stubborn, defensive, and emotionally cold. If I had tabled the largest differences in these views of their peers from the high morale students' views about their peers, heading the differences would be boring (48%), emotionally cold (43%), and inconsiderate (39%).

Table 12-3 captures the depth of potential dropouts' frustrations with their peers by contrasting the percentages of Belmont's and Parkworth's low and high morale students' wishes for their peers. For example, 54 and 50% respectively of Belmont's low and high morale students wish their peers were more honest.

Table 12-3   Comparison of Parkworth's to Belmont's High and Low Morale Students' Wishes for Their Peers

Wish	% Belmont		Wish	% Parkworth	
	High	Low		High	Low
Honest	50	54	Caring	47	56
Caring	21	46	Feels for others	37	48
Friendly	21	46	Friendly	20	48
Self-disciplined	43	46	Genuine	27	44
Trusting	39	46	Honest	53#	44
Happy	21	42	Humorous	7	44
Loving	7	42	Tolerant	17	44
Responsible	39	42	Accepting	57#	40

Difference is inconsistent with the pattern

Low morale students' frustrations with their peers is consistently greater than high morale students'. The abbreviated table does not portray the full extent of their frustration, especially with their interpersonal relationships, e.g., 38% of Belmont's low morale students also wished that their peers were more considerate, empathic, sensitive, and sincere, among other traits. The same pattern held for Parkworth's low morale students.

My norms for public and independent students' views of and wishes for their peers show us how widespread is adolescent dissatisfaction with their peer relationships. [ASH 37D: Public and Independent Students WCL View of Peers]. (*Schools of Hope* proposed that such dissatisfaction has been increasing over the years and identifies some of the reasons for such changes). Table 12-3 tells us that even Parkworth's high morale students were not immune to more pervasive societal changes. The majority wished that their peers were more accepting; at least a third of them also wished that their peers would listen and be more cooperative, fair, open, and trusting.

Tracing Psychic Dropouts' Peer Relationships Back to Middle and Elementary School

Have you, as I have, wondered how early the patterned differences between low and high morale students begin to emerge? Recall from Chapter 5 that morale progressively declines from fifth to eighth grade, at which time it seems to stabilize. Can we trace the genesis of the psychic dropout mentality at least back to that time? Because of the large number of eighth graders necessary to replicate fully the study of psychic dropouts' inner world, I explore only their peer group relationships. By combining Bloomfield Hills' three eighth grades I secured a low and a high morale group that matched my selection criterion for high schools. The results confirmed those of similar high school groups. The high morale eighth grade students reported only favorable attributes about their peers, such as friendly, fun-loving, creative, and energetic among others. The low morale eighth graders consistently assigned unfavorable traits to their peers, such as putting others down, aggressive, defensive, show-off, and stubborn. They also believed that their peers were emotionally cold, impersonal, dull, inconsiderate, inconsistent, boring, and uncaring.

Can we trace the roots of student estrangement back even to fifth grade, the earliest grade for which most students can reliably describe their morale and culture? The morale and WCL forms for elementary schools paralleled the adolescent and adult forms. While their content remained the same, their wording was altered to be appropriate for a typical fifth grader's vocabulary and conceptual level.

To secure enough fifth and sixth graders I returned to Edina's study of its district's schools. By combining its five elementary schools' students, I identified large enough samples of low and high morale students who differed by 20 points or more from their collective mean morale score. The advantage of Edina's combined samples is that socioeconomic, educational backgrounds, expectation levels, community values, and other possible factors affecting morale were reasonably similar.

To date we have discovered exceptional continuity in the attitudes of psychic dropouts from four different schools from different parts of the country. Is there similar continuity between different age groups? I compare Edina's fifth-sixth graders to Bloomfield Hill's eighth graders. Like Tables 12-2 and 12-3, Table 12-4 compares the *greatest differences* between the high and low morale students' views of their peers. Elementary students are less discriminating and critical, so just as their morale scores are elevated so are the percentages of their views. Psychic dropouts' views and wishes are far more heterogeneous than their high morale peers. The high morale elementary students agreed at my 2/3 criterion on 69% of the positive traits in their list. The low morale students agreed on only 2%!

Table 12-4   Comparison of Fifth-Sixth and Eighth Grade Students' Differences in Their Views of Their Peers

% High Greater than Low Morale				% Low Greater than High Morale			
Grade	5-6		8		5-6		8
Honest	51	Cooperative	57	Put each other		Emotionally	
Good-natured	48	Hardworking	53	down	50	cold	34
Caring	45	Playful	50	Demanding	38	Impersonal	29
Considerate	43	Caring	49	Impatient	36	Dull	27
Does what is		Creative	49	No sense humor	34	Inconsiderate	25
right	41	Helpful	47	Show-off	34	Inconsistent	25
Fun	41	Energetic	46	Difficult to be		Boring	22
Helps others	41	Understanding	46	around	33	Doesn't care	20
				Dishonest	33		
				Inconsiderate	32		

The table tells us that 51% more high than low morale elementary students checked their peers to be honest. Again, the table's results scarcely need interpretation. High and low morale students of all ages live in very different interpersonal worlds. The implications of this bald conclusion for practical action to reduce dropout rates need interpretation. The basic question is: Do elementary students with low morale become high school psychic dropouts? Given the continuity of the patterned differences, probably yes. The longitudinal evidence has not yet been secured.

What are the sources of low morale? Most likely many—gender for one. Boys average lower morale than girls; more boys than girls drop out. Quality of interpersonal relations is another: Psychic dropouts are very sensitive to teachers and students whom they believe are emotionally cold, non-accepting, boring, and uncaring; high morale students are much less so. Impersonal large schools are another source of low morale. They dilute the growth-producing potential of human relationships, as the next chapter describes.

The repetitive theme of psychic dropouts' inner world is estrangement. They indeed are strangers in what they believe is an impersonal, non-caring, and unhappy land. Can we improve morale by altering a school's interpersonal learning environment? Probably; Model High School and others I know have. Preventitive intervention to alter students' peer relationships should begin at least by fifth grade—if not earlier.

What may be the effects of psychic dropouts' alienation from their schools, teachers, and peers upon their beliefs about themselves? What would you now predict?

High and Low Morale Students' Views of and Wishes for Themselves

Recall that we consistently attribute many more favorable traits to ourselves than we do to others. Belmont's and Parkworth's students are no different. Regardless of their morale, 70% or more could not agree that their peers had any unambiguously positive traits. But at least 70% of them could agree that they themselves had numerous positive attributes. What is diagnostic, however, is that high morale students described themselves as having twice as many positive traits than the low morale students believed they had.[2]

Both Belmont's and Parkworth's low morale students agreed about the strengths they wished they had. Respectively they wished, for example, that they were more academic (59 and 54%), dedicated

(38 and 29%), self-confident (35 and 38%), and self-disciplined (35 and 42%).

Our beliefs about our strengths and weaknesses can determine our behavior and so become self-fulfilling prophecies. Are there any consistent differences in the self-concepts of highly satisfied and dissatisfied students? Table 12-5 summarizes the principal differences by comparing Parkworth's high and low morale students to Belmont's.

Table 12-5   Comparison of Parkworth's to Belmont's %
Differences Between High and Low Morale
Students' Views of Themselves

| *% High Greater than Low Morale* | | | *% Low Greater than High Morale* | | |
Belmont	*Parkworth*			*Belmont*	*Parkworth*
Dedicated	40	21	Argumentative	42	20
Plans ahead	39	15	Defensive	39	4
Accepting	33	6	Impulsive	33	8
Academic	32	55	Individualistic	32	18
Happy	32	46	Rebellious	32	37
Self-disciplined	32	20	Moody	29	21
Conscientious	30	16	Not easily impressed	29	20
Cooperative	30	22	Adventurous	27	30
Helpful	29	17	Sarcastic	27	-4#

Four percent fewer Parkworth's low than high morale students
described themselves as sarcastic.

What self-attitudes and traits may consistently separate our most and least involved students? Clearly students of high morale believe that they can cope effectively with schools' academic demands. Their high morale score suggests they are called to and feel fulfilled in their academic role. Their greater happiness validates the SRS as a morale scale.

On the other hand, students with low morale have a self-image that will, if acted out, frustrate, even anger, most teachers. Comparing their view of their teachers with their picture of themselves suggests a recipe for trouble in and out of the classroom. Expecting one's teachers to be stubborn, critical, unfair, and sarcastic combined with beliefs that one is a defensive, moody, and unrestrained individualist predicts what? A battle of wills and a year-long argument and rebellious acting out of risk-taking behaviors. As the psychic dropouts tell us, they are not readily open to being educated, but they wish they were! That is the hope, if they have teachers who fit their ideal, who accept their individualistic persona, respond to their moodiness and rebelliousness with a cheerful, kidding, and humorous light touch, and make learning a playful, lively adventure. If they do not have such teachers, they may retreat into themselves, become passively negativistic, defy teachers to teach them, or provoke one confrontation after another—and so make school a much less boring adventure.

What does this exploration of the inner world of psychic dropouts tell us? I cite only a few thoughts that intrigue me; you may have gained others more relevant to your interests.

1. The SRS and WCL continue to be profitably useful in illuminating the relation between individuals and their social systems. In one sense, the results of our exploration of dropouts also validates both measures.

2. The patterned differences between high and low morale students from large and small, lower and upper middle class, New England, midwestern, and southern public and private schools, and elementary, junior, and high schools are remarkably similar.

3. Dropouts are recognizable, regardless of such differences, by their attitudes about their schools, teachers, peers, and their beliefs about themselves.

4. And this is an intuitive leap, there may be an underlying personality predisposition to become a dropout, regardless of type of school. Chapter 5 reported that low morale may be symptomatic of developmental immaturity, not just of a serious slippage or misfit between students and their schools' culture, which of course frequently occurs.

5. If we genuinely listen to psychic dropouts' views and wishes we may discover clues about the learning environment that might further their maturing. Developing and marketing a quick fix-type of "dropout prevention technique or program" may reach a few stu-

dents but probably not the type of psychic dropouts the chapter describes. Their personal issues are deeper, more systemically integrated with their characters. Only a school committed to the growth of students and not just to their minds may reach such students.

I recommended that each Belmont faculty adopt two in-coming ninth graders predisposed to become psychic dropouts and become their year-long, caring mentor-parent-advocate. I was most serious, though the faculty thought I was joking. Their solution? Get the ninth graders hooked on computers! Given how psychic dropout's relationships are so negatively conflicted with everyone, might not an impersonal computer be a more appropriate teacher for some? They can be programmed to not be stubborn, critical, argumentative, dull, unfair, sarcastic, and aggressive.[3]

But can computers be programmed to be loving, warm, caring, and happy, even joyful? Should not every elementary school have computers whose welcoming arms can reach out, touch, comfort, and hug every child at least several times a day? Until then, affectionately playful dogs could substitute, if janitors wouldn't go out on strike. But I am serious.

Governors, legislators, and educators who wish to reduce dropout rates may succeed with some students, but probably not with the much larger number of potential psychic dropouts. Leaders must first create more humane growing-up environments in which no student is a stranger in an alien school. The next chapter examines in depth how the culture of public and private schools differ. We now know their students do. Private school students have higher morale. Do their schools differ in their humaneness?

Chapter 13

—◆◆◆◆—

COMPARING CHOICES:
PUBLIC OR PRIVATE SCHOOLS?

Claims and counterclaims about the advantages and disadvantges of
a public or private school keep surfacing and resurfacing in the media and political debates. Governmental paid vouchers, especially to
religious schools, currently fuel the stormy arguments. The debates
focus almost exclusively on schools' test-achieving effects. The weight
of the evidence suggests that students in NAIS schools outscore students in Catholic parochial schools, who generally outscore students
in public schools.

A host of methodological problems in such comparative studies
muddy the interpretation of such evidence.[1] By the term "public
schools" do we lump poor minority Sandia with suburban affluent
Reagan? Or large schools with numerous curricular options in math
with small ones which offer few? Or parochial school's reputed homogeneous, though increasingly diluted, "family-community" culture with Adelphi's pure academic one? And how do we equate
aptitude, parental expectations, and a host of other factors that might
contribute to one type of school achieving its goals but another not?

"Private" schools include a number of different types of non-public schools. I have no information about Catholic parochial schools.
By "private" I refer to members of the National Association of Independent Schools which does include some religious schools. My
sample includes a few Episcopalian, some Catholic, but no Jewish or
Quaker schools.

Some commentators propose that a school's culture is a major contributor to academic test-score differences.[2] I know of no study that has objectively measured different schools' cultures to find out. Nor do I know of any that have objectively examined public and private schools' cultures and the character outcomes on which this book focusses.

The liability of the cultural measures (the morale surveys as well) whose results the chapter reports limits the generality of their norms and findings to suburbia's typical schools, including lighthouse ones like Edina, Bloomfield Hills, and Reagan. (Urban minority schools are not included.) The liability now turns out to be a potential methodological strength. My public and private school samples are similar socio-economically. They share suburbia's values. None are "at risk" schools. With the exception of possibly two public schools, none have a dropout "problem"—though all have a "psychic dropout" one. The schools consider themselves basically college-preparatory; they value their high percentages of students who attend college. Many parents attended college and reputedly value education. They have no or few children on government sponsored lunch programs. No school is plagued by toilet paper shortages. Few of the boys' bathrooms I visited are decorated by graphiti; I noticed none without doors on their toilets! In other words, many of the reasons cited to explain differences in outcomes for public and private schools do not exist either actually—or symbolically.

What my results can tell us is whether high school students from independent (though not private parochial) and suburban public schools describe themselves and their peers similarly. Do their faculties agree about their students? Do private and public school students and faculty view their schools similarly? How do students view their teachers? I seek to clarify independent and public school cultural similarities and dissimilarities. Only then can I more confidently compare their character outcomes and the sources of any differences we may discover in the following chapters.

Public and Private School Cultural Differences

What information does the WCL generate about the schools to discover whether and how their students differ in their personalities? Table 13-1 compares how independent and public high school students and teachers differ in their views about and wishes for each other and their schools. It orders the percentages of their *differences* from least to most for faculty and students. I used a 10% difference between public and independent students' views of each of the WCL's 150 words about, say, their views of themselves, to identify the number of differences in their self-concepts. Similarly, I used a 5% difference in their wishes to learn how much they differed in their hopes for themselves. Table 13-1 reports, for example, that public and independent students differed by 10% or more on only 7 or less than 5% of WCL's 150 words when they described themselves; they differed on 24 or 16% of the 150 words when expressing their wishes for themselves.

Table 13-1   Independent-Public School Faculty and Student Differences in Beliefs and Wishes Ordered from Least to Greatest Difference

% of Differences in Views of		*% of Differences in Wishes for*	
Themselves by students	5	Their schools by faculties	9
Their students by faculties	16	Themselves by students	16
Their peers by students	17	Their schools by students	17
Their schools by faculties	30	Their students by faculties	22
Their schools by students	44	Their peers by students	27
Their teachers by students	54	Their teachers by students	27

Do you find Table 13-1 as illuminating but provocative as I do? The principal generalizations about independent and public schools that I glean from the table are:

1. Their students come from the same population. They describe themselves similarly, i.e. differ by only 5%. They have somewhat similar wishes for themselves, i.e. they differ in 16% of their wishes.

2. Their teachers and students confirm that the typical student or peer most likely also comes from the same population, i.e. their descriptions differ by 16 to 17% and their wishes by 22 to 27%.

3. Though independent and public school faculties and students describe their schools differently, i.e., by 30% versus 44% respec-

tively, they agree moderately well about their wishes for their schools, i.e., 9% versus 17%.

4. Their students differ so radically in their view of their teachers, i.e., 54%, that their differences in their views of their schools probably reflect primarily their beliefs about their teachers.

An interpretive warning. Regard the findings and my interpretations as provisional hypotheses requiring more extended research, especially on students' views of their teachers about which more data are needed. [ASH 37-38: Public and Independent Stable and Provisional WCL Norms].

We now need substance to make more concretely meaningful the significance of Table 13-1's abstract conclusions. I examine first the content of the students' self-concepts. Differences between the public and independent students' personalities rather than between their schools might account for most of their differences in achievement test, morale, or ethical behavior which I analyze in Chapters 14 and 15.

Public and Independent School Students' Self-Concepts

How can the WCL be used to identify how similar and dissimilar public and independent students view themselves? To condense the results to manageable numbers, Table 13-2 reports *all* of the traits that at least 70% of either public, independent, Reagan, or Sandia students checked about themselves. It orders them by independent school students' most widely agreed upon traits. I include Reagan's and Sandia's students to contrast a reputedly strong with a weak public school's students. What conclusions would you draw from Table 13-2?

Table 13-2's 10 % criterion is a reasonable but strict test of independent and public students' dissimilarities in their self-concepts. Of the seven differences on the WCL's 150 words, more public than independent school students thought they were rebellious; more independent students thought they were ethical. But if I had used a 15% criterion to define a meaningful difference, I would have identified only three differences. For reasons I have discussed earlier, I used a lower criterion, i.e., 5 %, to identify meaningful differences in their wishes. If I had used a 10 % criterion, independent and public students would have differed on only one of WCL's attributes, i.e., at least 10% more of the independent than public students wished that they were efficient.

**Table 13-2   Comparison of Public to Independent (NAIS)
Students' Beliefs about Themselves**

| Attribute | % Students Describing Themselves | | | |
	NAIS	Public	Reagan	Sandia
Friendly	87	84	81	68*
Can say no	83	81	81	68*
Caring	80	84	83	66*
Capable	78	78	74	48*
Considerate	73	72	67	46*
Fun	73	78	77	64*
Honest	73	71	64	66
Accepting	72	67	67	54*
Feels for others	72	72	68	60*
Good-natured	71	70	64	48*
Humorous	70	73	75	40*
Can make decisions	67	71	71	64
Understanding	66	71	61*	72

* Differs by at least 10% from one or more other
schools' students.

Note that the independent, public, and Reagan students did not differ by 10% in all but one of their most prominent traits, i.e., understanding. Since they differed on fewer than 5% of all of WCL's 150 traits, I conclude that their students come from the same population and can be fairly compared to each other. On the other hand, the asterisks marking 10% or more differences between Sandia and public school students tell us that they come from different populations. We must be cautious about lumping Sandia with other public schools and then comparing, say, their test results. The results may be due more to differences in their students' self-concepts than to differences in their teachers' skill or schools' attributes.

I feel confident about the independent and public school faculty and student norms about their views of their schools and students. The extraordinary similarity of their students' self-concepts makes me also trust their data, even though based on only 1700 students. [ASH 38C: Public and Independent High School Students' Views of and Wishes for Themselves].

Public and Independent Students' and Teachers' Views of and Wishes for The Typical Student

More independent students and teachers believe that their typical peer has more favorable and fewer unfavorable traits than public students and teachers believe about their typical student. For example, more NAIS teachers and students believe that their students are academically oriented. More public high school teachers and students (including Reagan's and Sandia's) believe that their typical students are less academically motivated, e.g., 20% of NAIS but 46% of Reagan's and 57% of Sandia's faculty believe that their students are apathetic; 25% of NAIS but 43% of Reagan's and 66% of Sandia's students believe that their peers don't care.

The WCL can also identify intercultural similarities and dissimilarities in students' personalities. I compared public and independent school students' views with American international students' views of their peers. As diverse as the latter students are, their views are more similar to NAIS school students' views of their typical student. They disagree with NAIS students on 23 % but with public school students on 31% of the traits they assign to their peers. More than the NAIS students, for example, they believe that their peers are relaxed, sympathetic, open, self-confident and joyful. Fewer believe that they are academic, capable, ambitious, and aggressive.

Public and Independent School Students' and Teachers' Views of and Wishes for Their Schools

Table 13-1 reported that public and independent students do not differ as much from each other as they believe their schools differ. It also showed that public and independent high school students differed by 10% or more on 44% of the WCL's traits about their schools. Such a large difference between students who are basically similar looms as the touchstone to identify real differences between independent and public schools. Table 13-3 lists the 10 attributes of their schools where independent students *differed* most from public school students. It also lists the 10 attributes of their schools where public students *differed* most from independent students. I also compare Reagan's and Sandia's student differences to the independent students' views. [ASH 37A,B: Public and Independent High School Teachers' and Students' Views of and Wishes for Their Schools].

Table 13-3   Comparison of Independent (NAIS) and Public School Students' Differences in Their Views of Their Schools

% Greater by Attribute	NAIS	% Greater by Attribute	Public	Reagan	Sandia
Caring	20	Boring	28	12	39
Honest	20	Dull	21	1	39
Independent	20	Unfair	17	17	43
Friendly	19	Casual	15	11	-2#
Intellectually rigorous	19	Impersonal	13	8	1
Intense	18	Put-downs	13	8	6
Proud	17	Doesn't care	12	3	38
Thorough	17	Lacks energy	12	3	26
Ambitious	16	Emotionally cold	12	6	25
Considerate	16	Inconsiderate	11	7	13

#Thirty-six percent of NAIS's but two percent fewer (34%) of Sandia's students rated their school as casual.

To repeat once more how to interpret the table, consider boredom, the principal attribute of a school that distinguishes low from high morale students. Fifty-seven percent of public but 29% of independent school students view their schools as boring—the difference of 28% listed in the table.

Note that more public school students consistently view their high schools more negatively than independent school students do. More independent than public school students did *not* select even one unfavorable attribute to describe their schools.

Table 13-1 indicates that public and independent students differed by 5% or more on 17% of their wishes for their schools. Not surprisingly more public than independent school students wished that their schools were different. What distresses me are the consistently low percentages of students who had any wishes at all for their schools. Where are the dreams, the ideals, the passion, the fire to want their schools to be different? Educational reformers cannot count on students to prod their schools to change. As painful as schools must be to those who believe they are boring, dull, unfair, and inconsiderate, resignation and apathy appear to be their students' response. Does not the pattern of results suggest students feel no ownership for their schools as alive, growth-producing places in which to mature?

Even more troubling is that teachers agree with their students about their schools. Table 13-1 tells us that public and independent school teachers differed on 45 or 30% of their schools' attributes by 10% or more. Forty-four of the 45 are positive attributes. More public than independent school teachers did *not* select one of the positive attributes. Both independent school faculty and students agreed that their schools were ambitious, enthusiastic, considerate, empathic, demanding, intellectually rigorous, and intense schools. More public school teachers agreed about the forty-fifth attribute: Their schools were more casual.

Without overwhelming you with more percentages, I summarize the tone of all of the comparisons. Independent schools are viewed to be more spirited places that provide more demanding, interpersonally responsive, and growth-producing cultures. Their higher faculty and student morale confirms their more alive cultures.

For students, their schools more often than not are their teachers. What do they contribute to their students' morale?

Public and Independent School Students' Views of and Wishes for Their Teachers

Table 13-4's differences between public and independent students' views of their teachers are so provocatively revealing (and troubling to me) that they should be replicated. We may have unexpectedly stumbled on a reason heretofore not investigated why improving public high schools has been so futile. Table 13-4 samples only the largest discrepancies in perception to dramatize how differently public and independent students view their teachers.

**Table 13-4   Differences between Public and Independent
(NAIS) School Students' Views about and
Wishes for Their Teachers**

% Difference in Views of Teachers				% Difference in Wishes for Teachers			
Attribute	Public	Attribute	NAIS	Attribute	Public	Attribute	NAIS
Dull	29	Intellectual	30	Cheerful	16	None#	
Boring	27	Enthusiastic	29	Caring	15		
Humorless	19	Energetic	28	Friendly	15		
Dictatorial	18	Caring	27	Fun	15		
Emotionally cold	18	Intellectually rigorous	27	Energetic	13		
Impatient	16	Excellence	26	Happy	13		
Lacks energy	16	Feels for other	24	Accepting	12		
Impersonal	15	Deep interests	23	Humorous	12		
Inflexible	15	Genuine	23	Trusting	12		
Defensive	13	Accepting	22	Joyful	11		
Doesn't care	13	Creative	22	Easy going	11		

Independent students had no wishes greater than 5% of public school students' wishes.

Let's first be clear about what the table reports. Consider boring. Sixty-four percent of public school students described their teachers as boring; 37% of independent school students also described their teachers as boring. The difference is the 27% that Table 13-4's first column reports. Table 13-4's differences do *not* tell us how many public students believed that their teachers were boring. [ASH 38B: Public and Independent High School Students Views of and Wishes for Their Teachers report the actual percentages].

How shall we interpret the table's devastating finding that public high school students so consistently view their teachers so much more negatively than independent students view theirs? Keep in mind that the results describe students' beliefs about teachers in reputedly exemplary suburban public schools, not about teachers in Wentworth's, Sandia's, and Washington's schools. Quite bluntly, does not the table suggest that more public than independent school students view their typical teacher to be burnt out, even dead?

What accounts for these differences which suggest many public schools are dysfunctional social systems that may adversely affect "the attitudes, the aspirations and the motivation" of those who work in them? Note one of Table 13-4's differentiating themes: quality of interpersonal relations. May not the results clarify and extend the research evidence, documented in *Schools of Hope,* that large, impersonal, and emotionally cold schools are unhealthy places, especially for vulnerable students. Does Table 13-4 suggest that the conclusion may also apply to teachers' premature psychic burnout? Might not Deming say at this point, "Stop blaming teachers. Examine how their school organization may block their healthy growth, limit their effectiveness, and reduce their morale?"

Pearl Kane has done just that. Studying New Jersey's charter schools' effects on their teachers, she concludes that their small size "contributes to building a sense of community" in which teachers sharing a "common educational philosophy. . . and working toward the same goals . . . find their work more satisfying . . . the majority of the teachers we met were growth seekers, willing to put forth increased effort for a satisfying professional life."[3] An echo of Model High School's similar findings?

The chapter has examined the *beliefs* of students and teachers, not their *behavior*. Not just public and independent school differences in size but also their differences in number of students taught each day may contribute to Table 13-4's dismal comparisons. How reasonable is it to expect the typical teacher teaching between 130 to 160 students five times a week to be cheerful, caring, energetic, and happy every day? As one public school teacher said of the table's results, "Give me the same number of students that your NAIS teachers teach each period for 180 days and then redo your study." Public and independent students' beliefs do parallel, however, achievement test findings. The next two chapters pursue public and independent schools' students' differences in ethical *behavior*—more strictly, students' descriptions of how they act in specific ethical situations. I search for attributes of their schools that might account for the differences. They frame the book's larger purpose: How to hold schools honestly accountable for creating a facilitative interpersonal learning environment and fulfilling their school-wide character values.

SECTION VI

———◆———

Rethinking Character Education

Chapter 14

—————•◦•—————

DISCOVERING DIFFERENCES IN

ETHICAL BEHAVIOR

Adults have always been exercised by what they believe to be youth's waywardness. Today's adults are no exception. Societal consensus about what is right and wrong has been changing, some say crumbling, especially since the 1960s. *Schools of Hope,* relying on WCL data, described the changing character of students; it identified some of the sources of their (and their parents') changing attitudes about morality.[1]

Parents, commentators, and politicians loudly and incessantly call schools to educate children to be more moral. Another national conference is held, then another and another. The flurry then dies down, only to rise again and then again. National educational organizations establish year-long committees on moral education. Individual schools review again their mission statements. A few courageous ones like Adelphi actually try to discover whether they have the climate that encourages moral development. But nothing ever seems to change for long. In fact, I have detected very little significant change in the past decade in our understanding of moral education. I know of few researchers who have studied in depth the conditions that must be present for it to "take." Of course, the issue of character education will never go away. It will be resurrected again and then again as long as children grow up amid rapid societal changes.

I fear that those who call for moral education and list their prescriptions misunderstand and so obscure more significant underlying sources of our moral confusion. Are they really asking the right questions? Their prescriptions— daily pledges of allegiance, morning prayers, and censorship of library books— may answer yesterday's questions. I doubt they do so for today's. If prescriptions have not worked in the past, should we not at least requestion the diagnosis? More profound underlying societal changes fuel our moral confusion not touched one whit by such prescriptions.

One historically momentous and irreversible source of moral confusion is the change in male and female relationships. Their associated meanings of maleness and femaleness are being permanently altered. Women, spurred by their oppression's suffering, are moving world-wide to redefine the meaning of equality and their opportunities for fulfillment. Male dominated organizations as diverse as Texaco, the Catholic Church, the Army, Virginia Military Academy, and Tech University struggle to understand and grudgingly adjust.

This, the first of three chapters, explores what the WCL and a measure of ethical behavior tell us about public and independent schools' gender differences in ethical behavior. It also illustrates how the personality roots of one virtue, acceptance and tolerance of those who differ from us, can be explored in more depth. Chapter 15 identifies a school's attributes which contribute to ethical maturation. Chapter 16 then reflectively compares the principal contributors to ethical maturation; it then suggests a few steps schools could take to prepare boys and girls to live more ethical and so more successful and happy lives in the future.

Measure of Ethical Values

In 1990, the parents of Minnesota's Edina's prestigious lighthouse school district asked it to help their children act more ethically. The committee did not know of my research on healthy growth and its associated values. However, it independently identified similar core values from its collective experience that the model of maturity identifies: honesty, responsibility, caring, courage, commitment, and tolerance. The committee then took the next step which most such committees seldom take. It described specific behaviors that characterized each value. A school- and community-wide strategic action plan to encourage the development of its core values completed the committee's work.

In a talk to Edina's parents I off-handedly challenged the district to secure base line information to determine the effectiveness of its planned programs. The administration unexpectedly turned the tables on me. It challenged me to develop measures of each core value defined by the committee's pool of examples.

The Ethical Value Questionnaire or EVQ consists of two parts, one consists of 18 items measuring how frequently a youth behaves ethically, the other of 5 items assessing degree of comfort relating to different types of people. Three items define each of the six ethical values. For example, students responded to the statement, "How would you rate yourself helping someone who really needs help" (Caring) or "Doing your homework as well as you can" (Commitment). They checked one of five categories: "All of the time," "Most times," "More often than not," "Sometimes," or "Rarely" for each behavior. Each item is scored from five (most frequent) to one (least). Each value's three items can be summed to give a total score of 15. A perfect or total ethical value score is 90.[2] [ASH 42: Description of Ethical Value Questionnaire— EVQ].

The EVQ's second part contains a frequently-used social distance scale. It measures degree of comfort in accepting others who differ from one self in increasingly intimate relationships. I explore its results later.

The Edina Study

Edina surveyed anonymously its fifth and sixth graders' morale. One half of them completed their abbreviated WCL form about their school and the other half about their peers. An ethical value scale parallel to the EVQ has not been created for elementary school students. Edina anonymously surveyed its junior and high school students more fully. After indicating their sex and grade averages, they rated the frequency of their participation in four types of co-curricular and community service activities, the number of hours worked each week on their homework and for money, number of times in the past month they had drunk alcohol and used drugs, and finally how much their parents cared about and supported their acting ethically. The EVQ can be altered by including a similar statement asking students to rate their teachers' care for and support of their acting ethically. After completing the background, SRS, and EVQ surveys, 1/4 of the seventh through twelfth graders completed one of the WCL's four basic targets, e.g., School, Self.[3]

All faculty completed its parallel morale scale, and the two Word Check List targets of School and Typical Student.

How Validly Can Ethical Values and Behavior Be Assessed?

Are you now asking the question I asked of the AAUW study? What independent evidence now suggests what the EVQ in fact measures? Ethical values and behavior are most slippery to objectify for study.[4] I had no access to judges knowledgeable about each student to validate the students' self-ratings. So I relied on researchers' more pragmatic and conventional practice. I defined what a test is by what it predicts.

Regardless of their school, sex, or grade level, students who describe their behavior to be highly ethical, in contrast to those who don't, reliably have higher morale, devote more hours a week to their homework assignments, get better academic grades, participate more frequently in co-curricular and community service activities, work fewer hours for money during the school week, drink alcohol and use drugs less frequently, believe that their parents and teachers expect them to be more ethical and caring persons, and report being more comfortable with people who differ from them. Model's faculty rated its more ethical students to be more mature. [ASH 21: Assessing Model's Effects on Its Students' Ethical Competence].

This broadly sketched portrait of a good school citizen describes the more ethical student in *every* school I have studied. Not every facet of the portrait, however, has been surveyed for every school's students. Its pattern agrees remarkably well with the patterns found about the lives of virtuous adults.[5] The EVQ validly measures self-reported ethical behavior as it is expressed in good school citizenship behavior. [ASH 22: Interpreting Ethical Value Questionnaire's Ethical Indices].

Gender Differences in Ethical Values

Table 14-1 summarizes public and NAIS gender differences found to date for different grades. The table is incomplete. Edina did not survey its seventh graders' ethical behavior. I also have too few public middle school students in my sample to feel comfortable interpreting their behavior in detail. I include primarily Edina's eighth graders to show the consistency in ethical patterning across the ages.

Table 14-1   Ethical Norms for Public, Reagan, and NAIS Middle and High School Boys and Girls

	8 Edina		9-12 Public		9-12 Reagan		7-8 NAIS		9-12 NAIS	
Ethical Values	Boys	Girls	Boys	Girls	Boys	Girls	Boys	Girls	Boys	Girls
Honesty	11.1*	11.6	10.6	11.2	10.4	10.9	11.9	12.2	11.8	12.2
Responsibility	11.0	12.2	11.8	12.2	11.4	12.3	12.2	12.6	12.0	12.5
Caring	11.6	13.0	11.4	12.9	11.6	12.8	12.3	13.0	11.4	12.1
Courage	11.9	12.6	11.4	12.4	11.4	12.1	12.2	12.8	11.7	11.8
Tolerance	11.7	13.2	10.9	12.8	10.8	12.7	12.6	13.2	11.2	11.9
Commitment	11.5	12.4	11.2	11.9	11.0	11.6	12.1	12.6	11.5	11.8
Total Ethical Value Score	68.9	75.0	67.3	73.4	66.5	72.2	73.5	76.4	69.7	72.3

* The maximum score for a value is 15 and for all six values 90.

I regret the too crowded table, but it helps when learning how to interpret more holistically to have as full a map of findings possible in one place.

Reliability of Gender Differences

Our question now must be: Is the 9-12th NAIS gender difference in the last column for Commitment, for example, of only .3 points a chance difference? Or is it, given the thousands of students involved, most likely to be found upon subsequent repetitions with other similar boys and girls?[6] For both public and NAIS middle and high school students for *every* core Ethical Value (except Courage for NAIS 9-12 grade boys and girls), girls reliably report acting more ethically than boys report. The odds are exceedingly small that the pattern (as well as of specific score comparisons) is due to chance. Similar gender differences for all ethical values have since been confirmed by several thousand other girls and boys from college preparatory boarding, rural, suburban, and more racially diverse urban schools. That the gender differences are so consistent for so many different schools confirms that they are real and very general. Boys and girls do consistently differ in their ethical relationships. Please don't ever forget, however, that there are some boys who are more caring than some girls and some girls who are more courageous than some boys.

Table 14-1 also permits us to ask if each sex acts more ethically in one value area than another. Specifically, in which areas do boys report acting more and less ethically? Note that NAIS boys believe that they act more responsibly but much less tolerantly of and caring about others. These differences are statistically so reliable that, again, the odds that they are due to chance are infinitesimal. The same conclusion holds for NAIS girls' reported greater responsibility but lesser courage and commitment.

By now you have probably already discovered the table's other principal patterns: The independent school boys and girls report that they act more ethically than public school boys and girls do. Middle school boys and girls report acting more ethically than their corresponding high school peers do. The NAIS high school boys report their greatest decline in ethical behavior from middle school boys to be in caring for and tolerance of others (too limited data from public middle school boys makes use of the Edina data too risky for similar comparisons). Other patterns are not as consistent.

Comparisons of public and private students' ethical behavior.

Table 14-1 for the first time enables comparisons of how boys and girls from reasonably comparable socio-economic, college preparatory public and independent schools differ in *ethical behavior*. We now tread on controversial political ground. Beware of advocates of publicly funded vouchers for private schools who may be tempted to use the results to uncritically advance their political cause. Three underlying assumptions of the currently acrimonious political debate must yet be thoughtfully examined before advocates can use the results *honestly*.

First, do private school boys and girls report acting more ethically than comparable public school boys and girls report?

Second, if so, why? Chapter 15 explores one of the possible "whys" by asking whether private and public schools differ in their moral climates. Jerome Hanus, a professor of government at American University,[7] claims that their difference in moral climates is the principal justification for vouchers.

Third, and much more difficult to answer rigorously, how decisively can private and public schools affect not just students' achievement test but also ethical behavior? Chapter 16 compares the "whys" of ethical behavior to intuitively judge their relative influence.

Table 14-1's results answer the first question about NAIS and public school gender differences quite straightforwardly. Statistically, NAIS boys reliably report acting more ethically than public school boys report in *every* core ethical area except for caring, about which they do not differ. (They also rate themselves to be more comfortable interacting with others who differ from them.)

Public school girls reliably report acting more ethically over-all than NAIS girls report. Moreover, the pattern of ethical differences between them (while highly improbable that they are due to chance) is confusing and contradictory. NAIS girls describe themselves acting more honestly and responsibly but less caringly, courageously, and tolerantly than public school girls report. They do not differ in their commitment to academic work.

I included Reagan's results in Table 14-1 to provide a more rigorous comparison. Recall that Reagan stands out even among my elite schools as a reputedly sterling school of unexcelled resources. The NAIS boys continued to reliably report acting more ethically; the girls did not consistently. NAIS girls reported acting more honestly, responsibly, and being more committed; Reagan's girls reliably reported being more caring, courageous, and tolerant.

Can advocates of vouchers now claim research demonstrates that private schools offer ethical salvation to our society? (I dramatize the issue to provoke a judicious interpretive answer to the exaggerated claims some advocates of vouchers make. My point is that research findings must be examined critically and holistically.) My answer? Definitely not! Why? For two reasons.

First, NAIS schools are most atypical "private" schools; their results cannot be readily generalized yet to the several thousand parochial and other privately funded schools' students. They are expensive; their teacher-student ratios are small; their parents are generally well educated. Students from other types of private schools may come from a different population.

Second, no comparable studies of other types of private schools have been done to demonstrate any alleged ethical superiority of their students. Let us say, for example, parochial school students report acting more ethically than *comparable* public school students. Can we then assert parochial schools have a greater impact on character than public schools? No. Might not their students' ethical behavior be due more to their shared Catholic parental up-bringing than to any attribute of their schools? Comparing the ethical behavior of Catholic and non-Catholic students in parochial schools might provide an answer.

What may cause gender differences in ethical behavior?

Numerous influences affect ethical behavior. Chapter 15 explores the effects of schools' moral climate, teacher modeling of ethical values, teachers' and students' emotional commitment to ethical behavior, and students' peer culture. Chapter 16 examines other influences for which I do not have direct evidence. Bio-hormonal, familial, and socio-cultural influences are other obvious influences.

Ethics are about how we should relate to others; the route to becoming more ethical is by way of maturing in our personal relationships. A deeper understanding of gender differences in ethical behavior must therefore also examine males' and females' interpersonal attitudes and skills. My entry into this occasionally polemical and confusing topic is by way of the ideas of masculinity and femininity. Individual males and females possess different amounts of both *stereotypic* masculine and feminine traits. Collectively, however, males and females reliably differ from each other in how much of their sex's associated traits they possess. For example, three judges who knew well each man whom I have studied for 40 years rated the men to be reliably more masculine than feminine (on most of 20 traits that other researchers have identified to describe each concept). Judges who knew the women well, whom I have studied for 25 years, rated them to be reliably more feminine than masculine on most of their stereotypic 20 traits.[8]

Such gender differences do not emerge as sharply when males and females describe *themselves*. The public and NAIS boys' and girls' descriptions of themselves did not differ on most of the WCL's 150 traits. When they did, they differed most on the traits typical of their sex. Table 14-2 orders the boys' and girls' self-descriptions by the genders' public school ratings. It includes the WCL traits most similar to researchers' identified traits for each gender. If you are trying to improve your diagnostic skill, take the time to examine the table carefully. It contains a critical key for understanding gender differences in ethical behavior.

Table 14-2 Public and Independent (NAIS) High School Boys' and Girls' Self-Descriptions of their Masculinity and Femininity

| | Masculinity Traits | | | | | Femininity Traits | | | |
| | % Public | | % NAIS | | | % Public | | % NAIS | |
	Boys	Girls	Boys	Girls		Girls	Boys	Girls	Boys
Adventurous	73	64	70	62	Caring	93	72	85	76
Decisive	73	73	74	62	Feels for others	84	56	81	65
Athletic	71	50	66	54	Loving	81	51	73	51
Competitive	71	51	67	57	Understanding	79	61	73	62
Aggressive	60	46	50	48	Cheerful	78	51	73	50
Ambitious	58	59	64	66	Giving	71	44	66	56
Courageous	57	44	51	47	Sympathetic	63	33	63	56
Independent	46	58	57	60	Warmth	57	29	52	37
Self-reliant	36	35	41	38	Expressive	51	38	57	39
Individualistic	31	39	45	45	Personal	41	29	42	30
Average	57.6	51.9	58.5	53.9		69.8	46.4	66.5	52.2

Reagan's average masculinity and femininity scores for its boys were 57.7 and 43.3 and for its girls 51.9 and 68.2.

Table 14-2's average scores leave little room for equivocation. In their schools, boys are boys are boys. They do not differ in their average masculinity scores. Their similarity cannot therefore explain why public school boys report acting less ethically than NAIS boys report.

I had not anticipated that almost as many girls as boys would describe themselves as masculine regardless of their type of school. Few students typically describe themselves negatively on the WCL.

The majority of girls rate themselves on average to be masculine. They are, I suggest, comfortable with and value such traits as assets. Their androgyny helps explain why feminists I know reject terms like "masculinity" as too simplistic for describing personality differences between the genders.

It is Table 14-2's femininity scores that provide the piece of our jigsaw puzzle that clarifies the genders' sources of ethical behavior. First, girls are girls are girls in their expressive and interpersonal strengths regardless of their type of school. Only 2.5% more public-Reagan than NAIS girls describe themselves in feminine terms. Their femininity does not seem to be a persuasive reason for the public and independent school differences in their ethical behavior.[9]

Second, Table 14-2's most illuminating result for me is the boys' (including Reagan's) femininity self-concept. It differs from the girls' by almost 20%. The girls' averaged masculine self-concept differed from the boys' by less than 5%. Girls are obviously more comfortable with their masculine selves than boys are with their feminine ones. Only a minority of boys accept feminine expressive and interpersonal strengths as part of their self-concepts. The majority are conformed by their gender's masculinity straitjacket.

Table 14-2 tells us that when they do differ, girls do not differ from boys as much in stereotypic masculine traits as boys differ from girls in stereotypic feminine ones. Girls have more androgynous self-concepts. The roots of these differences are deep, as a study of three-to-five-year-olds' play patterns found. Girls who play with stereotypic masculine and feminine toys, like blocks and dolls, are popular with both boys and girls. However, boys who also play with both are not accepted by other boys. The researchers concluded, "Males have a much more rigid definition of appropriate sex role behavior."[10] While such gender differences are widely known, how they affect a youth's adult ethical behavior has only recently been discovered.

How do gender and femininity differences explain ethical behavior?

I have found from my adult studies three relevant and provocative facts about virtue and its relation to gender.[11] First, virtuous men and women succeed more in every area of adult life (maritally, parentally, sexually, vocationally—though neither more nor less in income) than less virtuous men and women do. They are also physically and emotionally healthier, happier, and more mature. These findings parallel those of ethical adolescents. Recall that compared to less ethical ones they are better school citizens, are more satisfied with school and their work as students, succeed more academically, and may also be more mature. For the first time we have complementary evidence validating every major religion's claim that virtue is a path to successful living and well-being. And for the first time we also have scientific evidence that valuing character education may produce effective, healthy, and happier adults.

Second, the men and women and those who knew them most intimately agreed that the men acted less ethically than the women. Adolescent gender differences in ethical behavior are neither unstable nor peculiar to the teen-age years; they persist into adulthood.

Third, for *both* men and women, ethical behavior is associated with their feminine interpersonal traits. The core traits that typically define masculinity, such as aggressivity and competitiveness, are not related to measures of ethical behavior for either males or females. However, the core traits that define femininity, such as understanding of and sensitivity to others' needs and sympathy, reliably contribute to ethical behavior for both.

For me, the implications of these results have profound consequences for schools and society. Could it be that the critical contributor to ethical behavior is not gender per se but the expressive and interpersonal character traits traditionally associated more with females than with males? To be ethical males must be androgynous. Females don't need to be androgynous since masculine strengths are irrelevant to being ethical. Given the more sharply constricted American meaning of maleness than of femaleness, boys may be less educable than girls for moral education.

To rephrase the issue more precisely, masculine males and females must work harder to become more virtuous than feminine females and males need to unless they are androgynous.[12] The majority of public and NAIS boys describe themselves to be masculine as the majority of girls describe themselves to be feminine. Boys' testosterone, limited interpersonal skills, and macho-reinforcing peer environment that devalues sensitivity, compassion, and emotional expressivity make them more vulnerable to acting less ethically.

This line of argument also helps explain why NAIS boys reliably *act* more ethically than public-Reagan boys. Though neither more nor less masculine, the NAIS boys are more interpersonally feminine (though not much more expressive, loving, and personal), and so more androgynous overall. Recall that regardless of sex, adult virtue is reliably associated with such feminine interpersonal but not with typical masculine traits.

I now leave the table's other patterns for you to deduce their implications in order to illustrate another way to analyze ethical behavior. I will dig more deeply into the personality of boys and girls who are multiculturally intolerant. I elect this rather than one of the other virtues to study in depth. Its contemporary relevance is paramount for our society now and for its future. The approach and questions the WCL provide may model how you seek to understand in more depth each of the other virtues.

The Multiculturally Intolerant Youth

America is a microcosm of the world's diversity; the majority of its people will be of color in the 21st century. Acceptance of and empathy, tolerance, and respect for others who differ from ourselves are emerging as core ethical values for which American schools need to educate.

Bloomfield Hills' Parent Teacher Organization, recognizing the necessity of these values for its own community, asked me to conduct a weekend workshop on how to educate for tolerance. My predictably empirical self suggested I first understand how tolerant its students believed they were. Then, as I did for psychic dropouts, I identified very tolerant and intolerant students to explore how their inner worlds differed, if at all. Like the AAUW researchers, I relied on their self-ratings but then built a context of other information around them to understand what their ratings of tolerance predicted. Assuming that the roots of prejudice went at least as deep as the pubertal years, I surveyed all of the district's three middle schools' eighth graders. This chapter reports what I found and have since discovered from surveys of seventh through twelfth grade boys and girls in independent and public schools. I refer to the one international school for which I have information to explore whether more direct experience with diverse cultures affects tolerance.

The Measure of Multicultural Intolerance

The key methodological problem was to identify students' degree of intolerance for people who differ from them. The EVQ's Tolerance score consists of three statements which each student rated on five-point scales:

- Number of times a month you "used racial or sexist put-downs."
- Frequency of "accepting people who differ from you in their religion, race, sex, or life style."
- Frequency of "making an effort to include strangers or persons who differ from you in what you or your group are doing."

The optimal score of the three items was 15.

The EVQ's social distance scale asked each student to rate on a similar five-point scale, "How comfortable would you be with persons who are handicapped or differ in race, life style, or sex preference when . . .

A. in class together

B. studying or working with each other

C. hanging out together in a group

D. going to a movie together

E. becoming close friends with

The total score for complete comfort or total emotional acceptance for the five degrees of increased intimacy was 25.

Though the tolerance and acceptance indices differ in form, their scores predict each other at very high levels of certainty for both public and NAIS middle and high school students. So I combined the two to give an overall Multicultural Acceptance Index. Students who fully accepted others received a score of 40.

What Does the Multicultural Index Predict?

Bloomfield Hills' eighth graders who emotionally accept others have reliably higher morale and abstain from alcohol and drugs. Reagan's ninth to twelfth multiculturally accepting students also have reliably higher morale, drink alcohol and take drugs less frequently, devote more hours to their homework, and participate more frequently in extracurricular activities. But what I want to illustrate is how the survey materials may be used to go more deeply into the personalities of tolerant and intolerant persons defined by the combined Multicultural Acceptance Index.

Gender Differences in Acceptance of Multi-Cultural Diversity

Table 14-3 reviews the tolerance and acceptance scores, and their combined Multicultural Index, of boys and girls of different ages from different types of schools.

Table 14-3   Tolerance and Acceptance of Diversity in Public, Independent (NAIS) and an American International School's 9-12 Students

	Public 9-12 Boys Girls	NAIS 7-8 Boys Girls	NAIS 9-12 Boys Girls	International Boys Girls
Tolerance	10.9 12.8	12.6 13.2	12.7 13.2	12.7 13.1
Acceptance-Comfort	17.5 20.5	20.0 21.9	20.0 21.6	20.0 21.8
Multicultural Index	28.4 33.3	32.6 35.1	32.7 34.8	32.7 34.9

How trustworthy are the differences in tolerance and acceptance of others? Given the large number of students in each group, except the International school, even small differences are likely to be true differences though they may not be of practical significance. As an interpretive guide for your own judgment, the small number of International boys and girls do not differ reliably. The several thousand public and NAIS boys and girls do. The odds are less than one in 10,000 that their difference is not a true one. Reagan's boys' and girls' mean acceptance scores were similar to the public school norms. And as is true for the public school students generally, Reagan's girls reliably differed from its boys in being noticeably more acceptant of others.

What intriguing ideas, if any, do you find in Table 14-3? The ones I found are:

1. Girls accept people who differ from them more readily than boys do.

2. The roots of prejudice go deep into middle school. Efforts to increase students' acceptance of others must begin by seventh grade at least.

3. Students, both boys and girls, in independent schools tolerate and accept others who differ from them more than students in public schools do.

4. Both boys and girls with extensive experience in international schools with many diverse types of students are neither more nor less multiculturally acceptant than NAIS boys and girls.

Sources of Multicultural Intolerance

The multicultural acceptance of eighth graders.

I turn now to the Bloomfield Hills' eighth graders and Reagan's high school boys and girls for insights about the personalities of students intolerant of and rejecting of those who differ from them.[13] Remember that the students anonymously completed stapled packets of all the surveys so that their EVQ's could be associated with the WCL target they completed.

I relied on the Multicultural Index to select the most and least tolerant and acceptant students. I selected enough to be able to compare reliably for the eighth graders their views of their peers and schools and for the high school students their views of themselves. Immediately I encountered a methodologically troubling but revealing finding. About three times more boys than girls were multiculturally intolerant and about three times more girls than boys were tolerant. These ratios were not peculiar to the Bloomfield Hills' middle and Reagan's high school boys and girls. The ratios hold for other schools also.

Table 14-4, which describes the largest differences in the extreme eighth graders' views of their peers, convincingly shows that tolerant and intolerant students' interpersonal worlds are quite different.

Table 14-4 Comparison of Tolerant and Intolerant Eighth Graders' Largest Differences in Their Views of their Peers

More Tolerant than Intolerant%		More Intolerant than Tolerant%	
Considerate	49	Doesn't care	56
Giving	43	Put-downs	38
Competitive	38	Verbal	38
Friendly	37	Strong convictions	34
Adventurous	35	Emotionally cold	28
Can say no	35	Irresponsible	27
Feels for others	32	Show-off	27
Artistic	32	Stubborn	27

Differences in Their Views of Their Schools

Anticipates consequences	31	Dull	32
Can say no	28	Moody	28
Fair	28	Lacks energy	26
Happy	28	Sarcastic	20
Enthusiastic	27		
Ambitious	26		

Since tolerance co-varies with morale, Table 14-4's pattern of tolerant and intolerant students' views is similar to that of high and low morale students. Both psychic dropouts and prejudiced students are estranged from their peers and schools. What idea comes to mind about why so many more intolerant than tolerant students believe that their peers don't care, put each other down, and are emotionally cold? Or why so many more multiculturally tolerant students believe that their peers are considerate, giving, and empathic? Might these views be projections of the students' own personalities? Could it be that if others believe we don't care, put others down, and are emotionally cold people that they will react similarly to us? Cold people create cold environments. If we accept and empathize with others will they tend to accept and feel for us?

If the idea has merit, how might prejudiced people react to educational programs that seek to directly counter their prejudice by reasoned argument? With stubbornness and dramatic, over-exaggerated, and heated defense of their views? Or to programs that alter students' relationships with them to reduce their interpersonal alienation? Sometimes the long way around is the shortest route. Do the wishes of intolerant students for their peers open answer's door? Many more of them than tolerant students wish that their peers were more accepting, honest, joyful, and possibly fair and empathic. Research on integration in the armed services favors this answer. Working cooperatively with another to complete a mutually beneficial project will more likely reduce prejudice than will direct confrontation.

Believing that school is dull, sarcastic, and lacks energy is scarcely a recipe for increasing an intolerant student's educability. Intolerant eighth graders are still potentially educable. While very frustrated by school they have not yet given up on it. Large percentages of them wish that their schools were more adventurous, accepting, and fun. They also wish that their schools were more intellectual, trusting, cheerful, and joyful. The tolerant students have few wishes for their schools which they already feel compatible with.

The table tells us that intolerant pubertal youth are not very happy or, possibly, healthy. Just as the predisposition to be a high school psychic drop-out may take root in the pubertal and perhaps earlier years, so may personality continuity rule for intolerant eighth grade students. If so, then I predict they will have self-rejecting and interpersonally immature self-concepts throughout high school.

The self-concepts of intolerant high school students.

Comparing Reagan's multiculturally accepting and rejecting students confirmed my prediction. The pattern of the differences is so consistent I cite only a few of the largest differences. At least 20% and more intolerant than tolerant boys and girls think of themselves as defensively masculine, aggressively rebellious, sarcastic, and as impatient. The tolerant boys and girls disagree with the intolerant ones on so many positive but similar traits that I can summarize the differences in two sentences. Multiculturally acceptant students believe they have many stereotypic feminine interpersonal strengths. A third and more of them than their intolerant peers believe they are understanding, sympathetic, loving, considerate, and

empathic boys and girls; they create warm and accepting relationships with others.

Who may be the principal contributors to these interpersonal
differences? No question: the girls. The many more intolerant and
rejecting high school boys made it possible to compare them more
fairly with tolerant and accepting boys. Again the evidence is overwhelmingly clear. Many more multiculturally tolerant boys than intolerant ones describe themselves favorably. Forty-four percent more
believe that they are flexible and self-educating; 41% more that they
are good-natured, excellent; and more than a third that they are warm,
accepting, open, and cheerfully giving boys. Confirming the earlier
results, noticeably more intolerant than tolerant boys think of themselves as rebellious, impatient, athletic, and masculine.

The pattern of traits of the intolerant boy suggests that he has low
self-esteem and is interpersonally immature. His pervasive low self-
esteem suggests he is predisposed to becoming emotionally unhealthy.
Extreme prejudice can be a sickness when it is a projection of one's
own inner divided and rejected self.

Parents such as Edina's look to their schools to educate their youth
morally. America's democratic and increasingly multicultural society
needs citizens who accept, respect, and value others who differ from
them. It looks to its schools to educate its citizens to be so. Is their
hope justified? The next chapter illustrates how we can now begin to
evaluate that hope's promise.

Chapter 15

IDENTIFYING A SCHOOL'S MORAL CLIMATE, STUDENTS' EDUCABILITY FOR MORAL EDUCATION, AND PEER CULTURE'S EFFECTS

Anecdotal and some research evidence identify schools as potential contributors to students' character—their interpersonal and ethical behavior. Some claim that England won its wars on Eton's cricket and soccer fields where so many of its leaders had played. Adults frequently identify teachers as having significantly influenced them when younger. They typically cite their characters' attributes more than their minds' qualities to have been their schools' principal contribution.[1]

A half century of research has demonstrated that colleges can alter students' character as well as minds.[2] But not all colleges affect students' character. Of the hundreds studied, only a few have been found to produce distinctive, enduring effects on their students' relationships and values. Researchers remain undecided about the attributes of schools that contribute most to character maturation. One reason is that measures have not existed to assess schools' potentially more formative attributes. Studies of how middle and high school students mature are rare. Studies of their school's contributing attributes and enduring effects on their alumni are so scarce as not even to be visible—at least to me.[3]

For years I intensively studied how students became liberally educated or mature in one college—Haverford—which earlier researchers had identified as affecting its students' values.[4] Systemic institutional attributes rather than specific curricular and teaching practices contributed most to the maturation of students' character. Freshmen, seniors, and alumni agreed. The most formative influences were the college's values consistently implemented in the students' academic and social honor codes. An a-religious alumnus English teacher said of the college's effects, "Quaker ideals came through more strongly than I realized. Just their lingering impact. It is with me all of the time. I don't think the [intellectual] content stayed with me. That's mostly gone. But the values have remained."[5]

The principal institutional contributors to the college's effects were its

1. small size that encouraged ownership of and identification with its communal purposes,

2. intellectual and religious tradition and faculty expectations that were congruent with its students' values,

3. quality of relationships required by the students' formulated and enforced social and academic honor codes, and more generally,

4. coherence between its purposes and means to achieve them.[6]

While specific faculty, courses, and practices, such as religious services, affected some students, their effects on students' character were magnified and stabilized by the college's moral climate.

Our survey methods now make it possible to examine schools' systemic attributes to identify their contribution to their students' character. The chapter compares public and private schools' *moral* climates, and their teachers' and students' emotional commitment to and so educability for moral education. It concludes by examining how supportive of ethical growth is the students' peer learning environment .

Distinctive Moral Climate

Chapter 13 identified public and independent schools' differences as their teachers and students judged them. A quick review of that chapter would be helpful. It provides the context within which to interpret this chapter's findings focussed on the *moral* attributes of schools.

Every school's and college's mission statement that I have analyzed professes to educate for character. Even Tech included one character attribute—honesty—in its catalogue. But do schools have a climate of consensual values necessary to affect their students' character? Table 15-1 summarizes the judgments of faculty and students

about their schools' moral climates. It orders them by NAIS' and
public school teachers' averaged ratings for the WCL's ethical words.

**Table 15-1   Faculty and Student Judgments about the Moral
Climate of Independent (NAIS), Public and
Reagan High Schools**

Ethical Values	% NAIS Fac	% NAIS Stu	% Public Fac	% Public Stu	% Reagan Fac	% Reagan Stu	% Average NAIS+Public Fac	% Average NAIS+Public Stu
Dedicated	73	60	64	45	68	58	68.5	52.5
Caring	73	54	64	34	54	45	68.5	44.0
Responsible	55	47	42	32	33	38	48.5	39.5
Fair	53	38	40	32	26	37	46.5	35.0
Honest	50	50	36	30	19	29	43.0	40.0
Integrity	40	25	30	16	24	24	35.0	20.5
Deep moral sense	35	29	22	17	15	22	28.5	23.0
Courage	20	20	14	20	7	19	17.0	20.0
Average Value	49.9	40.4	39.0	28.3	30.8	34.0	44.4	34.3

Some teachers are skeptical that their students know what values
such as integrity, even deep moral sense, mean. But then what does
such ignorance say about the moral character of their schools and
faculty? Others argue that courage is a school's least appropriate or
relevant ethical value. But is it, in fact? Some NAIS schools fear that
to take a strong stand, even to a parent demanding that the head change
a child's grade, may alienate some of their paying clients. Some public schools fear, even if only a few parents demand that *Huckleberry
Finn* be removed from the English curriculum, their communities'
retaliatory anger at the polls. However, even if we eliminate courage
from the list, only 54% of NAIS and 42.6% of public school teachers
describe their schools as moral institutions.

More distressing, an average 40% of NAIS and 28% of public
school students at most believe that their schools witness model values. How can a school affect the character of its students if they believe, in spite of their school's rhetoric, that it is not fair or honest, or
that it doesn't stand up for moral values when attacked? How effective can specific curricular or other programs targeted to teach ethical values then be?

Table 15-1 leaves little doubt. Only a minority of both faculty and students judge their schools to have a noticeable moral climate. Neither the typical independent nor suburban public school has succeeded well in creating the climate most likely to contribute to character maturation. Schools like Adelphi and Reagan which have severely competitive academic cultures may actually squelch healthy character growth. If their academic values are not integrated with expectations for character excellence, they risk socially isolating their students and predisposing them to cheat and indulge in other forms of unethical behavior.

Of course there are schools whose moral climate is palpable, more often than not because of their religious traditions. ASH: 46 provides a diagnostic exercise to decide if St. Andrew's, a small NAIS boarding school, is a school of hope. A remarkable 70% of its students identified the school as having a moral climate's values. And both its boys and girls reported acting more ethically than the average NAIS boy and girl on every moral value. St. Andrew's avoided the risks that committed religious schools face: suppressing healthy growth during the critical period of value re-formation.

Schools concerned about educating for virtue risk becoming imprisoned by their own ideological rhetoric. One well-known fundamentalist college required its faculty and students to sign pledges of commitment to its faith. Its faculty and board were shocked to discover that only 15% of its students believed that their peers were ethical and had any integrity. Holding one's institution objectively accountable can be an act of courage and a prod to new growth—or at least to judiciously reflect upon its culture as the college then did.

As you might expect by now, the gender differences in reported ethical behavior parallel similar differences in perception of schools' moral climate. Predictably, public-Reagan schools' girls view their schools to be more moral than their boys do. NAIS boys and girls do not notably differ in their views of their schools' moral character. Paralleling the trend in Table 15-1, more NAIS than public schools' girls and boys view their schools to have stronger moral climates.

A school's perceived moral climate is the result of several attributes: its tradition, especially that part which is still alive and strengthened by its rituals, its head's modeling of and depth of commitment to ethical values, and its faculty's character and associated emotional commitment. I have no evidence about the first two but do about how students view their teachers' character.

Teachers' Perceived Moral Character

Chapter 13 discovered that the largest difference between NAIS and public schools was between their students' views of their teachers. Students perceive the same differences about their teachers' moral character. An average of 54% of NAIS but only about a third of public and Reagan students attribute ethical traits to their faculties. [ASH 23: Students' Beliefs about Their Teachers' Moral Character]. Some public school students' disenchantment with their faculty's moral character was deep. Ethical values grow out of our relationships. Twenty-four percent more NAIS than public school students believe that their teachers are empathic, 22% more accepting, and 21% more trusting. But 21% more public school students believe that their teachers are defensive—not a trait that opens students to moral persuasion.

By averaging NAIS and public-Reagan students' views of their teachers' specific moral attributes, it is possible to determine which attributes are more and less visible to their students generally. A bare majority of students believe that their teachers are dedicated and honest. Slightly less than a majority believe that they are fair and responsible. Teachers' least visible ethical traits are the depth of their moral concern, integrity, and courage. Ethical values are "caught from" more than "taught by" those who model such behavior and whom we respect. So we have another clue to understand why more NAIS than public school students report acting more ethically.

Table 14-1 showed that Reagan's faculty did not agree about its school's moral climate. The majority of its students did not view their teachers to be models of virtue. Does this not provoke a question about how its academic single-mindedness may affect its students' healthy growth and future success? What happens to students who secure mind's great powers but are not challenged to consider for what purposes they should be used?

Gender Differences in Judged Teacher Moral Character

Let us now press our understanding further about how teachers' modeling of virtue is related to students' behavior. Adult models of virtue may inspire and support acting ethically but may do so differently for females than males.

Given the persistent gender differences in ethical behavior, I had expected that boys and girls would view their teachers quite differently. But such was not the case, when I used a 10% difference in boys' and girls' perceptions of their teachers to index a meaningful difference. Public school boys and girls agreed on 98% of the WCL's 150 traits about their teachers; NAIS and Reagan boys and girls agreed on 88% and 90% respectively.

Boys were more critical and girls more favorable about their teachers. Both public and independent school boys agreed that their teachers were more fractious: argumentative, not easily impressed, and put them down. Public school girls believed their teachers were competent academicians: planned ahead, completed their plans, and were helpful, demanding, verbal, and well-informed. On the other hand, NAIS girls viewed their teachers as models of virtue: empathic, respectful, giving, caring, listening, and understanding.

Not surprisingly, more girls than boys consistently viewed their teachers as acting ethically, perhaps because their more developed empathic interpersonal skills made them more sensitive to others' personalities and expectations. Being raised to please others and accommodate to their expectations may contribute to girls' teachers' greater influence on them than on less sensitive and more critical boys. [ASH 24: Boys' and Girls' Differences in Perception of Teachers' Moral Character]. What was unexpected, however, is that boys and girls did not differ more markedly in their overall views of their faculty's ethical behavior, i.e., 3.5% difference for NAIS and public school boys and girls and 2.5% for Reagan's. Faculty modeling of virtue may contribute to students' ethical behavior; it just doesn't contribute more than a modest amount, if that much, to the ethical behavior of one sex more than to the other's. So we must search for other faculty attributes that may contribute more to girls' than to boy's ethical behavior.

Faculty Emotional Commitment to Ethical Values

Experienced teachers have endured a succession of new heads, each of whom has engaged them in another year-long debate about their school's mission. They also have participated in interminable school improvement committee meetings. Many are cynical about the results of one more debate or committee. "Nothing will change in the long-run," they tell me. Why? Because too often the faculty does not emotionally own or is not emotionally committed to the revised goals. Teachers play their principals' or legislators' games but continue to do their job as they have always done it. Implementation of a school-wide goal or new plan should begin with the goal or plan to which the largest numbers of teachers are *emotionally committed.*

Table 15-2 maps the relative commitment of the different faculties to ethical values as goals for their students. Recall how I measured emotional commitment. The WCL assumes that decisions made under the pressure of time are likely to be more emotionally than thoughtfully and rationally based. Adding the table's percentage of NAIS teachers who believe that their students are honest, 53%, to the percentage of those who wish they were, 21%, indexes the importance or "aliveness," one might say, of honesty to 74% of teachers.

Table 15-2   Independent (NAIS), Public, and Reagan Teachers' Emotional Commitment to Ethical Values as Goals for Students

Ethical Values	% NAIS			% Public			% Reagan			% Average NAIS+ Public
	Actual	Wish	Total	Actual	Wish	Total	Actual	Wish	Total	
Caring	50	26	76	42	32	74	35	41	76	75.0
Honesty	53	21	74	26	34	60	22	42	64	67.0
Responsibility	41	28	69	28	37	65	17	42	59	67.0
Deep moral sense	12	44	56	5	49	54	2	53	55	55.0
Dedicated	26	28	54	15	41	56	9	44	53	55.0
Integrity	29	21	50	15	30	45	13	33	46	47.5
Fair	34	16	50	28	17	45	15	13	28	47.5
Courage	17	25	42	8	22	30	6	19	25	34.0
Average Value	32.8	26.1	58.9	20.9	32.8	53.7	14.9	35.9	50.8	56.0

You may be surprised by what Table 15-2 tells us. The majority of several thousand teachers, regardless of their type of school, does not describe typical students to be noticeably ethical. The only exceptions are the 50 and 53% of NAIS teachers who believe that their typical student is caring and honest respectively. Public school teachers, and certainly Reagan's, are even more disenchanted with how ethical their typical student is.

Since our beliefs predispose us to act as if they are true—for they define what reality is for us—they can become self-fulfilling prophecies. Students who want to please and fulfill a respected adult's hopes and expectations may be spurred to act ethically. Today's perceptive students sense very quickly if they are not trusted to be honest, caring, or responsible. So some cheat, act cruelly and irresponsibly, thus confirming our beliefs about the stereotypic student.

Whereas NAIS, public, and Reagan faculties do not differ dramatically in their total emotional commitment, i.e., differing by only eight percentage points, you may also be surprised that only 56.3% (average of NAIS 58.9% and Public 53.7%) of teachers believe their students act ethically *and* wish that they would. Some find such results to be unbelievable and so fault the method. If asked directly, of course all of us want young people to be caring, honest, responsible, and decent human beings, perhaps even more so than to be outstanding scholars. But then why so much resistance by faculties to assuming sustained responsibility for moral education? Because, as Table 15-2 suggests, educating for virtue marshals only a bare majority of faculty's emotional commitment.

Table 15-2's differences between NAIS, public, and Reagan's teachers' emotional commitment to ethical goals parallel their students' perceptions of their teachers' character. Recall that only a modest majority of NAIS students, though about 15% more than public school students, attributed ethical traits to their teachers. And now Table 15-2 also confirms that only 59% of NAIS teachers are themselves emotionally committed to educating their students to be more ethical.

Does such commitment affect students' ethical behavior? We know that parents' commitment does. Children who believe that their parents expect them to act ethically and support them in doing so do in fact act more ethically. NAIS students (no information is available for public school students) who believe that their teachers expect and support ethical behavior in fact reliably act more ethically. However, parental expectations of and support for their children's ethical behavior contribute reliably more than teachers' to their students' ethical behavior. The conclusion that I draw is that teachers who model ethical values to which they are emotionally committed as goals for their students can modestly affect their students' ethical behavior. Parental influence is, however, a far more important contributor to their children's ethical behavior.

Moral education may achieve some modest success if it is initiated appropriately and implemented following the research-based educational principles described in *Schools of Hope*. But to succeed requires a faculty's emotional commitment to its goals. Does not Table 15-2 tell us, however, that moral education is only a palliative public relations slogan in the typical school's mission statement? How could moral education be made more than a sop to parents? By more consciously educating for those values to which the most faculty are emotionally committed. Regardless of the type of school, caring, honesty, and responsibility consistently capture the largest number of faculty commitments. The NAIS and public school faculties in my sample tell us that they are the values moral education should begin with.

But not for Reagan's academically focussed but more disillusioned and resistant faculty. While it also wants its students to become more ethical, it is less willing than other faculties to assume responsibility for educating them in ways to become so. Why? For contented faculties like Reagan's their views of and hopes for their schools (in contrast to their hopes for their students) are more likely than not to be projections of their views and hopes for *themselves*. The school is the faculty. Of all of the faculties I have studied, Reagan's is the least committed to ethical values as goals for its school—and for themselves? Compared to 62% for independent and 54% for other public school faculties, only 39% of Reagan's teachers are emotionally committed to its school developing a moral climate. Realistically, 39% is too small a core group of faculty to have a noticeable effect on the school's culture. It would not be too small a group if it contained all of the teachers' most respected and charismatic leaders. After all, Jesus's few disciples changed the western world.

Most new parents believe that they can make their children into what they wish. They soon discover that even their infants can be stubbornly willful. Later they find that their middle schoolers are frustratingly intractable. They are resigned to their adolescents being rebellious and negativistic to their parents' ethical expectations. Teachers also know well how students can frustrate their best intentions and expectations. How educable are high school boys and girls for moral education? Do they differ in their ethical self-concepts and emotional commitment to ethical values?

Students' Educability for Moral Education

Students' educability for a school's goals contribute to how well it realizes its hopes. Admission officers have honed their procedures to predict quite well how educable their applicants are for their schools' academic expectations. Would any argue that they can predict as well a student's educability for their schools' character goals?

What are the types and attributes of students most likely to be educable for moral education? To date we have discovered some clues. First, girls more than boys. Second, androgynous boys. Third, multicultural tolerance and psychological maturity. Fourth, good school citizenship behavior including community service activities. Fifth, those with ethically concerned and supportive parents.

What can the WCL tell educators about those attributes that *they* can affect: students' concept of themselves as ethical persons and their emotional commitment to acting ethically. Adolescence is a transitional period; it is a time of heightened vulnerability and so high potential for growth; it is the critical period for the re-formation of one's self-concept and values. Bloomfield Hills' Model High School showed us its students began to think of themselves as autonomous learners. Haverford College influenced its students to think of themselves as ethical persons of integrity. Schools of hope can transform that potential into actuality.

Gender Differences in Ethical Self-Concepts

Chapter 13 reported that independent and public high school students did not differ in most of their beliefs about themselves. The only exceptions were that more independent school students viewed themselves to be academic, intellectual, sophisticated, genuine, and more relevantly, had integrity and a deeper ethical sense. Table 15-3 examines in more detail the gender differences in students' ethical self-concepts for both types of schools. It orders them by boys' *averaged* declining percentages.

**Table 15-3   Independent (NAIS), Public, and Reagan
Boys' and Girls' Ethical Self-Concepts**

Ethical Trait	% NAIS Boys	Girls	% Public Boys	Girls	% Reagan Boys	Girls	% Average NAIS+Public Boys	Girls
Caring	76	85	72	93	71	96	74.0	89.0
Honest	72	75	63	79	56	72	67.5	77.0
Fair	62	57	47	54	58	60	54.5	55.5
Courageous	51	47	57	44	51	50	54.0	45.5
Dedicated	55	59	52	55	43	55	53.5	57.0
Responsible	54	63	50	68	42	60	52.0	65.5
Deep moral sense	44	51	25	44	29	50	34.5	47.5
Integrity	<u>46</u>	<u>38</u>	<u>20</u>	<u>22</u>	<u>26</u>	<u>32</u>	<u>33.0</u>	<u>30.0</u>
Average Value	57.5	59.4	48.3	57.4	47.0	59.4	52.9	58.4

The table's results about the students' *self-concepts* conform quite well with the patterns of specific ethical *behaviors* found with the Ethical Value Questionnaire—a very different type of measure. Both reciprocally confirm the validity of the other. Recall that NAIS and public-Reagan girls *act* more ethically than boys. They do not consistently differ among themselves in all of the ethical values. NAIS boys do consistently *act* more ethically than public-Reagan boys in every ethical area.

Table 15-3 also revealingly confirms the same patterns for the *self-concepts* of girls and boys. Girls have more ethical self-concepts than boys. Whereas independent and public school girls do not differ in their ethical self-concepts, boys do differ—even strikingly so. Only a minority of public and Reagan high school boys describe themselves to be ethical persons, due almost exclusively to not believing that they do have integrity and a deep ethical or moral sense.

What these ethical terms mean to adolescents is problematic. Public and Reagan girls and boys do not differ in their beliefs about their integrity—the only ethical attribute NAIS and public school girls differ noticeably in. Why? Might it be that integrity is not part of the lexicon of the public schools? Or of their parents? I don't know.[8]

Table 15-3 also tells us that NAIS and public school girls do not differ noticeably in the strength of their moral sense. Boys do. Seventy percent of public school boys do not believe that they have a strong moral sense; 56% of NAIS boys agree. Why such a discrepancy? Probably for several reasons. One may be that NAIS boys accept their feminine interpersonal strengths more than public high school boys do. Let's search further for other reasons.

To evaluate the relative effect of students' character and type of school upon their ethical behavior, we now need two other pieces of information: 1) boys' and girls' emotional commitment to ethical goals for themselves and 2) the nature of their peer learning environment.

Students' Emotional Commitment to Ethical Goals for Themselves

Unless people are emotionally (not just rationally) committed to a goal, little self-generated and sustained effort to achieve it will result. I measured the boys' and girls' emotional commitment to ethical values for the different schools. [ASH 25: Boys' and Girls' Emotional Commitment to Ethical Goals for Themselves]. Not surprisingly by now, girls are more emotionally committed to being ethical than boys are. Their emotional commitment is more similar than boys' is for NAIS and public-Reagan schools. NAIS, public, and then Reagan boys in that order are increasingly less committed to ethical values.

So how educable are students for moral education? Reassuringly, schools could count on about 2/3 of their students to be receptive to and supportive of a moral education. If the schools' climates valued and respected girls' equality, their voices could provide persuasive support for educating for caring, honesty, and responsibility. Strengths more than weaknesses provide the most favored paths to change and growth. More than 3/4 of both boys and girls believe they are caring persons. Curricular and teaching strategies that appeal to, rely upon, and use caring attitudes and skills could be the most efficacious lever for encouraging the development of other values, e.g., "Because we are caring persons, we accept and value others who differ from us and don't act in ways, like cheating, that hurt others."

The remarkable similarity of NAIS and public-Reagan's girls' emotional commitment to ethical values again highlights the importance of gender's contribution to ethical development. But again, we are faced with the issue of why independent and public school boys' ethical commitment so consistently lags behind girls'.

Though individual students may believe that they are caring, honest, and responsible, if they believe that other students are not, then their peer learning environment can erode their moral sense and especially their integrity. The less mature students may act in ways that contradict their ethical self-concepts.

Coherence between one's self-concept and one's peers' values could decisively either contribute to or hinder character maturation. That NAIS more than public and more than Reagan boys describe themselves as ethical suggests that their peer learning environment becomes increasingly inimical for public and especially for Reagan's boys' ethical maturation.

Peer Learning Environment's Contribution to Ethical Behavior

Our understanding of girls' and boys' ethical development remains incomplete. We must understand their views of their peers' and then of their peers' ethical values.

Students' peer culture may have several effects faculties may not be aware of. It can affect motivation. For example, 15 to 40% more NAIS than public-Reagan girls and boys believe their peers are academically capable. A matriculating capable and competitive NAIS student instantly learns that striving to live up to academic expectations is his peer group's norm. More NAIS students describe themselves as ambitious than their public school counterparts do. Their peer culture encourages them to devote more time to homework, which they in fact reliably do. Is a similar peer dynamic present that contributes to gender and school differences in ethical behavior?

Table 15-4 orders independent and public school boys' and girls' views of their peers' moral character by the averaged boys' beliefs.

Table 15-4   Independent (NAIS), Public-Reagan Boys' and Girls' Views of Peers' Ethical Behavior

Ethical Trait	% NAIS Boys	% NAIS Girls	% Public Boys	% Public Girls	% Reagan Boys	% Reagan Girls	% Average NAIS+Public Boys	% Average NAIS+Public Girls
Caring	36	43	27	41	33	35	31.5	42.0
Dedicated	42	59	20	33	28	41	31.0	46.0
Responsible	40	48	20	27	19	38	30.0	37.5
Honest	33	42	20	20	22	23	26.5	31.0
Fair	24	30	24	26	20	27	24.0	28.0
Courageous	19	26	28	33	31	35	23.5	29.5
Integrity	28	28	13	13	13	12	20.5	20.5
Deep moral sense	23	21	11	13	7	16	17.0	17.0
Average Value	30.6	37.1	20.4	25.8	21.6	28.4	25.5	31.4

The table confirms several themes. First, only an average of 25 to 31% of boys and girls view their peers as ethical. For boys, slightly less than a third view their peers to be caring and dedicated; for girls, more view their peers as dedicated and caring but also responsible. Table 15-3 showed us that a majority of both boys and girls view themselves as ethical in most value areas. Clearly then they must look to themselves rather than to their peers for ethical support. Unless their peer culture is modified, it may negatively affect many students' ethical maturation. Most students might welcome stronger adult expectations for and support of their ethical behavior. Such expectations would be congruent with their educability, and they could encourage students to develop the autonomy and its derivative value of courage to resist their peer culture's values.

Second, the results again flesh out the ethical differences between the genders and types of schools. More girls than boys view their peers as acting ethically. More NAIS students' believe that their peers support their ethical behavior than public school students do. This is the case, even though only about a third of NAIS students believe that their peers act ethically. The results confirm my hypothesis that NAIS students are more academic. More than public-Reagan students, they believe their peers are dedicated, responsible, and honest—values closely associated with academic life. More NAIS than public school girls also believe their peers have these academic-type strengths. This pattern fits the findings that NAIS girls reliably *act* more honestly and responsibly, and are more committed when compared to Reagan's girls.

As I have noted, ethical values, which concern how we should get along with others, evolve out of the ways we learn to relate to others. Schools' principal lever for furthering the ethical growth of students is to alter the quality of their relationships with each other and the schools' adults.

Why is there such a large gulf between the majority of students who believe that they themselves are ethical and the small number who believe their peers are ethical? Table 15-5 examines their peers' traits that may erode students' ethical behavior and limit schools' power to further students' ethical maturation. The table includes every trait that the majority of at least one of the three types of students believed its peers demonstrated. It lists in declining order the averaged percentages of boys who believe that their peers demonstrate disruptive and hurtful behavior. I include the students' own self-ratings for such traits.

Table 15-5   Students' Views of Their Peer's Most Troubling Traits

| | View of Their Peers | | | | | | | | View of Self | |
| | *% NAIS* | | *% Public* | | *% Reagan* | | *% Average NAIS-Public* | | *% Average* | |
Trait	*Boys*	*Girls*	*Boys*	*Girls*	*Boys*	*Girls*	*Boys*	*Girls*	*Boys*	*Girls*
Critical of each other	52	65	51	59	53	66	51.5	62.0	34.3	38.7
Sarcastic	52	47	54	62	47	60	53.0	54.5	53.0	31.4
Defensive	43	40	57	61	47	54	50.0	50.5	48.3	49.0
Put each other down	36	32	52	54	51	57	44.0	43.0	14.3	9.0
Doesn't care	25	22	51	47	45	41	38.0	34.5	21.0	13.3
Rebellious	27	28	49	51	44	48	38.0	39.5	32.7	28.7
Average	39.2	39.0	52.3	55.7	47.8	54.3	45.8	47.3	33.9	28.4

I was not surprised by the large number of students who report that their relationships are hurtful and produce defensiveness. After all, they are growing up in a sit-com, put-down, sarcastic, and violent society. No wonder so few students describe themselves or others as genuine. Not feeling accepted by or trusting others, they know that they and others must play defensive roles, such as being cool.[9] Nor was I surprised that students' ethical behavior, self-concepts, and peer environment parallel their beliefs about how troubled their peers' relationships are in NAIS, Reagan, and public schools in that order.

What perplexed me, however, were the differences in boys' and girls' beliefs about their peers that did *not* parallel their ethical behavior. Perhaps because of girls' greater interpersonal sensitivity and expressiveness, they may be more vulnerable to others' critical and sarcastic comments than boys may be? Boys can more easily shrug off nasty put-downs than girls can. Put-downs are more typically, though not always, males' currency for expressing affection. A hit on the arm, poke in the chest, and demeaning verbal repartees may really communicate affection. American society does forbid a boy to tell or demonstratively show another that he likes him, except perhaps on the athletic field.[10] But gossiping, cattiness, and exclusionary acts by girls are personalized, even interpretively exaggerated, as hostility and rejection.

Larger percentages of public-Reagan than NAIS boys and girls believe that their peers don't care or are rebellious. Such beliefs may reduce their morale and satisfaction with their schools and roles as students. Feeling good about one's self, peers, and school contributes to being more educable not only for a school's academic but also its ethical expectations.

What kind of peer learning environment do students want that might narrow or bridge the gulf between their ethical selves and a nonsupportive peer moral culture? Identifying every WCL word that at least a third of either sex wished for their peers resulted in a most eloquent message in its clarity. [ASH 26: Boys' and Girls' Wishes for Their Peer Relationships]. They want a more humane peer environment. They want peers who are honest, accepting, considerate, caring, empathetic, trusting, have a deep moral sense, and can say no. Aren't students saying, "Don't ignore character?" Their wishes provide a specific agenda for schools committed to providing an environment that supports healthy growth. It may also identify the type of personal relationships that must be present if specific moral education programs are to "take."

I write "may also identify" because the students' wishes seemingly contradict the hypothesis that altering students' peer learning environment could be a powerful strategy for creating a school's moral climate. The students' wishes do not parallel the ethical patterns we have so consistently discovered. An average of 7% more girls than boys want more humane and especially accepting peers. Yet girls are more ethical by far than boys. Six percent more public than NAIS girls want more ethical peers. Yet public-Reagan girls generally score higher on the Ethical Value Questionnaire than NAIS girls. NAIS boys do not differ essentially from public-Reagan boys in wishing that their peers were more ethical. Yet, NAIS boys consistently act more ethically than public school boys.

Might the pattern of results reflect more gender-related issues? Girls are more concerned about their peers' acceptance. Their identities are shaped more by their role relationships.[11] NAIS girls believe that their peers are more ethical and less fractious than the public-Reagan girls. They don't feel their peers' lack of acceptance as acutely. And regardless of the type of school, boys do not value the interpersonal traits as importantly.

To explore the relation of ethical behavior to the students' peer culture, I identified the NAIS school whose students behaved most ethically as the EVQ measured it. More than twice as many students viewed their peers to be ethical than Table 15-4 reported. Only an average of 7%, compared to an average of 33% for NAIS-public school students, wished that their peers differed on the traits I just mentioned. This link between ethical maturation and a humane peer culture supports my hypothesis, but the link needs to be studied more rigorously.

The next chapter seeks a broader perspective about moral development, its more influential determinants, and their implications for moral education.

Chapter 16

———●•●———

REFLECTING ABOUT MORAL EDUCATION'S CHALLENGES

The historic goal of liberal educators has always been and should be maturity or human excellence. Maturing or healthy growth includes the development of mind, character, and self. Maturing results in the development of the core virtues such as honesty, compassion or caring, tolerance, integrity, commitment, responsibility, and courage.[1] To focus exclusively on the development of mind, as the Reagan faculty did, risks distorting students' healthy growth. Mind without virtue can produce psychopathy. Virtue without mind can result in powerlessness.

Virtue as "moral excellence" or "moral sense" is not identical with specific ethical behaviors. A youth for whom virtue is the core of his or her identity will not answer when asked "Who are you?" by replying, "I am a male or female, middle or lower class, white or black." Instead, the youth will assert, "I am a moral person seeking to act with integrity."

Analysis of the Ethical Value Questionnaire shows that a more pervasive general attitude undergirds students' ratings about specific ethical behaviors. I labeled it "deep moral sense" in the WCL. Students with such a moral sense score high on all the specific ethical values such as caring, honesty, and responsibility. Students with a less developed moral sense may score high on responsibility and courage, moderately on caring, and low on commitment.

Our contemporary ethical crisis results from replacing an integrative and governing moral identity with more pragmatic values adjusted for immediate situational demands. Psychologists faultily justify this replacement by citing studies of children, not studies of mature persons. Less mature persons don't act honestly in varied situations.[2] More mature persons can and do.

Moral educators' primary goal should be the development of a deep moral sense or identity as a virtuous person. It should not be just academic honesty or even caring, as some feminists insist.[3] Teaching a youth the empathy necessary to care for others may be, however, the best opening to develop a moral sense.

Is moral education, when defined by specific programmatic goals to increase, for example, responsibility, *the* answer to our societal crises of dishonesty, drug use, teenage pregnancy, suicide, and violence? No. Specific programs depend upon their schools' supportive, systemic moral character for their effectiveness. Instituting an academic honor system in schools without a visible moral climate is not likely to succeed. Even for the most favored schools surveyed, like Reagan, the majority of their students did not believe their schools were moral institutions. Nor did they believe their teachers were highly moral persons. Nor did they (and the majority of their teachers as well) believe their typical peer was a deeply ethical person.

Lest my harsh judgment be misunderstood, I do not doubt that some individual schools, including colleges, some teachers, and perhaps even some local peer cultures encourage the maturation of a moral identity. Furthermore, I do not doubt schools' *potential* to produce good or virtuous people. After all, the majority of youth are ready for moral education. Most schools do not have the culture, perhaps the will, to create the climate necessary to bring out their virtues' latent potentials.

To fulfill that potential, educators need to consider more thoughtfully the principal contributors to a moral identity—the source of specific ethical behaviors. They need to assess and understand their schools' systemic contributing attributes as well as their students' educability for moral education. Then they must make an emotional commitment to moral education and initiate the sweeping changes in attitudes, relationships, and their school climates such a commitment demands.

Toward a Perspective about the Contributors to a Student's Moral Identity

You may disagree with my judgments about the relative importance of different contributors. You can rightly object that I cannot unequivocally identify "contributors" which imply events that "cause" ethical behavior. I don't want to belabor the interpretive issue, but it is important to keep in mind. *Parallel occuring events do not necessarily mean one causes the other.* My information is basically correlational. It identifies parallels, not causes. Because NAIS students act more ethically than public school students does not mean I can unequivocally claim that differences between the schools caused the ethical differences. They may have occurred for other reasons. Like what? Perhaps some differing parental attitudes I am unaware of. It is the accumulative consistency of the *pattern* of parallels that persuades me to write about "contributors."

The surveys' tabled patterns, not just their specific tabled results, also confirm what other researchers have reported. Ethical development is influenced by numerous factors, including one's biological inheritance, familial and cultural values, self-concept, as well as by schools and peers. I have only minimal evidence, though, about the effects of students' religious commitments, none at all about TV and music on their ethical behavior and moral sense. Since some of my judgments about schools' attributes are novel and have not yet been replicated by other researchers, you may weigh them differently.

Biological Inheritance as a Contributor to Ethical Behavior

The contribution of our evolutionary biological inheritance to our ethical behavior and more generalized moral sense cannot be ignored.[4] The pattern of sex differences in ethical behavior is just too consistent to believe that it is *only* the product of sociocultural expectations.

Why are boys so much more vulnerable to lapsing morally than girls? Whatever severely troubling behavior we examine, males reign supreme: Males make up 85% of more than one million Americans in prison; they sexually harrass, rape, and produce babies out of wedlock and more often than not then desert them; they more frequently steal, get drunk, fight, dominate, physically haze, and even torture and kill each other. In every culture in every epoch. And there are similar types of behavior in most species, particularly our closer DNA relatives with whom we share more than 98% of our genes—chimps, monkeys, gorillas.

Let's grant that females have always provoked trouble also, though less overtly disruptive to others: They gossip, lie to please, deceive, manipulate, coyly tease, and seduce. Freed from their former societal restraints, are not more women beginning to follow in the more blatant unethical footsteps of men: harrassing and sexually propositioning males, abusing and deserting, even murdering their children for their careers, shoplifting and stealing, compulsively gambling and drinking, driving more recklessly?

From studying how men and women develop through their adult years, I no longer discount males' and females' biological differences as one reason for their differing ethical values. Recent research reports sex differences in brain activity in arousing situations. More well-substantiated evidence exists about sex hormones. Estrogen, for example, contributes to nurturing behavior; testosterone to aggression, lust, competitiveness, and, I predict, when measured, dominance also—traits at the core of maleness in most cultures. Male more than female hormones are interpersonally and ethically disruptive. Our femaleness and maleness, femininity and masculinity, are rooted in our biology. They shape the quality of our relationships with others, which ethical values have always guided and regulated. So one might say that our moral sense is ultimately grounded on our biology. Testosterone is to courage as progesterone is to caring. However, our hormonal inheritance is limited and modifiable. Beyond a certain threshold level, for example, increases in testosterone do not increase sexual desire and performance.[5] Studies are needed about the relation of its increases to the aggressive and competitive behavior which provoke ethical crises. I have no direct evidence about how different testosterone and estrogen levels may, if at all, predispose boys' unethical and girls' ethical behavior.

Sociocultural and Familial Contributors to Ethical Behavior

Sociocultural values obviously affect our relationships and ethical behavior.[6] That both NAIS and public school boys think of themselves as typically masculine but NAIS boys report more caring behavior shows just how variable and modifiable our biological heritage can be. Moral educators, however, should not ignore that boys are likely to be less educable than girls for their essentially "femininizing" programs. Boys' reactions will be more variable and unpredictable. Their "natural" maturational route will be more competitive, aggressive, and adventurous.

Parental Expectations

Sociocultural values directly affect youths' values by way of parental expectations of their ethical behavior. The NAIS and public school parents' educational and socioeconomic background were similar and quite homogeneous. Their similarity permitted parental attitudes to emerge in their own right as powerful contributors to the NAIS and public students' ethical differences. The consistent magnitude of the correlations between parental expectation of and support for students' ethical behavior for every school is too great to judge otherwise. They are probably the most immediate and decisive contributor to students' moral sense.[7]

Predictably, girls reliably believe more than boys do that their parents expect them to act ethically regardless of their type of school. In contrast to public school boys and girls, both NAIS boys and girls reliably believe that their parents have higher expectations of their ethical behavior.

Like biological contributors, sociocultural and familial influences are also limited and modifiable. Not all the differences in NAIS and public students' ethical behavior can be attributed to their parental expectations. I explored the ethical behavior of *only* those students who believed that their parents *fully* expected them to be ethical. Though NAIS and public school boys and girls did *not* differ in their beliefs about their parental expectations, they still reported acting more ethically and tolerantly. Parental expectations, therefore, may not be decisive in and of themselves as contributors to ethical behavior.

On what types of ethical behavior do parents exercise their greatest influence? For both sexes in NAIS and public schools, they most effectively teach their children to tell the truth and to do their best in their academic work. Where do parents fall down most in teaching their children to be ethical? In learning to accept others who differ from them and in not using racial and sexist put-downs.

For example, the intolerant and rejecting Bloomfield eighth graders as well as ninth to twelfth graders believed that their parents did *not* expect them to care about and be tolerant of others. I have found this finding in so many other schools that we can assert that parental attitudes are probably critical contributors to the development of prejudice. While not a novel finding, it reinforces common sense. To educate for multicultural tolerance schools need parents on their side. The absence of wide-spread parental expectation and support will severely limit, even doom, any sustained moral education program to reduce prejudice.

Religious Belief and Participation

Parental participation in religious activities contributed to students' ethical development in my samples. Students who believed both parents were religious reported acting more ethically than those who reported that only one or no parent was religious. Students who identified themselves as religious and voluntarily participated in religious and service actitivies also reliably reported acting more ethically. Though religious adults in my longitudinal studies were more ethical, more ethical people were not necessarily religious in either behavior or commitment.[8]

The contribution of parental religiosity to children's tolerance is more complicated. If you pushed me to make a judgment, I would expect that religion's contribution to tolerance and acceptance of others would be nil or at least ambiguous. Fervently held religious beliefs have for centuries bred intolerance, rejection, or death of non-believers. Yet, every major religion values compassion and acceptance of "sinners." I have too limited evidence, however, to judge religiosity's *relative* importance as a more general influence on the ethical behavior of most youth.

Parents frequently ask what hope do my studies of young people have for our society's seeming moral psychopathy. We are evolving away from authoritarian religious and prescriptive moralistic standards of right and wrong. These gloomy transitional years disturb and confuse our youth and ourselves. But evolving to where or what?

Toward a universal or generalized understanding of morality as core ethical values or principles undergirding more mature interpersonal relationships?[9] What ethical values? The values that the Edina parents and the model of maturing identify: honesty, empathy and compassion, integrity, steadfastness or commitment, and courage, among other core values. These values are not only essential to becoming a successful and happy adult.[10] They have also become indispensable requirements if modern society is to function. For example, the globalization of our economy compels honesty if it is to work. Bond traders must be scrupulously honest and trustworthy when they instantaneously move billions of dollars electronically around the world. The world economy would collapse if they did not keep their word and could not be trusted. The international community is inching toward establishing universal human rights, trespassers upon which can be brought to judgment by any court.

Like our biological inheritance, changing sociocultural values and parental up-bringing, expectations, and religiosity influence ethical maturation—but not exclusively. So we must search further for other contributors to ethical development.

Students' Character as a Contributor to Ethical Behavior

Students' character, actual and ideal self-concepts, and maturity are the next most important contributors to a moral sense. Given the centrality of our identity as males and females to our behavior, it is not surprising that their associated traits of masculinity and most prominently femininity are associated with ethical behavior. A recent review of research firmly confirms males' predisposition to be sexually aggressive and more involved in anti-social activities,[11] so hindering the development of a moral sense.

Since our self-concepts can become self-fulfilling prophecies, it is sobering to learn that only a bare majority of boys (51%) and girls (59%) think of themselves as having a generalized moral sense. More indicative of their educability, however, are the 60 to 70% who are emotionally committed to moral excellence as a vital option for their lives.

Psychological maturity in adults predicts virtue. Maturing expands the arena in which freed choices are made. It makes available a larger variety of attitudes and skills for making more mature value choices. More mature adolescents are more educable and act more ethically than less mature ones. However, these findings need to be replicated.

Students' Emotional Commitment to Moral Education

A neglected but important contributor to the potential ethical development of students is their own emotional commitment to ethical values. Although only 23% of teachers believe that their students show any moral sense, an average of 60% of boys and 70% of girls are emotionally committed to ethical values. The majority of girls, though not of boys, are committed to a deep moral sense. When tension between students' ethical self-concepts and their beliefs about their peers' ethical behavior is so painfully great, students are potentially educable for adults' moral leadership—if only the schools' adults sensitively implemented what is now known about the most effective ways to nurture character maturation.[12] If teachers were more committed to moral education, they could count on more educable students than they may realize.

School as a Contributor to Ethical Behavior

Schools and their associated activities, such as co-curricular activities, command thousands of hours of students' growing up space. They could powerfully strengthen the development of a moral identity. Studies of Haverford College alumni revealed its power to do so.[13] Given the readiness of adolescents for questioning and reforming their ethical values, I had expected that secondary schools would also develop a moral sense in their students. My survey results from more than 10,000 students in our country's most favored secular and religious schools consistently suggest their effects may be moderate at most.

Why? Though concerned about their students' moral behavior, most schools had not created the kind of moral climate necessary to support their concern. Only 34% of their students believe that their schools have a moral climate. Only 41% believe that their faculties have an ethical character. Only 33% of boys, though 48% of girls believe that their teachers have a deep moral sense. While possessing the potential to contribute to moral excellence, few schools apparently fulfilled it.

The pertinent question is: What attributes of schools may contribute most and which least to their students' moral sense?

Before listing schools' attributes that might contribute most to students' moral sense, I briefly review two methodological issues that limit my judgments.

Assessing the effects of schools' attributes requires adequate base lines by which to evaluate their direction and magnitude of changes in ethical behavior. Such information is not available. Judgments about schools' contribution to ethical behavior remain most tentative until confirmed by more well-controlled studies.

Understanding why the independent and public-Reagan students differed so consistently requires other evidence than their socio-economic comparability. We have some evidence. NAIS parents are believed by their children to have higher ethical expectations than public school parents are by their children. NAIS students also agree among themselves more than public school students do about what their parents expect.

We also have information about the comparability of NAIS and public school students' personalities. Overall, NAIS and public-Reagan students most likely come from the same student population. Certainly the girls are similar. The boys may be. NAIS boys differ by having more typical feminine interpersonal attitudes and skills that contribute to their ethical behavior. We know that virtuous adult males and females typically have such skills. Whether NAIS boys entered their schools with such skills and/or whether they are the effect of their schools remains a moot issue to which I return shortly.

Distinctive Moral Climate

Research suggests that the most important school attribute contributing to its students' moral sense is the distinctiveness of its moral climate. More NAIS than public school faculty and students believed that their schools have such a moral climate. The sources of such distinctiveness are several: traditions and supportive rituals, a respected charismatic visionary head, faculty selected to be simpatico with the school's values to which they are emotionally committed, parents supportive of and students educable for the school's values. Collectively NAIS rather than public-Reagan schools were more advantaged on the attributes most likely to contribute to an ethical sense. Their teachers and students believed that they have more distinctive cultures and moral climates. Their students viewed more positively their teachers who have more visible moral characters. Their teachers tended to be more emotionally committed to moral education.

On almost all counts public schools are at a disadvantage. Why? Their large size and the way they are organized. They bar creating just the consensual values and interpersonal relationships necessary to further character's healthy growth. Not one of numerous research studies on the effects of school size, which I have reviewed elsewhere,[14] contradicts this judgment.

Smaller-sized schools provide the opportunity for more personal less anonymous relationships as well as for more active involvement in the school's co-curricular life. Students meet their friends more frequently during the week. They also have more hours of contact with their teachers. More students can fill leadership positions. Proportionally more students participate in athletics and other co-curricular activities. Small schools therefore provide more opportunity for students to become responsible school citizens. Indices of citizenship are reliably associated with ethical behavior.[15]

Why do NAIS boys act more ethically and tolerantly than public school boys? Matching their parental ethical expectations reduces the odds that NAIS boys' greater ethical behavior is due to parental differences. I believe that it is due more to the effects of growing up in smaller-sized, more ethically distinctive NAIS schools. NAIS and public school girls' personalities are more similar because of their being gender-related than because of their schools' values. NAIS boys greater femininity and so ethical behavior are due more to their socialization in a safer, less macho troubling peer environment.

Happily, the tide is turning. Smaller schools are now in vogue—too late for the millions of vulnerable and marginal students who have been hurt by the effects of impersonal large-sized schools. Smaller charter schools could well presage a longer-term positive effect on students' ethical behavior *if they create the kind of moral climate that promotes students' healthy growth.*

However, the survey reveals another, though problematic, advantage of small-sized schools that may explain in part why NAIS students act more ethically than public school students. The students are more ethically homogeneous; their parents' ethical expectations are also. Even when I matched NAIS and public school parents' ethical expectations, NAIS students' ethical behavior was more homogeneous. As I have argued elsewhere, the most effective model for altering character is a monastery. Its communicants' values are widely shared. Its values are ever-present.

But why a "problematic" advantage? Because excessive homogeneity may block healthy growth. Excluding diverse and conflicting views and beliefs risks entrenching a parochial and "ideological" mentality. On the other hand, an unreflective pursuit of diversity in belief and values risks eroding the core values that define a school's distinctive moral climate. The governing principle should be the congruence between an institution's core values and liberal educators' goal of healthy growth or human, not just parochial, excellence. The greater ethical homogeneity of NAIS students apparently has not resulted in closed mindedness. Both NAIS girls and boys feel more comfortable with and accept diverse values and life styles than more ethically diverse public school students feel and accept.

The Moral Character of the Faculty

The next most important school attribute is the character of the faculty—the quality of its relationships with its students and each other and its collective ethical values. Now that we can measure how students view their teachers, we confirm another consequence of large size. Teacher-student relationships become more impersonal. More students become alienated and drop out psychically from their schools. Teachers lose their *collective presence* as a model of the school's values to students, especially in large public schools. Twenty percent more NAIS than public-Reagan students believed that their teachers model ethical values. Even then, only a slim majority of NAIS students believed their typical teacher models a moral sense.

Faculty Emotional Commitment to Moral Education

Today's perceptive students also sense what teachers say about themselves. Only a bare majority of high school teachers are emotionally committed to ethical goals for their students; more elementary and middle school teachers are so committed. Furthermore, students do not learn that teachers also struggle with ethical issues. Teachers have not created the kind of curriculum and classroom activities which provide students the opportunity to know them as valuing human beings.[16] NAIS more than public school teachers can be known more fully; they are not as specialized. Individual NAIS teachers teach more varied courses, coach, and may be more accessible to students.

Peer Culture as a Contributor to Ethical Values

The least powerful positive, possibly most negative contributor to adolescents' ethical development is their peers' believed character. Only 24% of boys and 30% of girls believed that their peers show any generalized ethical behavior or moral sense. Given adolescents' peer conforming behavior, their peer group may well have negative effects on their ethical development. Recall that 40 to 55% of NAIS and public-Reagan boys and girls believed that their peers are critical, sarcastic, defensive—traits not conducive to ethical development. Moral education must begin by altering students' interpersonal relationships. Once students believe that their peers (and adults) are accepting, trusting, and open, we know they will be more educable for our specific curricular and other moral programs.

Moral Education in Independent and Public Schools

We are now ready to return to Chapter 13's three questions that help frame the debate about taxpayer support for vouchers for private schools. There are numerous types of private schools. I confine my comments only to those that qualify for membership in the National Association of Independent Schools. No similar studies have been done on other types of schools, such as those initiated by the Christian right, Catholic parochial, segregationist, Afro-American, or Hispanic constituencies.

The first question is, "Do NAIS boys and girls report acting more ethically than comparable public school boys and girls report?" I have struggled to assess "comparability." The schools studied are comparable enough to answer the question fairly. My answer is "Yes."

The second question is "Do private and public schools differ in their moral climates?" Again, I answer "Yes."

The results suggest that the third question must be rephrased in three ways.

The easiest to answer is, "How decisively *do* NAIS and public high schools contribute to students' *moral sense* or identities?" "Very little" for NAIS and "Not at all" for public high schools.

The second rephrased question is not answered so definitely. It asks about a school's *potential* to affect behavior if a school creates an ideal moral climate. "How decisively *can* NAIS and public schools affect students' *ethical behavior?*" "Moderately" for NAIS and "Not very much" for public high schools.

The third question is the most difficult to answer. "How decisively *can* NAIS and public high schools contribute to a students' *moral sense or identity?*" My answer is "Probably not very much" for NAIS schools and "Not at all" for public schools.

Your answers may differ. Why do I make such a tough-minded, but I think realistic, appraisal? Specific behaviors are easier to alter than one's identity, though such specific behavioral alteration may not persist once one leaves the school. The best insurance that specific ethical behaviors will persist in other situations is to integrate them with other components of the personality. Ideally, a change in one's mind and character should be integrated with and anchored to the core identity of the maturing self. "I am a competent and virtuous person who seeks to act with integrity."

As now constituted, large public schools cannot provide the moral climate to have enduring effects on their students' character. The host of changes required would to be impractical. Resources for moral education should be targeted to affect specific ethical behaviors with modest expectations of success.

Small public schools, private as well, can have more ambitious goals for a moral education effort *if* they more thoughtfully pay attention to and implement what the surveys suggest. Biological, parental, and sociocultural contributors to a youth's self-definition as an ethical person are most influential. Little psychological space is left in which schools can maneuver to make a significant impact. Let us assume that parental support is forthcoming and students are educable for moral education—as the surveys suggest many are. Schools can then realistically expect their moral education programs to affect ethical behavior, perhaps strengthen some students' moral identity, and even convert the rare few into virtuous persons.

I would temper my stringent evaluations if schools more courageously stood for ideals that were compatible with maturity's core values. Though adolescence is the period to dream an ideal for oneself and for one's country, today's students no longer dream ideals. Only 29 to 34% of public and independent school students think of themselves as idealistic. Ideals fuel hope. How shall we create schools of hope for youths to live lives of hope in the future?

I do not believe it wise for taxpayers to support non-public schools. The danger is too great that ideological commitments will obscure, if not preclude, liberal education's core values and subtly usurp students' right to dream their own dreams. In 1967 I proposed in *Humanizing Schools* that all students should have the opportunity to become educated in any of their state's public schools. In 1994, *Schools of Hope* affirmed my support for publicly-financed, small-sized charter schools. If funds are available, they should be funneled to innovative small public schools that try to create a moral climate congruent with liberal education's core ethical values.

Implications for Boys' and Girls' Character Maturation

As Kohlberg tried to show with his "just" schools, the principal route to internalize students' virtue is to alter their relationships with each other and adults.[17] Centuries of parental admonitions, priestly exhortations, hand-slapping rulers, daily prayers and chapel services, and a semester course on ethical behavior are rather feeble ways to alter character permanently. They may open the road to salvation, however, if their recipients are already educable for their prescriptive ministrations. For youth sceptical of authoritarian proscriptions, moral education must begin by cultivating its roots: altering how students and faculties get along with each other and explicitly and consistently valuing the kinds of relationships out of which ethical behavior evolves.

As the results suggest, our critical moral issue is not the education of women, as important as that must be to address. It is, as the Executive Directors of the National Coalition of Girls' Schools, write,

> "Girls are not the problem . . . We will know that educators finally have gotten the message when we see schools taking steps to change boys' attitudes about girls and women."[18]

To which I would add, "and to strengthen girls' *courage* to challenge such attitudes."

What should we do to prepare girls and boys for the psychological world of the future? Girls will continue to find ways to utilize their more acceptable masculine strengths in their careers and relationships. Males will have less and less dominating control over them. Both will have to develop the *core* attitudes and skills now known to be necessary to fulfill well their vocational, marital, sexual, parental, friendship, and citizenship roles: caring, honesty, integrity, sense of humor, openness, tolerance, dedication, and the interpersonal skills of understanding, respecting, and empathy for others.[19]

Today's youth will be in ceaseless contact tomorrow with the emerging interdependent global world of diverse peoples and values. It will demand such virtues and interpersonal strengths. Girls will master the technological skills the information age requires much easier than boys will the ethical and interpersonal skills their future requires. We have learned that girls' self-concepts are more receptive to a variety of potentially adaptive strengths; boys' self-concepts are more constricted and may be more rejecting, especially of potential strengths they identify as "feminine."

Why? I have clues, some of which may upset you as they did a psychiatrist who heard me speak about them. I recall his disturbance, and smile about his thoughtful, though unnecessary, invitation to consult with him for personal therapy! More than boys, girls are comfortable with and accept persons who differ from them, including those with different sexual preferences or life styles. Some skeptics of the gender differences in multicultural attitudes I have found argue the differences are not genuine ones. They say if I had not included sexual orientation as one of the components in the Multicultural Acceptance Index, I would have found no gender differences. (I think not likely. The measure of tolerance did not include sexual preference but was very highly correlated with the acceptance questions.) But their argument is a legitimate and important criticism to be settled by empirical study, not by ideological belief. The study is a simple one for a school to do. My hypothesis is that boys who emotionally reject and are hostile toward blacks, for example, will also have similar emotional feelings towards gays and lesbians, even towards women.

The evidence has been clear for years that boys are more upset about accepting gay persons than girls are. Astin has annually sampled the attitudes of several hundred thousand entering college freshmen from hundreds of colleges for almost two decades. He reports a declining number of students year-by-year who believe homosexual relationships should be prohibited by law. Recently, only 21% of girls but 42% of boys agreed that they should be.[20]

Another study provides another clue about some males' estrangement from their impulses, against which they protect themselves by repudiating others who have accepted them. Male university students claiming they were uncomfortable when around gays became more sexually aroused viewing homosexual videos than students claiming they were comfortable around gays. Both groups did not differ in their responses to heterosexual videos.[21]

The last but less blatant clues are the personal traits of the three to four times more boys than girls who are most uncomfortable with those who differ from them. They are more troubled and hostile than the most acceptant boys. They are also consistently more negative about their schools which they believe to be dull, about their peers whom they believe do not care and use put-downs, and about their teachers whom they believe are not dedicated, hardworking, or helpful. The most telling clue is that 27% more of the least than of the most acceptant boys described themselves not only as masculine but also more negatively than the acceptant boys described themselves.

To me such clues suggest that the American stereotyped macho ideal of aggressivity, competitiveness, lustiness, and emotional self-sufficiency predisposes some boys to hostilely reject those whom they view as impaired, (handicapped), weak (females), incompetent (ethnic minorities), and feminine (gays). Might not rejection of others who differ from oneself betray a deep, unconscious alienation and repression of the same potentialities in oneself? Males' antipathy toward gays may be, as the third clue hints, a defensive way to bolster one's image of oneself as a healthy, strong, competent, masculine male. Educating such boys for multicultural values risks provoking defensive and possibly severe acting out. Adult sensitivity to and compassionate understanding that such prejudice may be fueled by insecurity, conflict, and strong emotions is necessary if such boys are to become more educable to other values.

A less provocative implication of the clues is that males estranged from their emotionally expressive and feminine interpersonal potentials are the ones most vulnerable to acting less ethically and more prejudicially. May it not be easier to educate girls' minds for a technological future than it will be to educate such boys' hearts for an interpersonally interdependent one?

I remain uncertain about how to educate boys to accept and strengthen their more stereotypic feminine interpersonal potentials *without devaluing their biological and historical male strengths.* How we answer and then implement this challenge may well determine if less polarizing and adversarial and more healthy and cooperative male-female relationships, stronger families, and healthier communities will be ours in the future.

I support those schools searching for specific ways to educate its boys to be more interpersonally empathic and its girls to be more courageous, without devaluing their biological strengths. What ways?

Place boys in positions of responsibility where they must help others in ways that don't demean their own maleness and don't encourage their greater use of put-downs. Collaborative learning, teaching and mentoring youngsters, peer coaching, and community service are obvious ways. They combine boys' self-perceived ability to be responsible with activities that could teach them how to care. However, we must help them *acquire the appropriate information and skills about how to care* using available curricular programs.[22] Opportunities to demonstrate the value of caring must be consistently provided *throughout their school years.* We must test if caring has been internalized as a value resulting in subsequent *self-initiated* caring behavior. One semester's required or volunteered community service effort is not enough to stabilize and then test a value's autonomization.

Educate girls to understand their own beliefs and strengths which they must responsibly assert and persuasively defend against criticism. Place them in situations in which they can be responsible but in which they may fail, so they can learn how to bounce back and persist with their commitment after mistakes and criticism. The 1996 teen-age Olympic gymnastic teams admirably modeled these strengths. Graduated Outward Bound and ropes courses providing physical challenges and competitive team sports are not enough, however. Girls need to learn how to apply their increased self-confidence and risk-taking values to increasingly more personal relationships. They could debate or defend independent project work in a public forum. By using anticipatory rehearsals and role-playing techniques, drama teachers could help girls respond to sexual harrassments and so fortify their courage.

Such programs are probably not enough, however, given the depth and centrality of their maleness to males' self-esteem and their accommodativeness to females'. It is a larger sociocultural dilemma not to be readily resolved. Our biological inheritance is too compelling and, I suspect, increasingly out of phase with the evolving type of society for which schools must educate. I have argued that more humane accountability standards and honest assesments can prefigure steps that may meet such standards. What first steps can schools take to educate for the character that the next millennium will demand of its young?

Steps to Implement Moral Education's Virtues

If on a path that speaks to their students and teachers' needs, the remaining steps will become visible and show the way.

1. Secure parental commitment to the core values that define human excellence. Work with parents and community leaders, as the Edina school district did, to identify shared core values. Ideally, I would include representative students in every step.

2. Courageously, rigorously, and honestly assess the school's moral climate. Be willing to hold one's school as accountable as the schools I have described did.

3. Thoughtfully and non-defensively analyze and interpret the assessment's results with students and parents. Use the book's relevant chapters and their normative results to bring perspective to your interpretations.

4. Establish priorities among the core values. Identify the values most students and teachers are emotionally committed to. Work to develop those.

5. Develop a strategic action plan to identify the priority conditions that need to be developed first before introducing specific programs.

6. Assume and expect that students want to be moral persons and are educable for considered moral programs.

7. Work with students to create the accepting, empathic, and trusting peer culture they wish they had. It can be done. Bloomfield Hills' Model High School succeeded.

8. Provide educative experiences, especially for males, to develop the interpersonal skills, such as empathetic and caring ones, that undergird ethical behavior.

9. Regenerate faculty's calling to the ideals that brought them to teaching. See *Schools of Hope* for practical suggestions about creating more trusting, adventurous, intellectually exciting, and alive faculty relationships.

10. Given the greater openness to moral education among teachers of younger children, begin experimenting with practical programs with them. Edina found its elementary teachers to be most responsive and imaginative in recreating their schools' moral climates.

11. Then, grade-by-grade, build on and reinforce students' ethical behavior and budding moral sense.

We now know much more about ethical behavior than we did even a decade ago. Do we have the wisdom to create schools of hope? Do we have the will to resurrect human excellence that includes character and academic goals in our schools? Do we have the grace to accept our victories and the courage to face our defeats? Do we have the commitment and patience to persist and persist?

SECTION VII

—◆•◆—

Holding Schools Accountable

Chapter 17

———••••———

ACCOUNTABILITY CREATES
UNDERSTANDING THAT PREFIGURES ACTION

This concluding chapter reflects upon two of the book's interrelated themes and their results: How can schools *honestly* hold themselves accountable for achieving their goals? What does assessing schools systemically suggest about evaluating proposals for improving schools?

Steps to Make Accountability Honest

To honestly appraise a school's achievement of its goals requires much more than the typical detailed appraisals demanded by accrediting agencies, departments of education, and legislators. It requires a deep appreciation of a school's systemic attributes: its members' collective morale and invisible but formative culture, which shape the quality of its outcomes. It requires a dispassionately honest search for ways to discover what a school's actual effects really are. It requires intuition and judgment, disciplined by carefully secured reliable objective information, to integrate and make sense of a school's uniquely patterned effects. And finally it requires the humility to accept that one can only approach the truth about a complex, dynamic, changing social system such as a school.

An honest evaluation of a school requires at least three steps, illustrated concretely by Model's efforts.

Step One

An indispensable *first* step is to understand the morale of a school's members as well as of its culture. Not just its leaders and faculty but also its students, secretaries, and janitors are responsible for a school's morale and culture and its improvement. Every person contributes to each other's morale and the creation of a growth-producing culture. Deming claims that these are generic, systemic attributes that make more probable the achievement of high quality. Absent such knowledge about an organization's morale and culture means efforts to achieve excellence will more likely go astray and produce only transitory results.

It takes courage to risk learning about the morale of one's students, teachers, and staffs and the meaning of the school's culture to each. The earlier chapters illustrated how risking such self-discovery can create, however, healthier and more "growth-producing cultures"—if a school's leaders commit themselves to explore ways with their faculties and students to implement their self-discovery's findings.

Step Two

The *second* indispensable step to making an honest accounting is to determine whether the school has achieved the *school-wide goals* published in its mission statement. The schools' adults—board, administrative staff, and faculty—are primarily responsible for achieving these goals. (Students become secondarily responsible only as they make the school's goals their own.) At this step of assessment, most adults ignore their school-wide goals. When challenged, few faculties can even collectively tell me all their published goals, especially character ones. For more than a decade, I have warned schools not to ignore what they promise in their mission statements. Disgruntled parents and angry students, hungry lawyers, and a litigiously-inclined society guarantee lawsuits. The charges: The school failed to increase Susie's self-confidence, Bob's desire to want to learn, Betty's critical thinking ability, and Harry's ability to work cooperatively.

Several practical reasons limit making an honest accounting of school-wide goals. As Model High School discovered, its goals were imprecisely defined and methods were not available to assess them.

Also other demands absorbed the faculty's time and energy; assessment was not "owned" and so commitment could not be emotionally sustained once funding had stopped. The "pay-off" of the assessment's efforts did not persuade the faculty of their value. Faculty believed it already knew how well its students were growing, especially in their mastery of the academic competencies. Reliance on more authentic demonstrations of their skills therefore made formal assessment less necessary.

Four other more important underlying reasons account for resistance to demands for accountability. Educators are intimately aware of the complexity and uniqueness of their students. They rightly resist the "two-decimal" mentality of those who develop and then interpret such methods to assess growth. Requiring too precise measurements of human behavior can lead to triviality. They predict remarkably few adult successes or outcomes in any case.[1]

A second and related reason for resistance is the common belief that the most meaningful human outcomes are not assessable in any case. I do not share this belief. We can assess what others may believe is "unassessable." Name a school's outcome for which students cannot be crudely ranked in terms of their growth.[2] All measurement essentially involves ordering. We can order students on any attribute reasonably reliably if we can clearly define its characteristics. What can be more elusive than integrity, compassion, and tolerance that the EVQ measured with some success?

A third reason for resistance to assessing characters' goals is that we have been brain-washed. We believe that only mind's development *really* counts in life. Yet, as I have reported, what does count for almost every adult outcome—well-being, marital happiness, parental fulfillment, virtue, vocational competence and calling—includes character traits. As I've said too many times, measures of character's maturation more powerfully and consistently predict a wider range of adult outcomes than any measure of mind's maturation does.

A fourth reason for resistance is ambiguity and confusion about the purpose of education and therefore of accountability. Christopher Cross, president of the Council for Basic Education, claims, "Accountability remains the most elusive component of standards-driven reform. The adults in the system scorn it. . . political and business leaders support it, as do parents until it appears that it will affect their children."[3] I advocate that schools be responsible and seek disciplined information about how well they have achieved their own school-wide goals. I have suggested some research-based standards for schools to evaluate how well they have created a growth-producing environment likely to produce healthy enduring effects in their students. Future research may alter and/or extend such standards as well as create acceptable methods to assess individual student growth. Because we do not now have such methods I don't advocate grading students on their character maturation for purposes of granting them a degree.[4]

Step Three

The *third* indispensable step for making an honest evaluation of a school's goals is to assess its specific academic as well as character goals for which individual departments and faculty are primarily responsible. Achievement tests assess specific curricular goals, such as mastery of foreign language, mathematical and scientific knowledge, and their associated skills. These are the *easiest* types of goals to assess objectively. They are the goals for which faculty acknowledge their responsibility to develop. So resistance to assessing their effectiveness is less. Grant Wiggins has critiqued traditional measures of individual student achievement and his suggested alternatives round out the issues of accountability for me.[5]

The most recent cure for our educational ills—a national curriculum and its rigorous assessment—challenges a systemic understanding of schools and their purpose to promote healthy growth.

Assessing National Curricular Standards' Potential Effects

What stance do you now take about such curricular standards? You have learned about morale, growth-producing cultures, students' views of their schools and teachers, Sandia's and Washington's inner worlds, psychic dropouts, gender differences in ethical behavior, the personality roots of multicultural intolerance, and Step One's and Step Two's requirements for an honest accountability.

Development of national standards can clarify departmental curricular goals. Though voluntary, they will most likely become psychologically mandatory. They will make abundantly clear what many believe students should know to succeed as adults, and on which they will be rigorously tested. They will most likely increase some students' and schools' test scores.

But how may national academic standards contribute to the creation of a healthy, growth-producing school culture? While I support efforts to clarify what students should know and be able to do, I also fear such efforts' potential to harm teachers' and students' healthy growth. They could become a procrustean bed. They could limit teachers' sensitivity to and creativity in responding to their diverse students' needs. They could turn faculty even further away from learning how to create healthy schools of hope.

Teachers of advanced placement courses, analogues of national curricula for high schools, warn me of another potentially disastrous effect. Despite the advices of the framers of a national curriculum, teachers may feel pressure to teach to their examinations. They could become even more rigorous didactic information-dispensers racing to complete the curriculum before what could in time become national examinations. Experimenting with teaching their academic disciplines in ways that could further the growth of their students' character could become too risky. Their course's and school's test scores might slip. The ultimate psychological effect of *injudiciously* used national standards could be, paradoxically, to reduce some students' educability, especially of America's millions of vulnerable students.

We need school "canaries" to warn us of the possible effects that the purification and standardization of the academic curriculum could bring. Recall how the healthiness of the effects of Broward's academic purification could be assessed. It had the necessary base line information to evaluate the systemic effects of its head's effort to narrow and intensify its curricular programs. Should not every school first secure Steps' One and Two base line information about their morale, culture, and school-wide goals and their norms *before* initiating Step Three's new curricular standards? Might schools then be able to monitor more objectively over time a national curriculum's positive and possibly untoward harmful effects on teachers' and students' healthy growth? The effects of a national curriculum warrant an empirical study, not a preformed, knee-jerk ideological reaction, either pro or con.

We are on the way to securing Step One's measures. We have a plethora of measures of some of Step Three's goals, though not of most of mind's strengths that *Schools of Hope* identified are necessary for adult success: intuition, imagination, judgment, synthesizing ability, and others.[6] Our most glaring lack is the availability of adequate measures to assess honestly Step Two's school-wide goals, especially the character attributes necessary for adult success and well-being. The Ethical Value Questionnaire is only an initial example of how assessments of school-wide goals could be developed.

I would not recommend that schools use measures of its school-wide goals to grade, for example, individual students' maturity and ethical growth for purposes of their graduation. Their trustworthiness depends upon students' anonymity and honesty in reporting on their own growth. They should be used *only* for meeting Step Two's needs: evaluating how well the school, not an individual student, fulfills its mission goals. We still know too little about how best to educate for character outcomes.

For example, Model found that its students did not become more ethical as the EVQ measured their self-reported behavior, nor did they become less ethical. How shall we interpret Model's failure to affect its students' ethical behavior? [ASH 21: Assessing Model's Effects on Its Students' Ethical Competence]. We know that Model had a moral climate and that its faculty had the type of relationships that could affect its students' ethical behavior. So why did Model fail? Perhaps the ethical competence needed to be redefined. Perhaps a more sensitive measure of ethical behavior was necessary. Perhaps the dual responsibility for students' growth shared with their home-based schools provided conflicting cultures, not the coherent "monastery" type of culture necessary to affect students' character. Perhaps, perhaps, and perhaps. Before abandoning the competence, Model needed to explore more thoughtfully these "perhaps." I was inclined to believe the students' dual allegiance and the diluted amount of time each had at Model to be the principal "perhapses."

Every school needs on its assessment shelf measures of its school-wide goals and the national and local norms it has confidence in. Such methods could provide a school with the means to honestly evaluate its effects. They could propel continued reflective self-renewal efforts. They also could serve to prevent a national standard's potential erosion of a commitment to human excellence while strengthening commitment to its component —academic excellence.

Steps to Create Schools with Healthy, Growth-Producing Cultures

In the spring of 1984, the Illinois State Board of Education invited me to speak to its board members. It asked me to assist its members evaluate the varied proposals that *A Nation at Risk* had spawned for improving their schools. They were confused about where to begin. They did not know which ideas were more or less promising. On what should they spend their taxpayers' money? I reviewed the relevant research literature and reflected at length on what my studies of schools had told me by that time. Most of the proposals for reform, as well as other new ones, are still on some schools' and the national agenda. They could be sorted into whether they dealt with different goals for students, teachers, or schools. I then evaluated each proposal's likelihood of achieving its goal by assigning one of three judgments: Low, Moderate, or High likelihood. The board members did not respond enthusiastically. I failed to order the proposals in terms of most-to-least-specific steps that they could take.

Perhaps they might react differently now. Have they since learned from the expenditure of billions of dollars and from thousands of fruitless debates that no simple, quick, and painless "fix" can improve social systems such as schools' patterns of relationships? In 1999, as I near the end of my consulting career, I return to the board's request. How now would I alter my 1984 judgments? What order of steps would I take to create more healthy schools of hope?

But first, it is time for you to hold yourself accountable for what you have learned from our hours together. Please take your final examination in a playfully serious way. Table 17-1 lists many of the reform movement's goals and proposals for achieving them. Your exam has two parts for you to appraise what you will take away from this book. Assume you are asked to answer the Illinois board members' question I was asked. First, rate in Table 17-1's first column the likelihood of each proposal for achieving its goal. Assign one of three ratings: Low, Moderate, and High. For example, if increasing the number of hours that students stay in school each day will *moderately* increase their test scores, then mark the proposal with a "M" for moderate. Keep in mind what you have learned about public schools' young people, especially Sandia's and Washington's. Now, assign in column two a rank of "one" to your highest priority step, "two" to the next, and so on.

Please then reflect about two questions: Why did you assign a Moderate likelihood for lengthening the school day? Because Japanese students spend more hours in school and on Saturdays and they score high on achievement tests? Or because you know of research that suggests spending more time studying results in increased achievement? The second question is, "What changes need to be made to achieve the proposal's moderate promise?" You might list as the more important ones that parents agree that their children should spend more time in classes and that teachers learn how to teach into the mid-afternoon and summers in ways that don't deepen their students' boredom.

Table 17-1   Steps to Create a Healthy School of Hope

For Students

	Likelihood	Step #
Goal: Increase tested achievement		
1. Longer school day-year		
2. Require more math, science, and foreign language		
3. Require minimum grade average to participate in co-curricular activities, including athletics		
4. Reduce teacher contact from 150+ to about 80 students per week for high school		
5. Hold students to higher expectations and develop more rigorous standards for graduation		
6. Require one semester of service to community on non-school time		

	Likelihood	Step #

Goal: Develop lifelong learning attitudes and skills

7. Provide more training in self-educating skills and more opportunity for self-directed learning

8. Increase sustained opportunity for experiential learning in and outside of school

9. Make computer and other technology accessible for every student

For Teachers

Goal: Attract and hold excellent teachers

10. Increase teacher salaries

11. Offer merit salary increases

12. Provide a differentiated or hierarchical career ladder

Goal: Increase teachers' competence

13. Require teachers to take qualifying tests of knowledge in area of specialty

14. Provide more flexible entry routes into teaching

Goal: Nurture teaching as a calling

15. Provide opportunities for released time to get sustained renewal experiences

16. Hold clear expectations, consistently and humanely applied, that each teacher is committed to continued personal growth as condition for maintaining contract

For Effective Schools

	Likelihood	*Step #*

Goal: Create autonomous, humane, simpler organized schools

17. Decrease size elementary schools to 300; middle and high schools to 400-600

Goal: Clarify school mission and create shared values

18. Create school climate that mirrors school's goals that are collectively shared and consistently implemented
19. Develop a noble vision of school's goals appropriate to demands of 21st century
20. Hold schools meaningfully accountable for achieving goals

Goal: Principals must be educational leaders

21. Principals should have more educational, personnel, and financial autonomy and be held accountable for achieving their schools' goals
22. Create collaborative interpersonal working relationships between boards, principals, teachers, and students

If you could not complete the exam or avoided the task by giving tied ranks, then don't plan to run for the next school board election where you must take a stand. If you could not justify some of your ratings and rankings, then educate yourself more broadly. If the task upset or made you angry, then lighten up and perhaps learn to be more playful.

Why not now compare your current judgments with those you made before you read this book? What of its ideas have you now made more your own?

The exam was designed to test the skills required to be an institutional diagnostician: dispassionate judgment to keep the school, not just a specific departmental turf or one's own needs and desires, in mind while weighing the proposals against each other; the ability to think systemically and contextually while identifying the dependencies of proposals upon each other; the intuition to discover an underlying logic that might help to order the proposals. Appendix C describes my playful rankings and Appendix D their justifications.

Did you, as I did, find the task daunting at first? So many qualifications. So many ambiguities. So many different kinds of students and schools. But as I compared the proposals to each other, an underlying logic emerged that made ordering the proposals easier than I had anticipated. But the complexity of the task means your rankings may be wiser or more productive than mine.

I puzzled why I had weighted so many of the meritorious specific proposals to be not very achievable. I then realized that their success depended upon other proposals the success of which depended in turn upon others'. Ultimately the "logic" of the sequence of dependencies led to a school's systemic attributes. They are where practicable and meaningful reforms should begin.

For example, what must a school be like if more required math and foreign language courses will contribute to higher test scores? What may be their effect on marginal students' motivation and healthy growth and the curriculum's art, music, and vocational electives? The proposal may require more individual coaching, which requires smaller classes, more inductive and experiential exercises, use of computer programs for teaching algebra to the psychic drop-outs so alienated from teachers, and increased opportunity for teachers to develop new strategies. Decisions about how to meet these other proposed reforms in turn depend upon who selects, assesses, and pays competent but scarce teachers in the future. What kind of teacher do we need to achieve our stated goals: technically competent but immature math teachers who don't relate well to students in a coaching role? Or less technically competent teachers who do get along well with and inspire students and who have the maturity to upgrade their

competence? Does the school value and provide resources for its teachers' self-renewal? What is its vision of the kind of faculty it needs to
model to students its school-wide goals? And on and on.

Have I made my point? Sizer says we must change schools systemically, not bit by bit.[7] I agree *only* if we understand schools systemically as interdependent social systems. We dare never forget that
schools ". . . are about people and about the way people behave and
interact with each other in groups. They are about the attitudes, the
aspirations, and the motivation of people in work situations."

An emotional commitment to and implementation of this understanding of schools is where we must take our first step.[8]

I chose the Model High School to begin this book, not because
it is a replicable and practicable institutional, even programmatic
solution for thousands of schools and millions of students. It isn't.
Its "success" inherently depends upon the character of its leaders
and teachers searching, in their coordinate way, to create a growth-
producing school culture. I chose it for a more practical reason: it is
a functioning lighthouse. Its beacon lights up and projects into the
future a vision, an ideal of human excellence. It illuminates what
schools **could** be for our children. That hope is what contemporary
efforts to hold schools accountable lack. That hope is why we need
more humanizing accountability standards.

Appendix A

MODEL OF MATURING STRENGTHS THAT CONTRIBUTE TO SUCCESS

Table A: Model of Maturing: Strengths That Contribute to Success

The Person's Strengths	Developmental Dimensions of Maturing					Visible Signs of Maturity
	Symbolization	*Other-Centeredness*	*Integration*	*Stabilization*	*Autonomy*	
of Mind	Aware of how own mind works	Empathically grasps others' view	Thinks relationally and sees the whole picture	Functions well and resiliently under stress	Educates self and can create novel solutions for varied situations	Increased mastery, competence, and power
of Character	Sensitively aware of and reflective about relationships and values honesty	Cares for and values others' welfare with compassion	Creates mutually cooperative relationships and consistently lives values with integrity	Relationships endure and values persist with commitment	Self-reliantly forms selective relationships and stands up for considered principles with courage	Increased ability to create intimate and loving relationships and freed energy for new interests and enthusiasms
of Self	Accurately understands self	Accepts self as fully human and understands how others see self	Self is so together that it is able to act naturally and spontaneously	Has strong sense of self and is confident about wants and needs	Affirms own worth and directs and controls own growth	Heightened capability for self transcendence, objectivity, and sense of humor

Appendix B

EXAMPLES FROM STUDENT ESSAYS ABOUT HOW THEY HAD CHANGED IN SCHOOL

(SEE ASH 29 FOR THE SCORING MANUAL)

Growth in Symbolization

Symbolization of Cognitive Skills

I am getting better at explaining what I am thinking to a group.	12 girl
I ask (why) about many things now which I never have done before.	11 boy

Symbolization of Interpersonal Relationships

I'm also able to understand where people are coming from— their point of view.	12 girl
I have much more insight into teachers. I have begun to see them as people with real lives as opposed to just being people who talk a lot.	12 girl

Symbolization of Values

Now I see things in a new perspective. I feel an inner desire to do well in school and to have a future that I can be proud of.	12 boy
Last year I had no goals. Through the year I began to realize that without goals, I am really working for nothing.	11 boy

Symbolization of Self

I have discovered that I need outside motivation to do well.	12 girl
School just brought the inner me closer to the surface.	11 boy

Growth in Other-Centeredness

Other-Centered Cognitive Skills

I'm more objective now because I'm forced to look at many facets of particular problems here.	12 boy
I'm much more of an empathic listener.	11 boy

Other-Centered Interpersonal Relationships

Model helped me depend on and trust others. 12 boy	12 boy
I have cared more about others' well-being rather than just my own.	11 girl

Other-Centered Values

I look at everything with a positive approach which enables me to see the good in everyone and everything.	12 girl
Maturing has taught me and showed me that it is important to be fair to everyone because we are all equal.	12 girl

Other-Centered Self

I can finally say I like who I am.	10 girl
I have become a more "mello" person.	12 boy

Growth in Integration

Integration of Cognitive Skills

Since I've been here I have noticed that my thought is more coherent—I don't stumble for words when I speak.	12 boy

Integration of Cognitive Skills (cont.)

I have developed the ability to use logic/reason especially in situations where I am normally very (too) emotional.	12 girl

Integration of Interpersonal Relationships

I learned how to be a team player. Instead of being able to benefit just me, I learned how to make others benefit.	12 boy
School has shown me that a teacher can truly be your best friend.	12 boy

Integration of Values

Before my values were all about having fun or getting things out of the way as fast as I could. But now they're more structured and responsible.	11 girl
Through work on philosophies, I have been able to take these ideas into the real world and use them in my everyday life.	11 boy

Integration of Self

I am getting closer to being satisfied with my inner self.	11 boy
I am happy with myself, my friends, my schools, and everyone in them. . . . I have never been so optimistic about people and school.	10 girl

Growth in Stabilization

Stabilization of Cognitive Skills

My working habits have become much more efficient.	11 girl
I approach a problem more head on and think it through much more thoroughly.	9 boy

Stabilization of Interpersonal Relationships

I believe these interactions helped me establish many   10 boy
 strong relationships with many students here.

Stabilization of Values

My determination has increased tremendously—I actually   11 girl
 apply myself to school and find self-motivation to stick
 it through.

I'm more motivated to learn as opposed to just finishing   9 boy
 and turning in work.

Stabilization of Self

I have more faith in myself to solve problems than before.   11 girl

I've gained more confidence in my actions; not afraid to   10 boy
 express my feelings and thoughts.

Growth in Autonomy

Autonomous Cognitive Skills

Before coming here, I was a traditional type learner,   10 boy
 taking the teacher's information and leaving it at that.
 Now I second guess everything and try to rethink it.

Autonomous Interpersonal Relationships

I'm a lot stronger than a year ago. I don't want to be in   9 boy
 the so called "popular group". I am popular 'cause I
 have friends. I wouldn't have said that a year ago.

I will not allow myself to be affected by peer pressure. I   12 girl
 know who my friends are, who care about me, and who
 I care about. I have learned that I do not need the other
 materialistic and false fronts in order to be the true
 person I am.

Autonomous Values

Last year I was following the flow but now I am a self-thinking individual.	12 boy
I am also much more adventurous than ever before. I'm willing to take more risks. I have become more free.	12 girl

Autonomous Self

I feel as if I could always be myself now and not have to put up a front.	12 girl
I feel now that a man has stepped out of a boy's body, and for the first time I alone am in control of my destiny.	12 boy

Appendix C

STEPS TO CREATE A HEALTHY SCHOOL OF HOPE

For Students

	Likelihood	*Step #*
Goal: Increase tested achievement		
1. Longer school day-year	Low	19
2. Require more math, science, and foreign language	Low	17
3. Require minimum grade average to participate in co-curricular activities, including athletics	Low	22
4. Reduce teacher contact from 150+ to about 80 students per week for high school	High	5
5. Hold students to higher expectations and develop more rigorous standards of graduation	Moderate	9
Goal: Develop character-citizenship		
6. Require one semester of service to community on non-school time	Low	16
Goal: Develop love of learning and lifelong learning skills		
7. Provide more training in self-educating skills and more opportunity for self-directed learning	High	8

Goal: Develop love of learning and lifelong learning skills (cont.)	Likelihood	Step #
8. Increase sustained opportunity for experiential learning in and outside of school	Moderate	11
9. Make computer and other technology accessible for every student	Moderate	12

For Teachers

Goal: Attract and hold excellent teachers by increasing morale

10. Increase teacher salaries	Moderate	15
11. Offer merit salary increases	Low	18
12. Provide differentiated or hierarchical career ladder	Low	20

Goal: Increase teacher competence

13. Require teachers to take qualifying tests of knowledge in area of specialty	Low	21
14. Provide more flexible entry routes into teaching	Moderate	14

Goal: Nurture teaching as a calling

15. Provide opportunities for released time to get sustained renewal experiences	Moderate	13
16. Hold clear expectations, consistently and humanely applied, that each teacher is committed to continued personal growth as condition for maintaining contract	High	7

	Likelihood	*Step #*
For Effective Schools		
Goal: Create more autonomous, humane, *** and simply organized schools***		
17. Decrease size of elementary schools to 300; middle and high schools to 400-600.	High	2
Goal: Clarify school mission and create *** shared values***		
18. Create school climate that mirrors school's goals that are collectively shared and consistently implemented	High	4
19. Develop a noble vision of school's goals appropriate to demands of 21st century	High	1
20. Hold schools meaningfully accountable for achieving goals	Moderate	10
Goal: Principals must be educational *** leaders***		
21. Principals should have more educational, personnel and financial autonomy and be held accountable for achieving their schools' goals	High	3
22. Create collaborative interpersonal work relationships between boards, principals, teachers, and students	High	6

Appendix D

EXPLANATION OF STEPS TO CREATE

HEALTHY SCHOOLS OF HOPE

Proposals	Reasons for Assigning Likelihood	Conditions to Increase Achieving Goal
	Proposals for Students	
	Goal to Increase Test Achievement Scores	
1. Longer school day-year	Misunderstand student motivation and what contributes to effective learning. Proposal will increase boredom and resistance to school.	More effective use of school time. Educate teachers about students' motivation. Expand teaching strategies beyond lecture and question and answer; use experiential teaching methods.
2. Require more math, science, foreign language	More of same is not doing well now. Little prospect to improve teaching in future. Foreign language is elitist requirement for those now not able to master English's basic skills. Students perceive as useless. No evidence increases multicultural tolerance.	More inductive, practical, and experiential classes needed for majority of non-math, non-science students. Language best learned when must use it. Changing Hispanic demographics makes language more acceptable. Why not Mandarin for 21st century college-oriented? Computer can accelerate learning of basic language skills.

Proposals	Reasons for Assigning Likelihood	Conditions to Increase Achieving Goal
3. Require minimum grade average for co-curricular activities	Reduce desire to attend school for marginal students. Research shows co-curricular activity contributes to later adult success. Requirement undercuts value of character traits important for later success in just the group which needs their development the most.	Make school more appealing by meeting psychic dropouts' needs, especially. Reward for multiple intelligences to bolster self-worth. Integrate arts-drama with ongoing academic courses for students who learn best with right brain skills.
4. Reduce teacher contact from 150+ to about 80 students a week	Close supervision-coaching of communi-cation skills requires fewer students and sus-tained guidance-detailed corrective feedback. Enables teachers to be more flexible, imagina-tive, adventurous, and caring.	Retrain teachers to be coaches so not just repeat with fewer students current didactic teaching mode. To be economi-cally viable, reduce teacher specialization and refocus educational goals on teaching students to educate selves.
5. Hold high expectations; develop more rigorous graduation standards	Research shows im-portance of high ex-pectations and experiencing conse-quences of one's deci-sions.	Retrain teachers in principles of mastery learning; form more flexible groupings; abolish chronological age groupings to provide more individualization of instruction. More varied assessment methods to meet variability in learning styles.

Proposals	Reasons for Assigning Likelihood	Conditions to Increase Achieving Goal

Goals to Develop Character and Citizenship

6. Require semester of service to community on non-school time	Research finds responsibility for growth of another increases tutor-tutoree achievement and other character traits. Excluding from school-time devalues goal; absolves teachers from character education.	Apply "service" principle from K to 12; each child responsible for growth of another provides more actively involving interpersonal learning of skills-attitudes needed for community service which could serve as test of growth of character.

Goals to Develop Love of and Skills for Lifelong Learning

7. Provide self-educating skills and self-directed learning.	Most appropriate goal for uncertain future which students could emotionally own. Relies on principle of active involvement and value of assuming responsibility for one's own growth.	While assigned high probability of achieving, actual probability very low. Train teachers how to teach children to be self-educating and create school and classroom climate enabling them to do so.
8. Increase sustained experiential learning in and out of classroom	Research shows active involvement in situations in which one must be responsible powerfully contributes to academic and character growth. Counteracts boredom and cynicism about classroom "relevance."	Rich history of experience exists among experiential educators about how to implement proposal. Deep resistance by most "academic-type" teachers requires major re-formation of values and understanding of effective student learning conditions.

Proposals	Reasons for Assigning Likelihood	Conditions to Increase Achieving Goal
9. Provide access to computer and other technology.	Could provide the resources to motivate psychic dropouts and more independent-minded students. Its full educational potential not yet known; has potential for changing traditional classrooms.	Research is needed to assess not just acquisition of information and skill development but effects on character. Use needs integration with students' interpersonal and ethical growth. Could encourage technological psychopaths.

Proposals for Teachers

Goals to Attract and Hold Excellent Teachers by Increasing Morale

10. Increase salaries	Necessary for predicted teacher shortage due to baby-boom "echo." Exclusive emphasis on salary as incentive risks defining teaching as a job rather than a calling.	Salary increase should be on basis of equity, not to buy "morale." Greatly expand salary range to alter perceived status of profession. More focus on developing teachers' calling essential.
11. Offer merit increases	Researchers find few successful plans. Negative trade-offs are large: ambiguity of what defines effective teacher; teachers distrust decision-makers; divisive to a cohesive faculty.	Teacher participation in defining "merit." Tying "merit" to achievement test score improvement too limited view of "merit." Tying merit to school improvement more likely to decrease teachers' resistance.

Proposals	Reasons for Assigning Likelihood	Conditions to Increase Achieving Goal
12. Provide career ladder	Visible career ladder may provide recognition and models of competence and inspiration. But trade-offs are similar to those for merit increases.	Joint teacher-administrator definition of the ladder could moderate some divisiveness. Master-teacher apprentice teaching relation with new teachers could provide model of excellent teaching as intermediate rung of ladder

Goals of Increasing Teacher Competence

Proposals	Reasons for Assigning Likelihood	Conditions to Increase Achieving Goal
13. Teacher exams in area of speciality	Viewed as demeaning teachers' professionalism. Not yet proved effective without teacher ownership of its importance. Goal's value is obvious but creates intense resistance.	Urge higher minimum academic-character standards for entrance into profession with longer probationary period for contract renewal be more widely accepted. See proposal #16 for more positive approach. Need to create a self-renewing school and peer climate.
14. Provide flexible entry routes into profession	Teacher applicant pool needs expansion to provide for more cultural diversity. Teaching competence depends upon rich and varied interpersonal skills and values.	Provision of closely supervised master-apprenticeships in model classrooms could increase acquisition of complex teaching skills and provide "on job" test of teaching potential in early years.

Proposals	Reasons for Assigning Likelihood	Conditions to Increase Achieving Goal

Goals of Nurturing Teaching as a Calling

| 15. Released time for self-renewal | Teachers need opportunity to be confronted with new challenges, not repeat another safe summer course. Growth encouraged by altering traditional roles and abandoning traditional habits. | Schools report teachers are unimaginative and don't take advantage of such opportunities. |
| 16. Commitment to one's growth condition for contract renewal | Unions and boards must confront potential negative effects of tenure and provide more positive incentives to continued professional and personal growth. (See *Schools of Hope*, Ch. 12) | Existing definition of "growth" as taking more summer courses devalues teachers' personhood and the goal of human not just academic excellence for one's self as well as for students. Exit-job counseling should be provided to aid teachers to make community contacts |

Proposals for Effective Schools

Goal of creating more autonomous, humane, and simply organized schools

| 17.Downsize elementary to 300; middle and high schools to 400-600 or smaller | This book's evidence and that of others so consistently shows the importance of this proposal that achievement of other proposals is contingent upon | Creative use of technology can provide resources small schools allege they need. "Small-schools-within-large school" not an adequate solution unless school has control |

Proposals	Reasons for Assigning Likelihood	Conditions to Increase Achieving Goal
17. (cont.)	successful achievement of this one.	of its space to create its own culture. Leaders must become more knowledgeable about inner dynamics of their schools—a purpose of this book.

Goals of clarifying school's mission and creating shared values

18. Create school climate that supports goals	This book's evidence and that of others so consistently shows the importance of this proposal that achievement of other proposals is contingent upon successful achievement of this one.	Increased understanding of school's climate and factors that affect it accompanied by methods for assessing it been found to be a powerful lever for encouraging school improvement.
19. Develop vision for 21st century	Emphasis on "back-to-basics," as important as they are, has robbed teachers of the nobility of the motivations and visions that called them to teach. Lack of shared communal values leads to reduced faculty commitment and synergies.	Schools must be alert to the trivialization of their goals and culture. They need to be ceaselessly challenged to keep alive the goal of human excellence that calls teachers to teach and sustains high morale.
20. Hold schools meaningfully accountable for their goals	Improvement in schools depends on knowledge of both short- and long-term effects. Self-renewing schools and	To be responsibly held accountable, schools need autonomy from bureaucratic dictates and resources to create their

Proposals	Reasons for Assigning Likelihood	Conditions to Increase Achieving Goal
20. (cont.)	teachers seek information about their cultures and effects. How else can they know what and how to improve?	own growth environments and a community's belief in and trust that they can. British-type visiting school teams can provide objectivity.

Goal of principals being educational leaders

21. Principal be more than administrator: a leader	Widespread agreement exists that principals are key to creating an effective school. As leaders they are more than just effective administrators. They are stewards of their schools' visions, sensitive creators of their cultures and growth-producing environments.	Principals need involving reflective experiences about educational issues and goals, understanding of systems, and awareness of youth' and adults' healthy growth. More summer courses on budget preparation are not the route to leadership. Boards' highest priority should be nurturing their principals' growth.
22. Create collaborative work relationships throughout school	School improvement depends upon creating productive relationships more congruent with the changing values of society about "ownership" and sharing of power.	Current adversarial relationships are wearying everyone and transforming teaching from a calling to a job. Nation needs to re-evaluate those board-union relationships that hobble improvement, prevent needed changes in staffing, and impede faculty growth.

Notes

Preface

1. Spady, 1998.
2. Heath, 1977, 1994a.
3. Heath, 1994b, chap. 5.

Chapter 1

1. Joyce, Wolf, & Calhoun, 1993; Brandt, 1992a, 1995.
2. Pike & Barnes, 1994, p. 28.
3. Deming, 1982.
4. Pennar, 1997.
5. Pennar, 1997.
6. Sagor, 1995.
7. Dewey, J. (1934), 1964.
8. Heath, 1968.
9. Heath, 1994b.
10. Joyce, 1993; Bonstigi, 1992.
11. Pike & Barnes, 1994, p. 25.
12. Deming, 1982.
13. Pike & Barnes, 1994.
14. Joyce, Wolf, & Calhoun, 1993.
15. Heath, 1994b.

16. Heath, 1994b.

17. Brandt, 1992b.

18. Brandt, 1992a, 1995; Schlecty & Cole, 1992.

19. Rothman, 1990.

Chapter 2

1. Alverno College Faculty, 1976.

2. Comment from Boughner's critique of the chapter, January, 1998.

3. Montessori, 1912; (1948) 1973.

4. Sizer, 1984.

5. Statements about the "reliability" of a result or effect are short-hand expressions to indicate that statistically the result or effect is highly unlikely to have occurred by chance. [See ASH 4: Developing Reliable Measures of Goals].

Chapter 3

1. The Hawthorne effect refers to a classic study demonstrating that participants in a novel real-life experiment involving close monitoring were motivated to improve their performance which declined over time once the experiment was terminated.

2. Heath, 1994b, pp. 80-83.

3. ASH 33C, 37B,D and 38B-D give students' complete normative results for both NAIS and public high schools.

Chapter 4

1. Heath, 1991, 1994a.

2. Heath, 1968, 1994a,b.

3. Heath, 1968.

4. ibid #3.

Chapter 5

1. Pike & Barnes, 1994, p. 28.

2. Smart, Kuh, & Tierney, 1997 review post-Deming 1980's and 1990's research to identify numerous other contributors to organizational effectiveness (e.g., ability to accquire resources, organizational health). Other contributors, such as institutional culture, quality of interpersonal relationships, and system openness can be assessed using Chapter 7's Word Check List.

3. Heath, 1994a, chap 11.

4. ibid #3.

5. Coleman, 1966, p. 23.

6. These results have been consistently found and statistically confirmed for most schools that I have studied.

7. ASH 33 includes both more stable and provisional morale norms. Such norms should be used cautiously. Table 5-1 includes the morale scores of 14630 students. The public school sample includes 7806, NAIS 3768, international schools 2479, and liberal arts colleges 577. A total of 4367 teachers contributed to the morale scores.

8. The international teachers' surveys were not consistently identified with their divisional identity and so could not be listed in Table 5-1. The twenty-five schools were located in North Africa, Europe, Middle East, Southeast Asia, Far East, and South America. Nine midwest, west, and eastern colleges' teachers participated.

9. For the statistically minded, p values for the pair-wise comparisons ranged from .03 for public vs. NAIS middle school faculty morale to .0000 for NAIS elementary vs. middle school and public vs. NAIS high school students' morale.

10. Only the four most satisfying items are listed because satisfaction with the next four to eight items was so similar that discriminating between them would be too arbitrary.

11. Munneke & Bridger-Riley, 1981.

12. Comparisons of teachers to business-professionals are based on the 28-item VAS. These VAS total scores were 101.9 for NAIS and 95.3 for public school high school and 102.8 for business-professional men.

13. For some clues about the possible causes of such differences, see Chapter 13 which compares the cultures of public and independent schools.

14. Heath, 1991, chap. 27.

15. American Association of University Women, 1991, pp. 3-4.

16. Numerous measures of self-esteem are available though not specifically designed to measure middle school children's attitudes. I have used an alternative type of bi-polar scale, called Self-Image Questionnaire, to measure self-esteem. Persons rate themselves on thirty favorable attributes that identify effective, successful persons. Very extensive studies of its correlates in America and abroad confirm its power to predict a host of other behaviors and personality traits, especially a person's maturity. See Heath, 1965, 1977, and 1991 for both theoretical analyses of self-esteem and its associated empirical correlates.

17. I am indebted to the superintendents of American schools for the opportunity to comprehensively study all of their schools in Saudi Arabia.

18. Harris, L. & Associates. The Metropolitan Life Survey of the American Teacher, 1997. NY: Louis Harris & Associates.

19. See Heath, 1994b, pp. 294-296 for specific curricular implications for the pubertal child.

20. Azar's summary of studies of transition from elementary to junior high school by Eccles, Midgely, Ames, Anderman, and Dweck agrees with my results. Academic grades decrease, interest and motivation decline, schools are more controlling, less challenging, and more competitive.

21. Assume that grade-by-grade students' views of their public and independent schools from varied cultures were available. Then

comparing transcultural grade-by-grade similarities between students' views of their schools' cultures might enable us to tease out possible developmental from cultural contributors to declining morale.

22. The AAUW study was a cross-sectional, not a longitudinal one. So its authors cannot extrapolate its conclusions into the students' high school or adult years. The only two intensive long-term studies of female development have found that adolescent girls' personalities are poor predictors of their future adjustment. Extrapolations are therefore risky, though less for boys whose adolescent personalities are more predictive. *Lives of Hope,* chap. 22 compares the adult development of males and females who had been studied for decades.

Chapter 6

1. Pike and Barnes, 1994, p. 28.

Chapter 7

1. Heath, 1981.

2. Toma, 1997, distinguishes between culture as a pattern of values and climate as shared perceptions of organizations. The chapter describes a practical method that taps into both culture and climate; it is beyond my purpose to enter into their conceptual issues; Kuh, 1993; Blackburn & Lawrence, 1995, report research demonstrating that faculty perceptions of their environment and satisfaction more powerfully predict faculty activities such as teaching, research, and service than traditional sociological and career variables.

3. Andrews, 1979.

4. Rutter, Maughan, Mortimer, Oustoon, & Smith, 1979.

5. Hardy, 1974, p. 502.

6. Tinto, 1997.

7. Mayhew, 1979, p. 28.

8. National Association Secondary School Principals, 1986; Pace, 1969; Smart, Kuh, & Tierney, 1997.

9. For a review of the epistemological and methodological assumptions of this phenomenological view of "truth", see Toma 1997. An example of how failure to take a constructivist multiple view of reality that has practical societal consequences can be found in Freeman, 1997.

10. Heath, 1991, 1994a describe the attributes necessary to fulfill an adult's principal roles successfully.

11. Grannon, Kulick, & Schenck, 1981.

12. Given their larger schools and numbers of students to teach, it is understandable why public high school teachers are not tuned in as well as NAIS teachers to their students' peer learning environment.

13. Public school students view their peer learning environment to be more unfavorable and less supportive than their faculties are aware, e.g., more sarcastic, show-off, rebellious, and aggressive. See Table 15-5.

14. Rothman, 1990.

Chapter 8

1. Astin, 1977.

2. Heath, 1977b.

Chapter 9

1. Pike & Barnes, 1994.

2. Goodlad, 1997.

3. Banner & Cannon, 1997.

4. Goodlad, 1997.

5. Heath, 1994b, pp.280-282, describes a workshop exercise that has helped teachers develop more trust with each other.

6. Heath, 1994b, chap. 13, describes a high school curriculum that drastically alters the typical teacher-student relationship so that faculty's self-educating and character strengths become more visible to students.

7. Derived from identifying the percentage of WCL's positive traits that Washington's faculty does not check that more than 20 percent of other public school faculties do check. [ASH 37C: Public and Independent Teachers' Views of Students].

Chapter 10

1. Heath, 1994b, chap 5.

2. Heath, 1994b, distinguishes between liberal education and liberal arts. Educational philosophers define liberal education in terms of mind and character attributes. Liberal arts refer to specific disciplines such as mathematics and history. There is no demonstrable or necessary relation between taking a specific liberal arts course and becoming liberally educated.

Chapter 11

1. Heath, 1994b, chap. 3 for the changing attitudes toward authority.

Chapter 12

1. Astin, 1975.

2. As the data reveal, the WCL offers a quick, though crude, way to assess a person's self-esteem. Since 1960, H. Gough, father of the Adjective Check List which provided the idea for the WCL, has used the ACL as a personality measure.

3. Archer (1998) reports that math achievement co-varies with teacher training in technology, how computer is used, and positive school climate. How critical school culture is to effective use of computer has not yet been studied in depth. .

Chapter 13

1. Rothman, 1991.

2. American Demographics, 1990.

3. Kane, 1998, p. 45.

Chapter 14

1. Heath, 1994b, chap. 3.

2. The EVQ can be revised by adding examples of other virtues that schools may wish to study that are integral to their mission. An unreported study of Quaker high schools adapted the WCL to assess key defining Quaker values included in the EVQ, [ASH 43: Examples of Additions to EVQ for Special Assessment Purposes.]

3. Since 1990, the entire battery of surveys has been given similarly to numerous public and NAIS schools. Some of the surveys have been modified slightly depending upon the information particular schools wished to secure.

4. Heath, 1991, found that men's and women's ratings of their ethical behavior and those of three judges who knew them most intimately did not agree well about how virtuous they were. However, a combined measure of self- and judge-rated ethical attributes, such as honesty, depth of moral sense, and caring, predicted many of their accomplishments and well-being.

5. Heath, 1991.

6. The NAIS 7-8 grade sample included 404 boys and 409 girls from nine southern, eastern, and western middle schools. The NAIS 9-12th sample included 1587 boys and 1325 girls from 11 southern, eastern, midwestern, and western high schools. The sample includes day, boarding, coed, and a boy's school. Only a few religious schools (primarily Episcopalian) are included. (No Jewish, Quaker, or parochial Catholic schools are included.) The public school sample included 1633 boys and 1641 girls from 7 comparable socio-economic affluent eastern, midwestern, and western public high schools.

7. Hanus, 1996.

8. Heath, 1991, pp. 374-375.

9. The one possible exception is that the public-Reagan and NAIS girls' differ most in their beliefs that they are caring. Recall that they differed reliably in caring as measured by their EVQ's ratings of their actual behavior. It is just such congruence in patterns that reciprocally confirms their validity. This result provokes this question. Might not the premier place that caring has in a female's identity be why feminists like Noddings (1984) argue its development should be education's principal goal? Feminists have had much to say about how men's core gender-related traits affect schools' goals and practices.

10. Knight, 1988.

11. Heath, 1991, chap. 19.

12. Some critics confuse androgyny with homosexuality. I know of no reliable evidence to demonstrate that androgynous men and women are inclined to a bisexual or homosexual identity. They may be. We just don't know.

13. I do not have comparable data from the Bloomfield Hills' high school students to check for the continuity in personality findings. Nor do I have a large enough sample of Model's students to identify the number of extreme tolerant and intolerant students for each of the WCL targets.

Chapter 15

1. David Mallery of NAIS's staff has asked teachers in his workshops to identify the teacher who influenced them most when younger and the gifts that such persons gave them. Teachers invariably identify character attributes.

2. Pascarella & Terenzini, 1991, summarize research on moral education.

3. Unfortunately, researchers studying colleges seldom also study middle or high schools and vice versa to identify developmental

and institutional continuities. The availability of generic morale and cultural surveys could provide an opportunity to explore such continuities.

4. Heath, 1968.

5. Heath, 1976.

6. Heath, 1968.

7. Given the small samples, a 10% rather than a smaller difference highlights more clearly the possible differences.

8. This is the only reliable finding that might suggest that the NAIS and public school parents may have different effects on their childrens' ethical behavior. I cannot check this hypothesis since I had no objective measure of the parents' ethical expectations. One could argue just as persuasively that growing up in a NAIS school's different moral climate sensitizes one to parents' expectations. Given Chapter 13's demonstration that independent and public school students were so similar, the hypothesis that the former's more pronounced ethical self-concept is due to their schools' influence is more credible for me.

9. Heath, 1994b, chap. 2 develops this theme in more detail.

10. Ibid # 9.

11. Heath, 1994a.

Chapter Sixteen

1. Heath, 1994b, chaps 6 and 8 provide the theoretical rationale identifying core values that maturing produces.

2. Hartshorne & May, 1928.

3. Noddings, 1984.

4. Hall & Barongan, 1997, critique the research on date rape and other forms of sexual aggression but ignore the contribution of sex hormones.

5. Robbins, 1996.

6. Heath, 1977, Appendix A describes methods for and results of comparing Italian, Turkish, and American cultural differences in valuing different relationships.

7. Eisenberg & Murphy, 1995.

8. Heath, 1991, chap. 19, 1994a, chap. 18.

9. Heath, 1994b, chaps. 3, 6.

10. Heath, 1994a, chap. 3.

11. Hall & Barongan, 1997.

12. Heath, 1994b, Appendix B identifies and chap. 14 illustrates how to apply 20 educational principles to further character development.

13. Heath, 1976.

14. Heath, 1972, 1994b, pp. 80-83.

15. Heath, 1994b.

16. Heath, 1994b, chaps. 13-15 illustrate how teacher-student relationships could be altered to reveal teachers as more valuing adults.

17. Power, Higgins, & Kohlberg, 1989.

18. Moulton & Ransome, 1996.

19. Heath, 1994a.

20. Astin, 1996.

21. Adams, 1996.

22. Heath, H. E. has developed a curricular program, integrated with the academic one, designed to systematically teach caring skills and attitudes, especially for elementary and middle school students. Conrow Publishing House, P.O. Box 1411, Bryn Mawr, PA 19010.

Chapter 17

1. Heath, 1994b, chap. 5 summarizes the available research evidence.

2. Heath, 1991, pp. 368-84 describe measures of such "unassessable" attributes as happiness, emotional health, and empathy; Heath, 1965, describes measures of ability to think conceptually, logically, and realistically in threatening situations.

3. Cross, 1998, p. 32.

4. See Gauld, 1993, who describes how Maine's Hyde school has self-consciously implemented its philosophy that "when you put character first, academic achievement naturally follows." Students do not graduate if they have not shown growth in their character as the school and students define it.

5. Wiggins, 1993.

6. Heath, 1994b, chap. 7 describes the principal attributes of the maturing mind.

7. Sizer, 1992.

8. Heath, 1994b, pp. 371-73, sketches the next praticable steps.

References

Adams, H. E. *The Chronicle of Higher Education,* 1996, August 9, A8.

Alverno College Faculty. *Liberal Learning at Alverno College.* Milwaukee, WI: Alverno Productions, 1976.

American Association of University Women. *Shortchanging Girls, Shortchanging America.* Washington, DC: American Association of University Women, 1991, pp. 3,4.

American Demographics. The school question: public vs. private. *Wall Street Journal,* 1990, Oct 2, B1.

Andrews, F. M. (Ed.) *Scientific Productivity. The Effectiveness of Research Groups in Six Countries.* New York: Columbia University Press, 1979.

Archer, J. The link to higher scores. *Education Week,* 1998, October 1, 10-21.

Astin, A. W. *Preventing Students from Dropping Out.* San Francisco: Jossey- Bass, 1975.

Astin, A. W. *Four Critical Years: Effects of College on Beliefs, Attitudes, and Knowledge.* San Francisco: Jossey-Bass, 1977.

Astin, A. W. in Shea, C. New students uncertain about racial preferences. *The Chronicle of Higher Education,* 1996, January 12, A35.

Azar, B. Schools the source of rough transitions. *Monitor,* American Psychological Association, June 1996, 14.

273

Banner Jr., J. M. & Cannon, H. C. The "Who" of Teaching. Commentary. *Education Week,* 1997, April 16, 56.

Blackburn, R. T. & Lawrence, J. H. *Faculty at Work: Motivation, Expectation, and Satisfaction,* Baltimore: The Johns Hopkins University Press, 1995.

Bonstigi, J. J. The Quality Revolution in Education. *Educational Leadership,* 1992, 50, 4-9.

Brandt, R. (Ed.) Improving School Quality. *Educational Leadership,* 1992, November, 50, No. 3.

Brandt, R. On Deming and school quality: a conversation with Enid Brown. *Educational Leadership,* 1992, 50, 28-31.

Brandt, R. (Ed.) Self-Renewing Schools. *Educational Leadership,* 1995, April, 52. No. 7.

Coleman, J. S. *Equality of Educational Opportunity.* Office Education, 1966, 23.

Cross, C. T. The standards wars: some lessons learned. *Education Week,* 1998, October 28, p. 32.

Deming, W. E. *Out of the Crisis.* Cambridge, MA: Massachusetts Institute of Technology. Center for Advanced Engineering Study, 1982.

Dewey, J. The need for a philosophy of education, (1934). In R. D. Archambault (Ed.), *John Dewey on Education.* New York: Modern Library, Random House, 1964.

Eisenberg, N. & Murphy, B. Parenting and children's moral development, In: *Handbook of Parenting.* Mahwah, New Jersey: Lawrence Erlbam Assoc. 1995, IV., ch. 10.

Freeman, K. Increasing African Americans' participation in higher education, *Journal of Higher Education,* 1997, 68, 523-550,

Gauld, J. W. *Character First. The Hyde School Difference.* San Francisco, CA: ICS Press, 1993.

Goodlad, J. I. Commentary. Producing teachers who understand, believe, and care, *Education Week,* 1997, February 5, p. 48.

Gough, H. The adjective check list as a personality assessment research technique. *Psychological Report,* 1960, 6, 107-122.

Grannon, P., Kulick, W., & Schenck, L. Effect of single and coed schools on maturing. Unpublished senior thesis, Haverford College, 1981.

Hall, G. C. N. & Barongan, C. Prevention of sexual aggression. Sociocultural risk and protective factors. *American Psychologist,* 1997, 52, 5-

Hanus, J. J. School vouchers, pro and con. They are fair and they are practical. *Education Week,* 1996, July 10, 60.

Hardy, K. R. Social origins of American scientists and scholars. *Science,* 1974, 185, 497-506, p. 502.

Harris, L. & Associates. *The Metropolitan Life Survey of the American Teacher.* N Y: Louis Harris & Associates, 1997.

Hartshorne, H. & May, M. *Studies in the Nature of Character.* New York: Macmillan, 1928, Vol 1.

Heath, D. H. *Explorations of Maturity.* New York: Appleton-Century-Crofts, 1965.

Heath, D. H. *Growing Up in College.* San Francisco: Jossey-Bass, 1968.

Heath, D. H. Survival? A bigger school? *The Independent School Bulletin,* 1972, May, 9-15.

Heath, D. H. What the enduring effects of higher education tell us about a liberal education. *Journal of Higher Education,* 1976, 47, 173-190.

Heath, D. H. Academic predictors of adult maturity and competence. *Journal of Higher Education,* 1977, 48, 613-632.

Heath, D. H. *Maturity and Competence. A Transcultural View.* New York: Gardner Press, 1977.

Heath, D. H. A college's ethos: a neglected key to effectiveness and survival. *Liberal Education,* 1981, 67, 89-111.

Heath, D. H. *Fulfilling Lives: Paths to Maturity and Success.* San Francisco: Jossey-Bass, 1991.

Heath, D. H. *Lives of Hope: Women's and Men's Path to Success and Fulfillment.* Haverford, PA: Conrow Publishing House, 1994a.

Heath, D. H. *Schools of Hope. Developing Mind and Character in Today's Youth.* San Francisco: Jossey-Bass, 1994b. (Paperback, Conrow Publishing House, 1999.)

Joyce, B., Wolf, J., & Calhoun, E. *The Self-Renewing School.* Association
for Supervision and Curriculum Development, 1993.

Kane, P. R. Charter schools: paying attention to ancillary findings.
Education Week, 1998, October 14, p. 42.

Knight, P. Sex-role stereotyping hits early in life, research finds. *The
Sunday Oregonian,* 1988, March 27, D7.

Kuh, G., Assessing campus environments. In M. Barr (Ed.) *Handbook of
Student Affairs Administration,* San Francisco: Jossey-Bass, 1993, 30-48.

Mayhew, L. B. *Surviving the Eighties: Strategies and Procedures for
Solving Fiscal and Enrollment Problems.* San Francisco: Jossey-Bass,
1979, p. 28.

Montessori, M. *The Montessori Method.* New York: Frederick Stokes,
1912.

Montessori, M. *From Childhood to Adolescence.* (1948), New York:
Shocken Books, 1973.

Moulton, M. & Ransome, W. Letter to Editor. All-girl math classes won't
solve the problem. *Education Week,* 1996, July 10, 47.

Munneke, G. A. & Bridger-Riley, N. K. Singing those law office blues.
Barrister, 1981, Fall, 10.

National Association Secondary School Principals, Comprehensive
Assessment of School Environments, Reston, VA: 1986.

Noddings, N. *Caring: A Feminist Approach to Ethics and Moral Education.*
Berkley, CA: University of California Press, 1984.

Pace, C. R. *College and University Environment Scales. Sec. Ed. Technical
Manual.* Princeton, NJ: Educational Testing Service, 1969.

Pascarella, E. T. & Terenzini, P. T. *How College Affects Students.* San
Francisco: Jossey-Bass, 1991.

Pennar, K. The ties that lead to prosperity. The economic value of social
bonds is only beginning to be measured. *Business Week,* 1997, Decem-
ber 15, 153.

Pike, J. & Barnes, R. *TQM in Action,* New York: Chapman & Hall, 1994,
chap. 2, p. 28.

Power, F. C., Higgins, A., & Kohlberg, L. *Lawrence Kohlberg's Approach to Moral Education.* New York: Columbia University Press, 1989.

Robbins, A. Androgens and male sexual behavior. From mice to men. *Trends in Endocrinology Metabolism,* 1996, 7, 345-350.

Rothman, R. Educators focus attention on ways to boost student motivation. *Education Week,* 1990, November 7, 1, 12.

Rothman, R. Debate on merits of public, private schools re-ignites. *Education Week,* 1991, Sept. 18, 1.

Rutter, M., Maughan, B., Mortimer, P., Oustoon, J., & Smith, A. *Fifteen Thousand Hours.* Cambridge, MA: Harvard University Press, 1979.

Sagor, R. Overcoming the one-solution syndrome. *Educational Leadership,* 1995, 52, 24-27.

Schlecty, P. C. & Cole, R. W. Creating "standard-bearer schools." *Educational Leadership,* 1992, 50, 45-63.

Sizer, T. R. *Horace's School: Redesigning the American High School.* Boston: Houghton Mifflin, 1992.

Smart, J. C., Kuh, G. D., & Tierney, W. G. The roles of institutional cultures and decision approaches in promoting organizational effectiveness in two-year colleges. *Journal of Higher Education,* 1997, 68, 256-281.

Spady, W. G. Educentric testing undermines America's future. *Education Week,* 1998, October 7, p. 36.

Stevenson, H., Azuma, H., & Hakuta, K. *Child Development and Education in Japan.* New York: Freeman, 1986.

Tinto, V. Classrooms as communities. Exploring the educational character of student persistence. *Journal of Higher Education,* 1997, 68, 599-623.

Toma, J. D. Alternative inquiry paradigms, faculty cultures, and the definition of academic lives. *Journal of Higher Education,* 1997, 68, 679-705.

Wiggins, G. P. *Assessing Student Performance. Exploring the Purpose and Limits of Testing,* San Francisco: Jossey-Bass, 1993.

Index

M

Marathon Elementary School, 76-79, 113
Marlboro School, 108-9, 115
Marshall School District, 83-86
Masculinity, 61, 184-88, 193-94.
    See also Femininity; Gender differences
Maturity, psychological:
    attributes in students, 46-50
    criteria of healthy school, 105-22
    limited by overdeveloped strength, 112
    measure of student's, 45-46
    MHS effect upon, 44-50
    model of, 45, 105, 243
    as predictor, 44-45
    relation to a school of hope, 104-5
    student descriptions of, 46-50. *See also* Autonomy; Empathy; Growth, healthy; Internal coherence; Reflective awareness; Stably resilient
Mayhew, L., 89
MHS. *See* Model High School
Middle school:
    Bloomfield Hills study of, 161-63, 188-93
    Edina study of, 161-63
    and ethical behavior, 181
    out of phase with development, 72
    morale decline in, 69-75.
    morale of students, 63-64, 73-74.
    See also Rosemont Junior High School
Minority schools: 12-14, 117-20, 123-37, 131-32.
    See also Sandia High School; Washington Junior-Senior

Minority schools: (cont.)
    High School; Wentworth High School
Model High School (MHS): 15-56
    and academic grades, 26, 42-43
    assessment limitations of, 18, 24, 28-31
    assessment of, 28-40, 41-51
    assessment as school of hope, 53-56
    authentic assessment, 22-23
    and community involvement in, 23
    compared to private schools, 38-39
    competencies expected by, 18
    competency effects, 41-44
    culture of, 33-34, 37-40, 230
    curriculum of, 24-25
    effect on ethical competence, 204
    effect on healthy growth, 36-37
    evaluation of assessment procedure, 233
    faculty morale, 27
    faculty-parental view of, 38
    as honest accountability study, 51-53, 232
    means to hold students accountable, 22-23
    principal maturing effects of, 23, 36-37, 45-50
    resources of, 25, 38
    structure and program, 23-25
    students, 33-35, 37-39
    students' morale, 35-37, 163
    University of Michigan study of, 32
    values and assumptions of, 20-23
    vision of, 17-23, 41
Montessori, 4, 7, 10, 19, 21, 22, 44, 130. *See also* Countryside Elementary School

R

S